Relating

Relating Faith

Modelling Biblical Christianity in Church and World

Robert Knowles

Paternoster:
thinking faith

Copyright © 2014 Robert Knowles

20 19 18 17 16 15 14   7 6 5 4 3 2 1

First published 2014 by Paternoster
Paternoster is an imprint of Authentic Media Limited
52 Presley Way, Crownhill, Milton Keynes, MK8 0ES.
www.authenticmedia.co.uk

British Library Cataloguing in Publication Data

A catalogue record for this book is available from the British Library

ISBN 978-1-84227-831-4
978-1-78078-080-1 (e-book)

Cover Design by David Smart
Printed and bound by CPI Group (UK) Ltd., Croydon, CR0 4YY

Contents

Foreword by Anthony C. Thiselton   xi

Preface and Acknowledgements   xiii

Abbreviations   xv

Part One: Relating Faith: Discipleship   **1**

1. Being Formed by God's Biblical Speech-Acts   3

    God's Biblical Speech-Acts   3

    How Westerners Block God's Biblical Speech-Action   4

    How to Be Formed by God's Biblical Speech-Action   6

2. Communion with Christ in the Central-Room   11

    Communion and Conflict: Becoming Different to the World   11

    Communion and Conditioning: Battle to Reshape the Christian   13

    Communion and Criticism: Openness to Challenge by the Real   15

    Communion and Compromise: Against Narcissism
      and Obscurantism   16

    Communion and Cultivation: Education and Being Interpreted   18

    Communion and Community: Promoting Gifts and Reconciliation   19

3. Love for God and Others: Biblical Lawfulness   21

    The Fig-Leaf: We Distort God's Law to Hide Our Sin   22

    Shame Laid Bare: God's True Law Exposes Our Sin   24

    The Fleshly Lawlessness that God's True Law Exposes   28

    The Fleshly Legalism that God's True Law Exposes   31

    The Demonic Oppression Associated with Fleshly Legalism   33

    The Downward Spiral: Fleshly Lawlessness and Fleshly Legalism   35

    Jesus' Life, Death and Resurrection Ministry as Satisfaction of
      God's Law   37

      God the Trinity and Jesus' divine nature   41

      Jesus' human nature and legal qualification as our
       penal substitute   41

Jesus' life: his earthly mission and our human
    predicament   42
Jesus' death: the legal forfeit that procures our
    justification   42
Jesus' resurrection: establishing the new covenant
    with believers   43
Jesus' exaltation: his enthroned redemptive mission   44
Four Further Points Related to Jesus' Satisfaction of God's Law 45
Justified by Grace, by Faith, apart from Law, but still under
    Christ's Law of Love   49
The Heart of God's Law: Love for God as Genuine Worship   53
The Social Outworking of God's Law: Lawfulness as Love for
    Others   56
    Love as biblically wise relating to others   56
    Biblically wise relating versus anti-intellectualism   58
    Repudiating sinful manipulative strategies   60
    Trinitarian inclusiveness that confers freedoms   62
    Helping others into the freedom of right relating   64
The Advancement of God's Law: Lawfulness and Human Laws   66
    Submission, testimony and refinement   66
    Qualified respect for human judgements   70
    Resonance, witness, love and wisdom   73
Part Two: Relating Faith: Church   **77**
4. Church Distorted by Modernity   79
    How the Church Blocks Right Relating, Gifts and Ministries 80
    Caveats in Defence of Church Leaders   88
5. Church Distorted by Postmodernity   90
    'Corinthian' and Postmodern Cultural Sins in Churches Today 91
    Corinthian and Postmodern Cultural Sins versus True
    Christian Spirituality   93
6. Distorted Church as the Main Cause of Church-Hopping   98
    Relational Problems as a Cause of Church-Hopping   98
    Relational pre-emptive manoeuvring   99
    Relational breakdown   99
    Relational sin   100
    Relational dissonance   100
    Relational difference   102
    Cultural Sinfulness as a Cause of Church-Hopping   103
    Narcissistic self-promotion   103

Materialistic self-diversion 104
Relativistic self-evasion 105
Distorted Theological Persuasions as a Cause of Church-Hopping 108
People can feel theological distortions 108
Platonic or traditional theological distortions 109
Charismatic theological distortions 111
Older-style liberal theological distortions 112
Post-evangelical theological distortions 113
Marginalization of biblical-relational Christianity 116
Distorted Church Structures as a Cause of Church-Hopping 118
Distorted church structures, infantilization and
blocked ministries 118
The silencing of true prophets and theologians 123
The resulting hungry flock: 'the bleating of the
lambs' 125
Distorted Styles of Worship as a Cause of Church-Hopping 126
Distorted 'freedoms' in worship 127
Distorted 'forms' in worship 130
Distorted Pastoral Practice as a Cause of Church-Hopping 133
Distorted pastoral practice: irrelevant 'abstract
salvation' 133
Distorted pastoral practice: too close to cult
dynamics for comfort 135
Distorted pastoral practice: inadequate for complex
issues 136
Distorted pastoral practice: divorced from
genuine prophetic discourse 138
Distorted Witness as a Cause of Church-Hopping 141
Horizons of Expectation and Consecration to God as Causes
of Church-Hopping 142
Are We Being Too Harsh on the Church? 144
Eight Final Suggestions for Positive Ways Forward 145
Part Three: Relating Faith: Mission **151**
7. Mission Distorted by Five Distorted Church Cultures 153
Reformaca 156
Evangelica 156
Charismatica 157
Liberalica 157
Post-Evangelical Neo-Pragmatica 158

8. Mission and What Evangelism *Doesn't* Involve   161
   Against Standardizing Disciples and Discipleship   161
   Against Standardizing Churches and Mission   162
   Against Embarrassing Breaches of Social Etiquette   164
   Against Obscurantist Sloganeering that Resists Biblical
     Wisdom and Apologetics   165
   Against Pseudo-Evangelistic Infantilization that Resists
     Content and Vocabulary   167
   Against the False Evangelistic Promises of Counterfeit
     Worship Cultures   168
   Against Fleshly Legalistic 'Evangelism at Spiritual Gunpoint' 169
9. Mission and Understanding Modernity and Postmodernity   172
   Rise of the Knowledge of God versus Death-of-God Utopianisms 172
   Turn to Relationality versus 'Play' and Conflict   178
   Rise of Historical Consciousness versus Historical Negationism 182
   Rise of Liberating Concientización *versus Historical*
     Relativism   187
   Linguistic Turn to Enfleshed Word versus Docetic-Rhetoricist
     Flux   191
   Rise of Democracies versus Fragmentation and
     Authoritarianism   195
   Rise of True Self-Awareness versus Avoidant 'Deconstructed
     Selves'   200
   Rise of True Interpretation versus Deceit over 'Impossible
     Objectivity'   205
   Today's Postmodern Spiritual Battlefield   209
   Modernity and Bad Postmodernity: Disasters and False
     'Solutions'   214
   Bad Postmodernity Deployed: Twenty-Five Resulting
     Problems   217
       Fivefold cognitive, relational and ethical
         disintegration   217
       Fivefold cultural 'fragmentation–authoritarianism'
         dipole   218
       Five problematic 'allowed rhetorics' that control
         speech   220
       Five problems resulting from modernity remain
         unaddressed   221
       Five problems associated with digital culture   222

Biblical-Relational Evangelism and Promoting Good
   Postmodernity   224
      What true mission to Western postmodern society
        does not look like   224
      The general characteristics of true mission to
        Western postmodern society   226
      The specific characteristics of true mission to
        Western postmodern society   227
Endnotes   229

Dedicated to David, Anna, Thomas, Matthew and Isla Knowles
– my brother and his family;
and to John R.W. Stott, Francis A. Schaeffer, Colin E. Gunton and
Leonardo Boff
– some more of my teachers in the Christian faith

Foreword

I am glad to have this opportunity warmly to commend Dr Robert Knowles' book. It will be of great practical help in implementing the way in which we read the Bible, including what we expect, and what we look for, and also our communion with God and church life. It rightly begins with an emphasis on speech-acts, which may sound superficially a theoretical subject, but which is of the utmost importance for practical Bible reading and Bible study. He also explains the multi-functions of language, which we find both in ordinary conversations and in the language of Scripture. But the book concerns not only Bible-reading, but also more widely communion with God and the life of the church. In our communion with God it is also important to appreciate what diverse functions of language can be used in how we address God, and how we listen to God's word. Not all language is information, but effective speech-acts of various kinds. To grasp this will enrich our prayers and our relationship with God.

Dr Knowles also grasps the nettle of the impact of postmodernism on Christian belief and practice today. He rightly notes that prayer and communion with God should militate against preoccupation with the self, which he calls 'narcissism'. He is also aware of the possibility of distorted communication, against which we must all be on our guard. In some circles the church is bedevilled with 'false prophecy'; in other circles, with distorted reading of the Bible. Dr Knowles also addresses the issue of justification by grace through faith, and both the importance and relevance, but also limitation, of the law. Christians should be neither legalist nor antinomian. He includes a useful section on church leadership, with a salutary warning about use of power. He even considers the peril of 'church-hopping'. Throughout the book he gives helpful practical examples, which include suggestions about reading specific biblical passages. He then returns, once again, to the peril of 'bad' postmodernity, and the possible insights that 'good' postmodernity may sometimes bring.

Emeritus Canon Professor Anthony C. Thiselton,
PhD, DD (Durham), DD (Archbishop of Canterbury at Lambeth),
Hon. DTheol. (Chester), FSJC (Durham), FKC, FBA

Preface and Acknowledgements

The essays in this book, *Relating Faith*, emerged from a far more extensive body of shorter writings that were written between early 2003 and early 2012. This was the period during which I also wrote the bulk of my large textbook on the theory of interpretation, *Anthony C. Thiselton and the Grammar of Hermeneutics* (Milton Keynes: Paternoster, 2012). The present essays, then, owe much to my engagement with, and are heavily influenced by, the thinking of Professor Anthony C. Thiselton.

At the same time, the present essays are more practical in character than my textbook, which is more theoretical. In *Relating Faith* I have often attempted to *apply* 'Thiselton' – to *demonstrate* that what Thiselton says is not at all abstract or 'merely academic', but of great practical usefulness and of urgent and even prophetic importance for Christian discipleship, for the church, and for mission in today's postmodern world.

Having said this, *Relating Faith* is not just 'Thiseltonian'. I deploy Thiselton's insights within a structure of my own that brings in numerous other insights from other thinkers. If *Anthony C. Thiselton and the Grammar of Hermeneutics* attempts to be utterly 'Thiseltonian' – in order accurately to expound and systematize Thiselton's formative and core thinking – then *Relating Faith* is more reflective of how I have attempted to incorporate many of Thiselton's insights into my own developing theology.

I would particularly like to thank the following persons for their encouragement and assistance in relation to the present work: Timothy Smith, Christian Jensen, Revd Ted Fell, Julie Robinson, Revd Kieran and Catherine Webster, Revd Richard and Rachael Matcham, Matthew and Helen Crockett, Mark and Julie McKee,

Revd David and Sue Morrell, Gerwyn and Ruth Miles, and Revd David Grove. Special thanks are also due to all those who have financed and/or who continue to finance my work as a whole – though they are too numerous to list here. I would particularly like to thank Revd Phil Hill, Revd Dave Cave, Revd Geoffrey Fewkes and Revd Pete and Wendy Orphan – successive pastors of Pantygwydr Baptist Church, Swansea – for continuing to allow their church to handle my finances. I would especially like to thank Eric Matthews, Paul Carter and the other treasurers at Pantygwydr for all their hard work. I hope that this arrangement might continue as I have other volumes in mind that I would like to write, God willing!

Special thanks are also due to Professor Anthony C. Thiselton and to Revd Kieran Webster. Professor Thiselton has been a great help and a source of profound wisdom and encouragement throughout the whole period during which *Relating Faith* was written. And it was during one of my frequent stimulating discussions with Revd Kieran Webster that the title, *Relating Faith*, emerged: faith is *relational* in that 'love for God and neighbour sums up the Law and the Prophets' and in that, in response to the Great Commission, we are to *relate* our faith in Jesus Christ *to the world as it actually is at the present time.*

I would also especially like to thank Dr Mike Parsons and Trisha Dale, my very helpful editors at Paternoster, and Authentic Media Limited, Paternoster's parent company, for encouraging me to publish this second volume. In particular, I would like to thank Professor Anthony C. Thiselton for the gracious Foreword that he has penned for *Relating Faith*. And, finally, I would like to thank my mother, Dorothy Knowles, for her love and support.

Dr Robert Knowles
Cardiff
March 2013

Abbreviations

CEN	*Church of England Newspaper*
CGrad	*The Christian Graduate*
CP&B	*CyberPsychology & Behaviour*
Chm	*Churchman*
CUP	Cambridge University Press
ExpTim	*Expository Times*
IVP	InterVarsity Press
JTS	*Journal of Theological Studies*
MUP	Manchester University Press
NLitHist	*New Literary History*
NTS	*New Testament Studies*
OUP	Oxford University Press
Rev EMB	Anthony C. Thiselton, 'Review of A. Hodes' *Encounter with Martin Buber*', *Churchman* 90.2 (1976), pp. 138-9
SJT	*Scottish Journal of Theology*
TAB	*Transactional Analysis Bulletin*

Part One

Relating Faith: Discipleship

1.

Being Formed by God's Biblical Speech-Acts

God's Biblical Speech-Acts

According to speech-act theory, all speech is 'communicative action' – for example, rebuke, promise, exclamation, report, warning, declaration, teaching, informing, naming, and so on. There are as many kinds of 'speech-action' as there are verbs![1]

The effects of different kinds of speech-actions are just as variable. Thus, a rebuke could be met with contrition, violent reaction, or indifference. Or, a report could cause various reactions, depending on what was reported and to whom. Thus, the report, 'Your wife is having an affair' could shatter a world; or the report, 'There's a ship in trouble off Beachy Head' could engender an RNLI response.

That is, speech-acts are 'self-involving'. Thus, for example, I could say, 'That warning from the Lord shook me up and I repented.' That is, God warned me, and my self-involvement was that I repented. Conversely, the Lord's self-involvement was that – through the biblical texts – he genuinely *was* warning me that he would discipline me if I did not repent immediately.[2]

In this example, then, I am actually being related to by the Lord through the words of Scripture. This is not like reading a novel, since I am being warned in real life. Proper Bible-reading is an experience of being addressed by the God who is not just 'in the text' but who is in the real world.

During proper Bible-reading, then, God harnesses the biblical texts as speech-actions in order to address me in my real world. The Holy Spirit in me seizes on a text in the Bible as I read it and says, 'This is you. Deal with the issue'; or, 'You're being afflicted in this way, but this situation is about to change'; or, 'Try looking at this matter differently', and so on.

How Westerners Block God's Biblical Speech-Action

But why don't many Westerners today experience God through the Scriptures in this way? Well, Anthony C. Thiselton argues that we Westerners, due to our philosophical heritage, often reduce the variable speech-actions of language to 'statements conveying information and concepts'.[3] Thus, Western Christians tend to view the Bible as 'information' and/or 'concepts' from God to 'learn', asking, 'What truths (i.e. concepts, or information) can we get from this?', or saying, 'Let's meditate on these truths so that our perspectives alter.'

And, partly, this is right! Biblical language *does* transmit statements that convey conceptual truths and/or true information. The problem, though, is that biblical – indeed all – language is multifunctional. Biblical language is not *just* 'truths' (i.e. concepts and/or information) even if it *includes* 'truths'.

Now, of course, a statement like 'Your son is dead' is world-shattering. But many statements are not this dynamic or impacting, and so reducing Bible-reading to 'reading statements' can often make such 'Bible-reading' repetitive, boring or dull.[4] That is, and additionally, this suppression of multifunctionality can stop the Bible from challenging our traditions, and can thus encourage a traditionalism that idolizes our current imperfect understanding of Scripture by setting this imperfect understanding of Scripture above better understandings of Scripture. But if even the Bible and the Holy Spirit can no longer challenge our existing imperfect biblical interpretations (unless God overrules this sorry state of affairs), then we are saying that 'We already think like Jesus', which is self-idolatry.

That is, reducing Bible-reading to 'reading statements' makes God seem like a remote boss who sends us instructions from Siberia. When the boss is away we feel that we can choose whether or not to respond to his instructions straight away. Given the absence of immediate relational interaction with the boss we assume some authority over the boss that we don't actually have.

When the boss is with us in the office, however, we respond immediately as a matter of right-relational reflex. We woud not say to
our boss something like, 'What eternal truths can I get from your
instructions?' if he were present with us in the office, but would
follow the boss's instructions straight away.

Western Bible-reading, then, often reduces Bible-reading to
'reading statements' so as to assume authority over God and over
Scripture, and is thus often idolatrous. Moreover, we get bored of
the sub-relationality of such Bible-reading. We quench the Spirit's
indwelling relational presence, and substitute doctrine *about* the
Spirit's indwelling.

That is, reducing the biblical texts to only statements 'Western-
er-style' precludes relationship with God through the Scriptures
by suppressing the great variety of biblical speech-acts that should
ordinarily be involved in immediate relationship between God and
us – even if God sometimes overrules this unfortunate practice.

Often, though, this practice becomes a Western device for
suppressing the threat of an immediately-at-hand God so that we
can seek to control our own destinies in sinful 'modern' autonomy
from God. As interpreters *of* Scripture, rather than as those interpreted *by* Scripture, we Western Christians often effectively suppress
Christ's Lordship over our lives. We often sacrifice the immediacy
of a daily relational walk with God – which is especially medi-
ated by the Holy Spirit through the Scriptures – and instead seek
to experience God as a warm glow. We say, 'Just give me "truths"
from afar – "truths" that don't involve me in threatening immediate
relationship with you, oh Lord – just give me "data plus niceness".'

And even if we *do* want a proper relationship with God, then
it is still difficult to overcome our Western 'training'. Thus, for
example, much expository preaching reduces Scripture to statements and concepts 'to be applied' when, really, it should liberate
Scripture to function as all kinds of formational and transformational speech-acts from an immediately-present God. That is, we
shouldn't just ask systemic questions of the biblical texts; rather,
we should ask relational questions of the biblical texts. Whilst the
biblical texts *do* convey truths, they are primarily God's immediate relating to us – for 'love sums up the law and the prophets'.[5]

Our specific point here in the present chapter, though, is that
our overly Westernised devotional times need to be transposed

into a relational key. The following practical steps may help us to reshape our devotional times relationally – as follows.

How to Be Formed by God's Biblical Speech-Action

And so, first, it is useful to get hold of a Bible-reading plan. Using a Bible-reading plan ensures that we do not try to gain control over God's voice by just choosing passages that we like. The next six chapters in my Bible-reading plan are: Mark 2; 2 Corinthians 12; Jude 1; Numbers 2; 1 Chronicles 14; and Isaiah 59. Don't worry about there being six chapters to get through – this kind of devotional time can be spread over a few days.

Second, write down the next six chapters from your Bible-reading plan at the top of the left-hand page of a double page in an A4-sized journal, a bit like this:

Mark 2	2 Corinthians 12	Jude 1
Numbers 2	1 Chronicles 14	Isaiah 59

Third, before reading your six Bible chapters, think of the most pressing issue or question in your life at the moment, and write it out under the six Bible chapters that you have just noted down. If you can't think of anything immediately pressing, it doesn't matter. But, in all cases, pray, 'Please speak to me through your word, Lord', realizing that God may relate to you in a surprising way. The top left of your double journal page may now look something like this:

Mark 2	2 Corinthians 12	Jude 1
Numbers 2	1 Chronicles 14	Isaiah 59

Optional Question: e.g. What about the situation concerning my future ministry? What do you say, Lord?

Fourth, begin your Bible reading, noting down any references that stand out to you for whatever reason. You are not looking for a big experience (though you might have one), but for different kinds of self-involvement: are you sensing an encouragement, a warning, an unusual point, a rebuke, an uncomfortable point, something that resonates or grates with you, something that informs or teaches you (yes, that is still allowed!), or something that stands out to you for some as-yet-unspecified reason? It doesn't matter if you can't identify the specific kind of speech-act or self-involvement yet – just note down the references that stand out to you as you read them, such that the top left of your double journal page now looks something like this (though your chapters and verses will likely be different from mine!):

Mark 2:2,7,10–12, 13–17,22	2 Corinthians 12:4, 6,9–11c,15,19,21	Jude 1:1–3c,5,7–8, 10–11
Numbers 2:2a, 3d,7b,9d,10b	1 Chronicles 14:2, 8,10–12,14–17	Isaiah 59:1,cf.,2–4, 7–9,14–15

Fifth, revisit each of the chapters and verses that you have written down. Write on the left-hand page of your double journal page what you think the speech-acts are that God is performing in relation to you in the case of each verse. Here, you need to be suspicious of yourself. Are you writing down just what you want God to say to you in the case of any given speech-act under consideration? If you think you might be doing this, write something like, for example, 'You *want* to teach God's word', *not*, 'You *will* teach God's word.' The former of these utterances is God highlighting my desire; the latter of these utterances is a promise.

That is, there is an art to interpreting which kind of speech-act God is performing in each instance of speech-action being considered, since there is such scope for self-deception. Thus, the correct utterance might actually be, 'You *fear* that you will never teach my word.' Naturally, of course, some may prematurely charge this approach with being 'pietistic' or 'subjectivistic', but we will explain in our next chapter why this charge is misleading. Crucially, hermeneutics has proven that it is actually impossible for us to understand *anything* without our subjectivities being involved.

But how do you know which speech-act God is performing in any given instance under consideration? Well, as you go through more and more devotional times in this style, then certain themes will build up in how God is relating to you. Against the background of these themes, certain utterances will seem to be unrelated to previous conversation, or will seem to be at an odd tangent, or just spurious. Furthermore, our own biblical and systematic theologies become a better and better filter as they develop. Thus, in my case, given my training and gifts, the utterance, 'You will *never* teach my word' would (unless I am run over by a bus) be unbiblical, for biblical theology says, 'If one's gift is teaching, teach.'[6]

There is no substitute for trial and error at this stage. It is quite possible to construct an entire delusional world concerning 'what God has promised me'. And so, self-distrust and growing in biblical wisdom – and growing in our own biblical and systematic theologies – are the most important principles at this stage. Nevertheless, you should end up with three or more columns of speech-acts or utterances on your left-hand page underneath your verse references and your question (if you had one), looking something like this:

You will teach my word	God gave Paul experience of paradise	You are kept by Jesus
God can forgive your sins	Refrain from boasting whatever God does	God is bringing you mercy
etc.	etc.	etc.

Notice that, in the left-hand column, there is a promise and an encouraging assertion. In the middle column there is a report and a command. In the right-hand column there are two encouraging assurances. Crucially, these are not just statements, but are different kinds of speech-act. You could also number these speech-acts as 'utterance #1', 'utterance #2', 'utterance #3'. . . etc. if such numbering helped you to keep track of these speech-acts in the next stage of the process (see below). It would not be unusual for more than fifty speech-acts to accumulate over the course of an extended devotional time of this kind.

Sixth, by now, then, you should have several utterances or speech-acts written in three (or more) columns below your references. So, what is supposed to happen on the right-hand page of your double journal page? Well, this is where the process becomes very much an art again. What goes onto the right-hand page is a resolution of the themes that emerge from the immediate relational interaction that has just happened between God and you. On the right-hand page, the idea is that you try to re-organize the apparently unrelated utterances noted on the left-hand page. Often, when you do this, five or six recurring themes will emerge. But instead of writing, say, for example, 'utterances #1, #28, #12, #13', as we have had to do below due to space considerations, the idea is that you will have written out again, in full, the utterances that you noted down on your left-hand journal page but that, this time, you will have gathered those utterances together in a *different order* (hence the random utterance-numbers below) beneath the emerging recurring themes – i.e. in whatever order you noticed a link emerging between a given utterance and a given theme. So, your right-hand journal page could end up looking something like this:

(a) Theme: God judged you for sin:
    utterances #1, #28, #12, #13, etc. (i.e. utterances or speech-acts that reflect this judgement theme – NB you will have written these out in full!);
(b) Theme: Yet, once convicted, you behaved commendably:
    utterances #4, #65, #43, #14, etc. (i.e. utterances or speech-acts that reflect this commendation theme);
(c) Theme: So, now God's disciplining of you in relation to this matter is at an end, and deliverance is at hand:
    utterances #8, #9, #30, #17, etc. (i.e. utterances or speech-acts that reflect this promissory theme);
(d) Theme: Conversely, God will now judge those who treated you unfairly:
    utterances #3, #5, #9, #42, etc. (i.e. utterances that reflect this promissory theme);
(e) Theme: You, however, shall be raised up, vindicated and blessed; God will achieve his purposes for you:
    utterances #7, #56, #32, #16, etc. (i.e. utterances that reflect this promissory theme);
(f) Theme: So then, since God's salvation is at hand, don't lose hope and fall into sin, but persevere!

utterances #15, #24, #3, #46, etc. (i.e. utterances that reflect this exhortatory theme).

Of course, even at this stage, there is still plenty of scope for self-deception. Suspicion of one's own motives for hearing a certain kind of message from God should be paramount. Furthermore, as you grow in self-understanding, you may be able to filter out other personal traits, such as pride, undue fears, doctrinal weaknesses, and so on. This whole approach is an art that demands rigorous honesty with oneself. Indeed, trusted others should be consulted often – in order to help one to keep one's feet on the ground. Broadly speaking, though, a relational interaction with God may often involve some rebuke, some affirmation, some encouragement, some perspective-correction, some promise, some exhortation, and so on. But no two interactions are exactly alike, even if life-themes emerge. May God speak to you clearly!

2.

Communion with Christ in the Central-Room

Christians often speak of having 'devotions', or a 'quiet time', by which they mean a private time with the Lord Jesus Christ that involves both prayer and meditation upon biblical texts. My first chapter tried to refine this common Christian tradition. Here, in addition to what has been said above, I offer a further tradition-refinement of devotional practice. That is, in the present chapter, I offer a further devotional model that I call 'being in the central-room'. This model, like all other models, has difficulties and limitations, some of which I will highlight.[1] Yet, it still has value – and so I will explicate it, as follows.

Communion and Conflict: Becoming Different to the World

Imagine a large circular central-room, with Christ and yourself seated in the middle. This central-room is the 'world'[2] of your communion with Christ – with God. And this central-room is surrounded by peripheral – though still vital – rooms. These peripheral rooms are the various 'worlds' of daily life: work, family, church, recreation, and so on.

In the central-room, the conversation is comparatively *truthful*: the Holy Spirit activates biblical texts as speech-acts that address you; and you (hopefully) pray truthfully to God. And this central-room conversation is to be *private*: Jesus says, 'When you pray, go into your room, close the door and pray to your Father, who is unseen. Then your Father, who sees what is done in secret, will reward you.'[3] Conversely, in the peripheral rooms – i.e. in life's various spheres – the conversations are potentially less truthful and more public.

The Christian life, then, is a to-and-fro movement between the central-room and the peripheral rooms. As Christians, we seek to be in the world but not of it – to be defined by the central-room of communion with God. And yet, we still go into the peripheral rooms – into life's various spheres – but do so as Christians, seeking not to be completely defined by those spheres of life. And whilst we still commune with God in the peripheral rooms – in life's various spheres – other conversations are also happening in those peripheral rooms – conversations that are different from the conversation that pertains to the central-room, as noted above.

Thus, Christians inevitably face conflict. Conversation with God through the Scriptures involves the light of truthful, razor-sharp speech-actions, insights and assumptions that build, form, reform and transform our lives unto right pathways of thought and practice – and so peace comes, perspective returns, power flows, and our 'persons' are progressively reshaped. But, in the peripheral rooms – in life's other spheres – collisions occur between the discourse-world of communion with God and the discourse-worlds of work, family, recreation, church, and so on. Collisions occur between biblical and unbiblical assumptions, practices, ways of thinking and speaking, atmospheres, environments and tribal smells. These collisions, then, are not just a matter of collisions between world-views (though this latter kind of collision happens as well).

Therefore, since obedient and mature Christians are significantly defined by the discourse-world of the central-room of communion with God, then obedient and mature Christians live in tension with the world's worlds. The world also detects this tension such that 'everyone who wants to live a godly life in Christ Jesus will be persecuted'.[4]

This tension or collision of worlds is both internal and external. Philosophy says that language and thinking are intertwined,[5] and that language and practice are intertwined.[6] And so, in entering life's various fallen spheres, Christians, whilst seeking to be shaped by the discourse, thinking and practices that pertain to communion with God, collide with the discourse, thinking and practices that pertain to the world. Therefore, to the extent that Christians internalize the world's practices, language and thinking, they will experience both internal and external conflicts between at least two sets of ways of living, thinking and speaking: the ways of the central-room of communion with God and the ways of any peripheral room or world that has begun to reshape their lives.

Communion and Conditioning: Battle to Reshape the Christian

Thus, Christians are poisoned daily. In the central-room of communion with God, the atmosphere – the practices, language and thought-forms – is comparatively unpolluted. But in the peripheral rooms of fallen life the atmosphere is polluted or altered away from biblical norms in its practices, language and thinking: mere engagement with life's fallen spheres tends to re-programme, or reshape, Christians.

Indeed, Christians who are immersed in peripheral rooms long enough without being reset by breathing the pure air of communion with God can even cease to believe in the very existence of the world of the central-room. Communion with God becomes a memory of something vaguely 'other' that now seems unreal. Now, the 'real' seems to be the immediate environment of some peripheral room or other, which becomes the new 'central-room' for the backslider.

That is, the assumptions, practices, discourse and thinking of a peripheral environment can so reshape backsliding Christians after that environment's own image, that such Christians become blind to or forgetful of the reality of the divine. Such persons forget how to leave peripheral worlds so as to re-enter the central-room of communion with God; and this forgetting becomes a kind of addiction, trap or theatrical performance that forgets it's a play.

To those still aware of God, such persons seem punch-drunk or locked into a peripheral reality. Such persons, though, view quiet times as peripheral, optional activities 'on the side' – when in fact communion with God is not so much a 'time' as a different world or *place* that it takes time and practice to enter into.

It is communion with God that involves immersion in the real world, however. The world's 'worlds' pass away; but the world where God is worshipped endures forever, for 'his dominion is an eternal dominion' and 'the Scriptures must be fulfilled'.[7]

To those programmed by immersion in life's peripheral worlds, though, the 'real' world seems to be the secular world, the world of work, or of family, church, romance, recreation, fitness-training – and so on. The world you are most immersed in seems like 'the most real world' to you, for it is *this* world that most programmes you after its own image.

It is crucial, then, to keep returning to the central-room of communion with God. To be a Christian is to be shaped by immersion in the world of communion with God and its practices, discourse and thinking, which means being shaped by biblical worlds brought alive by the Holy Spirit. But, as Christians, we are also shaped by life's fallen worlds in which the practices, discourses and thinking are not biblical. We are pulled in two or more directions at once: time in the central-room shapes us one way; time in peripheral rooms shapes us in other ways.

And so, in order to avoid undoing their Christian shape, Christians need to return continually to the central-room of communion with God so as to allow God to deploy biblical speech-acts and criteria in order to objectify, evaluate and critique – and thereby to re-peripheralize – the practices, discourses and thinking of the more peripheral fallen worlds of life. Otherwise, Christians will be progressively poisoned by less-than-true practices, discourses and thinking. They may even potentially become so reshaped by Western life-worlds that they lose sight of the very existence of God, or of a place outside their immediate surrounds. They may thus become trapped in repeated worldly patterns, and then life's true biblical priorities will become obscured, de-ranked and marginalized. Only then does the quiet time seem like a pious extra. Communion with God, though, can only be dismissed as a fantasy by those who never enter into it.

Now, as we said, this model has its limitations. When I retreat to commune with God, I bring the world's conditioning with me, which pollutes that communion. That communion, there-fore, is not *just* unpolluted. Conversely, since God created the world, the peripheral rooms have much good in them, and are not *just* polluting. Thus, some would argue that the 'world' of, say, 'raising a family' was hardly either 'polluting' or 'peripheral'. And yet, it is still possible to compare and contrast more or less wise or worldly worlds or paradigms in or through which to do parenting. So our point stands.

That is, our life-worlds, our horizons, move under different influences.[8] Biblical communion with God moves us towards purification. Less biblical peripheral worlds do indeed tend to pollute and blind us in some ways, even if they also educate us in other ways.

Communion and Criticism: Openness to Challenge by the Real

In a postmodern world, though, we encounter a conflict of inter-pretations. Which of life's many spheres, worlds, discourses, texts, thought-forms, practices or paradigms *should* be the most central for right human living?

Well, Christianity and the Bible, if they are true, should compare favourably with other paradigms for human existence and with other claims made by other religious texts and by other tradi-tions of thinking. If Christianity and the Bible are true, then they will stand the tests of critical debate and of practical viability for living.[9]

Since the Bible itself espouses the roles of rationality and of experience, then our approach here does not exalt 'reason' or 'experience' over the biblical texts. Jesus himself says, 'If anyone chooses to do God's will, he will find out whether my teaching comes from God or whether I speak on my own.'[10] One can only become convinced that biblical and prayerful communion with God constitutes life's central-room by trying it and by allowing critical challenges from sources that are external to the world of that central-room. Conversely, those making peripheral worlds central should also allow criticism according to criteria that are external to their worlds, not least biblical criteria.

Such openness to challenge aligns with the scientific testing of hypotheses. Suspicion rightly arises when any truth-claims immunize themselves from external questioning. It is weak belief systems, authoritarian regimes and personality cults that cannot stand against scrutiny, and that refuse to be challenged by sources of challenge external to themselves.

Some, though, including dogmatic scientists, refuse such external challenges because they habitually evade self-criticism. They inhabit carefully constructed discourse-worlds, and train others – under threat of an ugly scene – to avoid conversational no-go areas, certain topics, or even single words that reflect life-issues that are crying out to be addressed. Even science can be an avoidance strategy. A refusal to be challenged, then, is a refusal to live in the room of a genuinely true world.

Admittedly, the psychoanalytical tradition says that patterns of self-deceit and delusion shelter us all from uncomfortable realities. Nobody's world or discourse is wholly true, but is at best distorted. Nevertheless, God calls us into an increasingly real – increasingly biblical – world in which our practices, discourse and thinking are increasingly shaped towards alignment with a truthful authentic humanity in which reality, convictions, actions and words 'correspond' in inner and outer consistency and integrity.[11]

Communion and Compromise: Against Narcissism and Obscurantism

Travelling towards the central-room of communion with God thus involves ongoing self-criticism that is not narcissistic. Narcissism involves a counterfeit journey of self-discovery that suppresses painful truths about sinful relational distortions. Hedonistic film stars are forever 'growing' through making their movies – but we know that their life-journeys and remarks often amount to narcissistic self-absorption.

Genuine movement towards the central-room of communion with God, then, tends to come through *others'* godly observations about our lives. Genuine self-criticism does not habitually put oneself down so as to solicit others' comforting affirmation in a manner that perpetually distracts them from giving us godly criticisms.

Genuine movement towards the central-room of communion with God, moreover, involves a self-critique that is increasingly straightforward: sin is called 'sin'. Having to have the most sophisticated analysis is just a ruse that attempts to disallow honest critique from others. Central-room discourse is concerned with real, often straightforwardly observable, patterns of relating.

Thus, many world-views and life-paradigms compete for centrality. But we should enquire as to which of them 'cuts most ice' when it comes to critical wisdom, openness to challenge, and straightforwardness of speech and of analysis in relation to real patterns of relating.

False-paradigm promoters resist challenges from truer-para-digm promoters by resisting challenge itself – their paradigms can survive in no other way. By contrast, truer-paradigm promoters welcome challenge, because either they have the critical power to answer the content of challenges, or else they want to be corrected. False-paradigm promoters get angry when threatened by truth; truer-paradigm promoters are threatened only by sins, and other-wise remain calmer.

So, set yourself to face everything, and you'll journey towards the central-room! Otherwise, you'll be clinging to whichever peripheral room suits your chosen self-deceptions, and you'll be insisting – or refusing to be challenged over the assumption – that *that* peripheral room is really 'central'. The journey to the central-room of communion with God, then, involves a journey towards truthful, enlightened, healthily self-critical, wise and straightfor-ward speech.

Such straightforward speech, though, is not the language of infants. Those who want churches to infantilize them with endlessly repeated neutered 'basics' are fleeing from the central-room of truth and maturity. They are directly disobeying Hebrews 6:1–3.

And yet, the straightforward speech of the central-room is not the pseudo-sophistication of sophistry either but, rather, is genuine wisdom.

The question is: what is a person trying to *do* with their language? Power abuse can play the intellectual, but also often seeks to keep language infantile so as to keep the oppressed from gaining the maturity that they need in order to expose their oppressors.

The journey to the central-room of communion with God, then, repudiates obscurantism or 'opposition to knowledge and enlight-enment',[12] and embraces education. For the time-being, God may well meet me where I am now. But, if I insist on remaining where I am now, then God may eventually refuse to meet me there.

Communion and Cultivation: Education and Being Interpreted

Naturally, for Christians, education involves Bible study. But in Chapter 1, we said that some approaches to the Bible actually hindered communion with God. Biblical language is not just a vehicle for making statements that convey concepts or information,[13] for God relates variably to us through biblical speech-acts so as to form or *build* us as Christians and as church.

If God uses the Bible to say, 'I forgive you', it looks relationally odd if I reply, 'What eternal concepts are conveyed by your act of forgiveness?' Viewing biblical language as primarily a vehicle for transmitting statements that convey concepts or information is an approach that evades a relational dynamic interaction with God[14] – even though biblical language does also communicate truths. We argued earlier that such an approach to the Bible was really a power-bid that sought to usurp divine authority. Such 'Bible study' is thus alien to the genuine education that pertains to the central-room of communion with God.

Therefore, ironically, it is the practice of viewing biblical language as primarily a vehicle for transmitting statements that convey concepts or information that falls into subjectivism and into false self-absorbed pietism, since this practice gives the interpretative authority to the *Bible reader*. By contrast, a relational approach to the Scriptures is neither subjectivistic nor falsely pietistic precisely because it submits Bible readers to authoritative divine relational address that includes, but that cannot be reduced to, transmitted content. Biblical truths, doctrine and systematic theology remain utterly crucial in a relational approach to the Bible precisely in that such an approach submits them to, and deploys them within, a formative relational dynamic in which *Christ remains Lord* – and, therein, additionally, prohibits their use as a mere tool of human power.

God uses the Bible to *trans*form his subjects, not just to *in*form self-arrogating modernists. It is modernists who reduce the Bible to cognitive content so as to avoid relational submission to God. Modernist Christians replace the central-room of *communion with* God with the peripheral room of *communication from* God, and so sidestep the genuine education that pertains to the former.

And so, whilst all education – whether in the 'natural' sciences or in the humanities – can facilitate communion with God, this is not what normally happens in the West. Rather, Western modernists (and postmodernists) set themselves up as the interpreters, not as the interpreted,[15] and then sublate all education into that delusional framework – the framework of becoming our own 'lord'. But Jesus says, 'Nor are you to be called "teacher," for you have one Teacher, the Christ.'[16] Naturally, of course, there are still human teachers; but these are to promote submission to *the* Teacher, Jesus Christ.

Education that leads to the central-room of communion with God, then, involves us becoming the interpret*ed* who submit to God's biblical interpretation *of* us. True education is not about becoming master, but about being mastered.

Being mastered, though, is not about being indoctrinated into an infantilizing cartoon view of reality, but is about embarking on a process through which our horizons are continually expanded towards an understanding of and submission to the real. And if biblical Christianity is true, then the reality that we gradually understand and submit to will be Christ-centred. This reality will become our central-room, and other life-paradigms will be shown to be peripheral and / or false.

Communion and Community: Promoting Gifts and Reconciliation

Practices pertaining to the central-room of communion with God centre on love, for 'love for God and neighbour sums up the Law and the Prophets'.[17] Our chapter on biblical-relational lawfulness (see Chapter 3) deals with love extensively, and so we may confine our attention here to just two points – as follows.

First, love is many things because it promotes the otherness of the other. In any particular church setting, love promotes diverse persons, giftings, callings and ministries – not an idealized or standardized formal blueprint called 'church community', but (in each instance) a particular community that is uniquely shaped by its unique members and their unique exercised gifts.

By contrast, a pastor who covets the 'audience'-'applause' generated by those who 'ape chat-show hosts' performs for 'the gallery',[18] and suppresses others' ministries. Rather than promoting others into their callings under God, he or she manipulates others into the diversion of applauding him or her every Sunday. To these ends he or she also distorts the content of the preached gospel, but then markets this as 'feeding Christ's lambs'. We will see later that Anthony C. Thiselton implies that such practices are a common occurrence in 'postmodern' churches. Certainly, such churches are not journeying towards the central-room of *corporate* communion with God.

Second, love that pertains to the central-room of communion with God seeks to be reconciled with others.[19] Communion with God does not always depend on such reconciliation, however, because sometimes others refuse to be reconciled with us.

Thus, sometimes, others are too dangerous to approach. Like Lamech, they want vengeance 'seventy-seven times' and, according to Jesus, are like 'pigs' and 'dogs' (i.e. animals who do not reflect on their *own* uncleanness) who will 'turn and tear you to pieces'.[20] We are commanded to restore kingdom-relating, not to collude with abuse regimes or with the brutalism of so-called chav culture.

At other times, such others are too injured to approach. Kingdom-relating always respects appropriate boundaries, which may mean 'no further contact'. Love does not impose or enforce 'reconciliation', but sets the other free. We will look at the issue of setting others free in more detail in our next chapter.

Let us no longer think only of *time* with God, but also of journeying towards the *place* where communion with God is perfected – the central-room of our lives.

3.

Love for God and Others: Biblical Lawfulness

Christians often struggle with the question of law, which is hardly surprising. Thus, on the one hand, Jesus says, 'until heaven and earth disappear, not the smallest letter . . . will by any means disappear from the Law', and 'unless your right-eousness surpasses that of the Pharisees and the teachers of the law, you will certainly not enter the kingdom of heaven.' Paul agrees, saying that 'we uphold the law', that 'Everyone must submit himself to the governing authorities', and that he himself is 'under Christ's law'.[1]

And yet, on the other hand, the writer to the Hebrews tells us that 'when there is a change of the priesthood, there must also be a change of the law', and that this change has happened, since Jesus' 'priesthood' – of 'the order of Melchizedek' – has now replaced 'the Levitical priesthood'. Moreover, Paul says, 'I myself am not under the law', and that we are 'not' 'justified' 'by observing the law'. Paul even argues that 'God . . . cancelled the written code', thereby 'disarming' demonic 'powers and authorities', and that 'the law of the Spirit of life set [him, i.e. Paul] free from the law of sin and death'.[2]

So then: does biblical law change or not? Is biblical law cancelled or not? Is there one biblical law, or are there two or more biblical laws? Are we under law or not? If biblical law is from God, then where do demonic powers fit in? And how do these questions relate to the question of our obedience to national and international laws, or to governments – or even to bosses at work, and so on?

The Fig-Leaf: We Distort God's Law to Hide Our Sin

Well, to begin with, we should note that, as sinful human beings, we tend to hide from our sin by promoting a distorted perception of what God's law is in at least three ways:

(a) We set aside God as 'Lawgiver and Judge', set ourselves up as lawgiver and judge, and thus try to make ourselves accountable only to ourselves. Thus, we break 'the first . . . commandment' which is that we should love God.[3]

(b) We set aside God's 'rights and wrongs', set up our own 'rights and wrongs', and thus try to make ourselves accountable only to our own distorted standards. In trying to redefine 'right and wrong human living' in this way, we are in effect trying to redefine our very identities.[4]

(c) We tend to judge others, but not ourselves, by our distorted 'rights and wrongs', so that sometimes we do not hold ourselves accountable at all. Thus, we break 'the second' 'commandment', which is that we should love others as ourselves.[5]

Note, though, that in breaking the first and second commandments in this way, we in effect try to redefine 'law' as 'rules' that are taken out of the framework of loving relationship with God and with others. Our 'law' becomes non-relational, or 'de-relationalized'. Moreover, in judging ourselves and especially others by false standards – and ourselves sometimes not at all – we tend to try to redefine 'law' as a tool that is intended to prove falsely to ourselves and to others that we are righteous, or as a tool that is intended to justify ourselves self-deceptively. Thus, to the extent that we promote a corrupt version of God's law, 'law' for us becomes a matter of non-relational rules – rules that, in addition, we tend to deploy as a tool of self-deceptive, self-righteous, self-justification.

Even those who claim to obey God do the same things. Thus, in trying – in effect – to usurp God's role as Lawgiver and Judge, the Pharisees broke the first commandment and set aside God's commands – replacing the latter with human traditions, and thus distorting the content of the law by embracing different 'rights and wrongs'. Judging others as 'more sinful' than themselves, they also broke the second commandment, becoming egocentric in elitist, self-righteous self-justification.[6] Thus, the Pharisees broke relation-ship with God and neighbour, but saw themselves as 'righteous' according to distorted, non-relational rules. They cancelled love in order to serve an abstraction of non-relational rules by which they self-righteously justified themselves.

In thus redefining 'right and wrong' non-relationally in order to serve their own self-righteous self-justification, the Pharisees distorted the content of God's law, stressing prohibitive avoid-ance of law-breaking more than the paradigmatic positive pursuit of law-keeping, stressing outward actions more than inward actions, and sometimes stressing more serious offences whilst glossing-over less serious offences.[7]

Thus, the Pharisees would carefully avoid ceremonial unclean-ness, but would carelessly neglect 'justice, mercy and faithfulness'; they would condemn adultery, but would be unconcerned about lust; and they would condemn murder, but would be unconcerned about vocalizing judgementalism.[8] That is, the Pharisees broke the second commandment which says that we should love others as ourselves: they obeyed their non-relational rules outwardly in order to win others' adulation and thus bolster their self-right-eous self-justification, whilst simultaneously treating others with contemptuous superiority.

Moreover, in breaking the first commandment to love God, the Pharisees broke communion with God, and thus became suscep-tible to demonic oppression by other spirits, which is why Paul associates their 'written code' with 'slavery' to demonic 'powers and authorities'. And yet, in their self-legitimization, the Phari-sees believed their own propaganda, and were blind to their sins whilst claiming to be able to see.[9]

Naturally, of course, those who do not claim to obey God fare just as badly as the Pharisees. As Western (post-)modernists:

- We too set ourselves up as lawgiver and judge, preaching Kantian or Nietzschean autonomy from God;
- We too cast that autonomy in ethical terms, reinventing our own rights and wrongs, and thus redefining what it means to be human;[10]
- We too tend to judge others but not ourselves, in self-right-eous self-justification – seeing ourselves as 'law-abiding

citizens' even though our relating to others is full of self-centred distortion;

- We too redefine 'avoidance of law-breaking' as 'law-keeping', straining out legal gnats and yet swallowing moral camels;
- We too stress outward 'crimes' but often care little about inward attitudes;
- We too often see only more serious law-breaking as 'law-breaking', being over-ready to gloss over less serious law-breaking as though it were a trivial matter;
- We too are often out of communion with God and are often oppressively enslaved to our written codes – sometimes even to demonic forces;
- We too believe our own propaganda, being blind to our sins whilst claiming to be able to see as 'advanced' 'modern' folks who are 'no longer in the dark ages'.

Shame Laid Bare: God's True Law Exposes Our Sin

Jesus, however, exposes the truth about God's law to the Pharisees, and also to us. Re-emphasizing love for God and neighbour, Jesus stresses that 'all the Law and the Prophets hang on these two commandments', and thus Jesus recentres the law relationally. Paul follows suit, arguing that 'love is the fulfilment of the law' and that, so far as our relationships with one another are concerned, 'The entire law is summed up in a single command: "Love your neighbour as yourself."' John agrees, arguing that since 'God is love', then Christians also should love each other, for Christians are 'children of God'.[11]

Jesus' positive or paradigmatic commands concerning love, however, do not replace or dismiss the prohibitive commands. Jesus, too, commands, 'Do not murder, do not commit adultery, do not steal, do not give false testimony, do not defraud.' Yet Jesus does indeed add the positive paradigmatic commands, 'honour your father and mother', and 'love your neighbour as yourself'; and Jesus rebukes the Pharisees for neglecting 'the more important matters of the law – justice, mercy and faithfulness'.[12] God's law is not only *prohibitive*, but is also *paradigmatic* – a paradigm or model for how we should live in a positive sense.

Jesus, like the Pharisees, also stresses outward obedience to the law when he commands, 'Do not commit adultery.' But Jesus then says, 'anyone who looks at a woman lustfully has already committed adultery with her in his heart.' Indeed, the law says, 'you shall not covet your neighbour's wife.' Thus, Jesus asserts that 'What goes into a man's mouth does not make him "unclean", but what comes out of his mouth, that is what makes him "unclean"' – for 'the things that come out of the mouth come from the heart, and these make a man "unclean". For out of the heart come evil thoughts, murder, adultery, sexual immorality, theft, false testimony, slander. These are what make a man "unclean"'.[13] God's law, then, is not only against *outward* crimes, but is also against *inward* crimes.

And Jesus, like the Pharisees, reaffirms the command, 'Do not murder'; but then he says, 'anyone who says, "You fool!", will be in danger of the fire of hell.' And Jesus affirms the command, 'do not steal.' But Jesus' brother James says: 'When you ask, you do not receive, because you ask with wrong motives', which include coveting, or wanting what is not one's own.[14] Thus, even asking God to collude with a larcenous desire before any larceny has even happened is law-breaking. Such strictness of standards is not legalism, but is a reflection of divine perfection. Legalism relates more to strictness of enforcement, to distorted standards, to self-righteousness, and to demonic oppression (see below). God's law, then, is not only against *more serious* crimes, but is also against *less serious* crimes too.

And so, the unavoidable outcome of our discussion so far is the conclusion that God's law sits in judgement on our law.

Jesus also exposes the self-exaltation that is at the heart of our distortion of God's law. Thus, Jesus rebukes the Pharisees, saying, 'You have a fine way of setting aside the commands of God in order to observe your own traditions!' The Pharisees 'nullify the word of God', specifically the command, 'Honour your father and your mother', 'for the sake of' their 'tradition', which promoted what was supposedly the giving of 'a gift devoted to God' instead of 'helping' one's 'father or mother'.[15] Thus, if challenged, the Pharisees marketed the tension *between* their law and God's law as a tension *within* God's law so as to pretend to be lawful by God's standards.

This 'non-listening to Scripture' that masquerades as 'listening to Scripture' is also typical of our own postmodern socio-pragmatic or neo-pragmatic culture. Such culture falsely markets its own power bids over Scripture as being 'a possible reading of the biblical texts', and does so by falsely dismissing any notion of objective access to the biblical texts. Such culture, moreover, projects out or disowns such power bids as being 'the problem of any who challenge our ways'. Such practices, though, are merely self-deceptive self-righteousness marketed deceitfully to others in a self-justifying manner. No wonder, then, that when Jesus faced the Pharisees in the first century, and when others face the neo-pragmatists today, then both Jesus and these others are faced not just with R. Lanham's and S. Fish's 'rhetorical man', but with the rhetorical man's demonic master, the 'strong man'.[16]

But why would we, in our neo-pragmatic culture, wish to exalt ourselves over God and over his law in this way, just like the Pharisees did? Well, in our case, it is because Western modernity (and also Western postmodernity) actively pursues humanistic utopias of which the 'middle-class dream' is only a small part. Actively, we build against God, for 'God made mankind upright, but men have gone in search of many schemes'. And yet, 'Unless the LORD builds the house, its builders labour in vain', for only 'If it is the Lord's will, we will live and do this or that'.[17]

We noted earlier on what we called the Western espousal of Kantian or Nietzschean autonomy from God – including ethical autonomy from God. Thus, Colin E. Gunton argues that the Western 'ethical will', largely following Kant, refers to the self, and not to the transcendent God. And E. Behler cites Harold Bloom's view that Western culture has undergone a 'Nietzscheanization'. Kant and Nietzsche, though, viewed it as childish to require a revealed ethics for guidance. And in our Western use of the thought of Kant and Nietzsche, 'adulthood' supposedly means our 'growing up so as to decide for ourselves' what 'right' and 'wrong' are.[18] In popular culture, moreover, this stance easily becomes the justification for hedonistic lawlessness.

Not surprisingly, then, Scripture teaches us a different view of adulthood – including ethical adulthood – when David writes:

cf. Jesus - be like children

The LORD is my shepherd, I shall not be in want. He makes me lie down in green pastures, he leads me beside quiet waters, he restores my soul. He guides me in paths of righteousness for his name's sake. Even though I walk through the valley of the shadow of death, I will fear no evil, for you are with me; your rod and your staff, they comfort me.[19]

True adulthood, including true ethical adulthood, does not believe in some humanistic 'utopian' fantasy about self-empowered autonomy in some kind of benign universe that we can easily master by imposing upon it some designer reality that includes a new 'designer' reinvention of 'human selves'. Rather, true adulthood, including true ethical adulthood, acknowledges our need for God's care, his providence, his healing, his ethical guidance, his protection from evil, and his comfort. This is not childish, but a matter of realism, since we are neither the chief Creator or designer nor the Master, but we are in fact – unless we are redeemed by God – easily enslaved to forces greater than ourselves (we are not at the top of the spiritual food chain).[20] It is God who designed and created us, and therefore it is God who determines, knows and reveals what our 'rights' and 'wrongs' are. Therefore, God will judge our views of 'sin', our views of 'righteousness', and our 'judgments' on the same. That is, 'he will convict the world of guilt in regard to sin and righteousness and judgment'.[21]

Summarizing: Jesus calls us back to a true understanding of God's law that sees God's law as being:

(a) *Theocentric*, or centred on God's authority, not on our pretentious self-exaltation according to a self-deifying paradigm of 'adulthood';

(b) *Realistic*, or true to God and to created reality, not to some humanistic utopian fantasy about a 'designer world' and about 'designer selves';

(c) *Given or revealed*, or created and made known by the transcendent God; and not socially, individualistically, or humanly 'designer-constructed' locally;

(d) *Relationally configured as love for God and neighbour* – i.e. not only as prohibitive rules but also as paradigmatic relations;

(e) *Concerned with disposition and attitude as well as with embodied actions* – i.e. both inward and outward;

(f) *Strict in relation to standards* – even if the notion of strictness requires qualification when it comes to enforcement (see below);

(g) *Accessible*, such that there is no excuse for simply projecting our own content onto Scripture and calling that content 'biblical';

(h) *Convicting*, or that which shows up our sin – particularly that which shows up our judgements about 'right' and 'wrong' as being the self-deceiving, self-righteous self-justification that they are; and yet also,

(i) *Somehow liberating* – i.e. not enslaving, being unlike the legalism imposed by demonic spirits.

The Fleshly Lawlessness that God's True Law Exposes

In the light of a true understanding of God's law, then, we find that we are thoroughly law-breaking, or prone to lawlessness. By showing us his true law, God shows us our true selves. That is, 'through the law we become conscious of sin.'[22]

Becoming conscious of sin, however, is not merely a matter of intellectually comparing and contrasting two things – namely God's law and ourselves – as though at a safe distance. Rather, the revelation of God's law *to* us causes something to react *in* us. Paul says, 'For I would not have known what coveting really was if the law had not said, "Do not covet." But sin, seizing the opportunity afforded by the commandment, produced in me every kind of covetous desire . . . when the commandment came, sin sprang to life and I died.' That is, 'in order that sin might be recognised as sin, it produced death in me through what was good [i.e. God's law], so that through the commandment sin might become utterly sinful.'[23]

In other words, it is as though God says to us, 'Don't sin, it kills you.' But the very mention of the word 'sin' reminds us sin-addicts of what we crave, and the craving springs to life again. We then feel compelled to indulge in that craving, to commit sin, and thus we end up yet again going through a process that, full-blown, leads to death.

Thus, by revealing his law *to* us, God stimulates the sin principle *in* us. We then sin, and so set off potentially deadly processes in and through our very beings. Both by experiencing this death-principle, and by comparing and contrasting our actions with God's revealed law, we realize both that we are utterly sinful and that we are in a deadly struggle with sin. In all this, God himself has not sinned, but has merely revealed the good to us, namely God's law.

Thus, we really come to know that we are sinners when, in precognitive reaction to God's law, we experience a deadly force operating within and through us that we find ourselves unable to hold back, such that we may even fear for our very lives. Paul is not comparing and contrasting matters from a safe distance when he says, 'evil is right there with me.' Rather it is as though, when driving through a safari park, we suddenly find that we are not safe in our cars but outside with the devouring lions. And just as lions only really become utterly lion-like *to you* when they've actually got their paws on you, so sin only becomes utterly sinful *to you* not when it is merely 'crouching at your door', but when it 'has you' in its deadly power. It is then that we shout, 'What a wretched man I am! Who will rescue me from this body of death?'[24]

But what exactly does our law-awakened lawlessness look like? Does it have a basic structure that we *can* objectify as though we were at a safe distance from it? Well, Paul analyses sin as follows:

(a) Rebellion against God;
(b) Wicked hardening of our hearts against God;
(c) Shunning relationship with God;
(d) Separation from God's life;
(e) Suppressing truth about God;
(f) Ignorance concerning God's life and truth;
(g) Insensitivity to God's life and truth;
(h) Susceptibility to oppression by 'the basic principles [or "elementary spirits" – i.e. demons] of this world' and to being deceived by 'hollow and deceptive philosophy';
(i) Foolishness or darkened understanding and heart coupled with futile thinking;
(j) Idolatry of creation;
(k) Being given over to the sensory realm;
(l) Experimentation – or inventing ways of doing evil;
(m) Addiction or slavery to sin and its 'cravings';
(n) Iniquity – especially lawless relating to others.[25]

That is, when we reject God's Spirit, we end up potentially at the mercy of demonic spirits, who can enslave us. When we reject God's law of relational wisdom, we end up developing counterfeit non-relational thinking and law. When we reject the Creator, we end up attempting to derive life from the creation alone, which distorts our relationship to the creation, such that this relationship becomes substance-abuse on a grand scale.

Sinful and demonically inspired thinking, then, would have us reconceptualize life in non-relational or de-relationalized terms – first with respect to God, second with respect to each other. But this leads to our substance-abuse of the whole of creation.

And so, R. Lundin, followed by Anthony C. Thiselton, speaks of Western 'orphaned' thinking that is born of isolation from right relationship with God: as Christians, we think of Jesus 'sustaining all things by his powerful word'; but how do Western concepts such as, for example, 'energy', 'biology', 'mind', 'body' or 'psycho-somatic' at all connote 'human being as responsive to the omnipresent life-giving Spirit of Christ'?[26]

The answer is that often they do not. As orphaned concepts, they are defined in such a way that a 'spiritual' aspect that should be internal to their grammar is *a priori* excluded. That these concepts normally have no connotation of susceptibility to influence by the transcendent Spirit of Christ, and thereby have no 'Spirit-related' aspect to their meaning, is a de-relationalization – i.e. an abstraction of these concepts' meanings from the notion of relationship with God – an abstraction that contrasts with biblical thought, the latter being reflective of relationship with God and neighbour.

That is, the doctrine of sin is mirrored in the development of Western thinking. Being de-relationalized or self-programmed as 'being-without-relationship-with-God', we Westerners are then thrown into a pattern that sublimates (i.e. redirects in a 'socially acceptable' way) the innate desire to worship God into an organic pattern of addictive substance-abuse in relation to the whole of creation – which is why modernity threatens us with ecological disaster. Bad relating leads to substance-abuse – whether at the level of the individual, or at the level of Western modernity's greed and exploitation of the world's created resources.

And so Paul, when confronted by God's law, finds a destructive and addictive sin-principle awakened within and through his very being, a sin-principle that he also analyses in terms of the above demonically promoted and de-relationalized structure, and that is as true of us in the West today as it has been of all sinners down the ages. And so Paul cries out: 'What a wretched man I am! Who will rescue me from this body of death?' Naturally, of course, Paul's *final* answer to this question is, 'Thanks be to God – through Jesus Christ our Lord!'[27] However, he only comes to this conclusion having tried out a different but futile solution to his 'lawlessness' problem first – as follows.

The Fleshly Legalism that God's True Law Exposes

That is, Paul first tries to solve the problem of his lawlessness by turning to legalism, only to find that this solution does not work. Thus he writes, 'I found that the very commandment that was intended to bring life actually brought death'; and he writes, 'I find this law at work: When I want to do good, evil is right there with me.' Through bitter experience, Paul finds that 'I do not understand what I do. For what I want to do I do not do, but what I hate I do.' Through bitter experience, Paul finds that 'I have the desire to do what is good, but I cannot carry it out'. Through bitter experience, Paul finds that 'what I do is not the good I want to do; no, the evil I do not want to do – this I keep on doing'.[28]

Paul thus realizes that even God's true law cannot deliver him from sin and its consequence, death. And so he concludes that, 'the law was put in charge to lead us to Christ'. Moreover, he concludes that, 'Now that faith [in Christ] has come, we are no longer under the supervision of the law'.[29] Thus, it is as though Paul experienced, in microcosm, the transition from the Old Testament to the New Testament. That is, in the Old Testament (or old covenant) we see a long period of time during which the people of Israel were 'under the supervision of the law' and were without 'faith' in Jesus Christ. Then, in the New Testament, faith in Jesus Christ was introduced. Similarly, in microcosm, we see that in Paul's life there was a time of his being 'under the supervision of the law', and of him trying to save himself repeatedly, but that this time was superseded by the new era of his faith in Jesus.

Thus, God's law reveals to us that we are prone to lawlessness, but also that we are prone to futile legalism. That is, God shows us that we are law-*breakers*. But God also shows us that we are unable – humanly speaking – to become law-*keepers*.

God does this in order to show us the depth of our plight. At first, God's true law proves that we are law-breakers. But then, in our ignorance, we think that the problem is superficial, and that it can be solved merely by our own efforts to become law-keepers. Next, however, we find that, to our dismay, we cannot become law-keepers by *God's* standards no matter how hard we try (though, as we indicated above, we reinvent 'law' in a distorted, watered-down form in order to try to convince ourselves that we are 'law-abiding citizens').

That is, we find that our attempt at law-keeping becomes a matter of 'putting on the necks of the disciples [i.e. upon our own necks in this case] a yoke that neither we nor our fathers have been able to bear'.[30] Since our first fallen instinct is to try to save ourselves by proving that we can be righteous, then not just Old Testament Israel, but also sometimes even the individual Christian, needs an object lesson in which the futility of attempts at self-salvation by law-keeping is driven home through bitter experience.

In other words, part of the purpose of the Old Testament period, after Moses and preceding Jesus, was to allow humankind in Israel to discover for itself the futility of its instinctive fallen response to revealed divine law. So strong is humanity's fallen drive to justify itself as being 'righteous', that often the only way for fallen human beings to give up on self-righteous self-justification is for them to have the bitter experience of repeatedly failing to achieve self-righteous self-justification. That is, self-justification attempts, being self-righteous all the way from the level of actions to the level of assumptions, are themselves sinful or 'fleshly', and so leave us trapped in the sinful patterns of the 'flesh'.

Thus, in one place, Anthony C. Thiselton writes: 'both legalism and lawlessness are 'fleshly' in so far as they both hold out a false promise of life on the basis of man's own efforts.'[31] Elsewhere, Thiselton cites Bultmann in this respect:

'The attitude which orients itself by "flesh" . . . is the self-reliant attitude of the man who puts his trust in his own strength and in that which is controllable by him'. It is 'a life of self-reliant pursuit of one's own ends'. This leads not only to man's 'boasting', but to his becoming a 'debtor' to the flesh (Rom. 8:12) in the sense that he falls under the power of this mode of existence. He becomes 'fleshly, sold under sin' (Rom. 7:14). Far from gaining the wholeness of authentic existence, 'I' and 'I', self and self, are at war with each other . . . innerly divided (Rom. 7:14–24).[32]

In other words, by revealing his law to us, God proves that we are law-breakers who 'pursue our own ends'. However, God also therein proves that there is something deeply problematic even with our law-keeping as well. Even our law-keeping is insufficient to deal with sin, and we find ourselves still trapped as 'divided selves' who are still under slavery to sin and thus to our own destruction. Indeed, the entire legalistic endeavour turns out to be self-righteous – yet another pursuit of our own ends – a form of 'boasting' in humankind. And so, the entire legalistic endeavour proves itself to be useless and futile when it comes to restraining the flesh – for, indeed, it is fleshly itself.[33]

The Demonic Oppression Associated with Fleshly Legalism

There is another dimension to this bitter experience, however: when we try to assume fleshly authority over our own salvation, that 'authority' is usurped – not only by enslaving fleshly sin-patterns, but also potentially by enslaving demonic spirits. Thus, it is not only 'the written code' that Christ has to 'cancel' when he redeems us, but 'the written code' as a weapon wielded by demonic 'powers and authorities'.[34]

In Galatians, Paul addresses Christians who are 'thrown' 'into confusion' by false teachers. These Christians 'are trying to be justified by law' because they have somehow 'been alienated from Christ' and 'have fallen away from grace'. Moreover, they are potentially, or even actually, 'enslaved by' 'elemental spirits'. If the Holy Spirit allows Christians to 'await . . . righteousness' such that they do not have to 'obey the whole law' immediately, demonic spirits seek to impose a 'burdensome' 'yoke of slavery' under which fallen Christians are compelled or 'required to obey the whole law' right now.[35]

The result is heavy oppression, for Paul asks, 'What has happened to all your joy?' Since such fallen Christians are 'alienated from Christ', then there is also a sense (if not an ultimate reality) of their remaining 'unforgiven' and of their 'not being at peace with God', for Paul warns: 'if you let yourselves be circumcised, Christ will be of no value to you at all.' Having 'fallen away from [a mode-of-being consistent with justification by] grace', such Christians keep 'trying to be justified by law' through obsessive attempts to gain peace with God through frantic legalism.[36]

Fortunately, this situation is reversible. Elsewhere, Paul says that, 'Israel . . . pursued a law of righteousness . . . as if it were by works'. Negatively, they were 'cut off' from the 'olive tree' of saving connection to God; but, positively, 'if they do not persist in unbelief, they will be grafted in . . . again'. Indeed, why would Paul even bother to write to the Galatians if they were eternally lost? Thus, it is the false teachers who 'will pay the penalty', not the Christians whom the false teachers 'throw' 'into confusion'.[37]

For faith in Jesus – itself a 'gift' – is to be central to our response to all sins, not just to 'all-sins-except-fleshly-legalism'. Neither legal works, nor righteous works, nor even our maturity, secures God's grace, for redemption came to Israel – who were 'in slavery under the basic principles [i.e. demonic spirits] of the world' *and* 'under law' – 'when the time had fully come', and through the actions of another, namely God's 'Son'.[38] Thus, B.R. Gaventa writes, 'what changes in the situation [to secure release] is not that humanity becomes mature but that God intervenes in the fullness of time.' Similarly, when Christians are handed over to evil spirits, it is only for a season.[39]

Of course, if a Christian has already been temporarily handed over to Satan for a season – and during such seasons Satan does not simply 'flee' when we command him to do so – then that Christian is also more vulnerable (during such seasons) to the temptation to fall into the bondage of fleshly legalism, since the latter is demonically promoted and inspired.[40] Nevertheless, if you have been duped into a demonically coerced attempt to be justified by law, you simply have to desist from that attempt, trust that Christ will redeem you by grace alone, pray for that redemption, and wait for

Christ to redeem you from the demonic oppression. Desist, trust, pray, wait – and, in *God's* timing, the season of demonic oppression will end.

Demonically inspired, demonically promoted and demonically coerced fleshly legalism, then, is the degeneration of the self-righteous attempt to be justified by obeying the whole of God's law (or at least a distortion of it) in the immediate present towards enslavement to the power of the demonic demand for immediate, absolute, legalistic righteousness as a precondition for a temporary peace – a peace that soon dissolves when yet another lack of absolute, legalistic, righteousness emerges under demonic accusation. It is easy to see how this scenario soon descends further into one marked by obsessive-compulsive behaviours.

To put it another way, then any attempt – even by Christians – at autonomy from God's grace insults the cross of Christ and grieves God's Spirit. God's Spirit may then chastise us by handing us over to other spirits for a season. These other spirits tempt us into lawlessness, and then accuse us into legalism. In this way, they propagate the deception that we, by ourselves, can procure life in autonomy from God, either by doing what we sinfully want (lawlessness) or by doing what we sinfully think we should (legalism). This entire lawlessness–legalism complex, however, presupposes autonomy from God and from each other, since it is de-relationalized. Thus, it breaks the first two commandments, contradicts our created relational nature, perpetually defers saving trust in God, hinders our redemption, and is thus destructive.[41]

By contrast, the Holy Spirit, having already given a better kind of peace to Christians who rely on God's grace in Jesus Christ, requires that we 'wait' for a future full righteousness that is not legalistic but, rather, is relational – even if we wait 'eagerly' as 'those who hunger and thirst for righteousness' and as those who 'will be filled'.[42]

The Downward Spiral: Fleshly Lawlessness and Fleshly Legalism

And so, we may now gather together some of the key points from our discussion above in summary form, as follows:

(a) God initially reveals his law primarily only outwardly (our consciences are corrupted as are our laws – see later, and above).

(b) Our sinful lawlessness reacts to this law, becomes amplified, and thus becomes more visible to us.

(c) In our persistent purblindness, however, we then think lawlessness is the whole extent of our problem.

(d) So, we react to our reaction, and attempt to become lawful by ourselves, motivated by (belief in the possibility of) self-righteousness.

(e) Thus, our attempt to become lawful is still a self-righteous attempt to assume authority over ourselves in autonomy from God, and thus continues to break the first commandment, leaving us alienated from and unable to love God.

(f) Being still alienated from God, our sinful natures or flesh remain fully intact (Paul would say 'inwardly uncircumcised'), and we remain vulnerable to demonic spirits (Jesus speaks of 'Satan', or the 'strong man').[43]

(g) Thus, despite our attempting to be lawful, we find we are still lawless.

(h) Moreover, despite our attempting to assume authority over ourselves, we find that the flesh and potentially demonic spirits usurp that authority, and enslave us.

(i) Thus, we find ourselves in a vicious circle: tempted into lawlessness, but accused into legalism.

(j) This vicious circle easily descends into a downward spiral – into an obsessive-compulsive oppression of ever-increasing lawlessness and ever-increasing legalism.

(k) This downward spiral adds individualistic self-serving introversion and withdrawal to the lawlessness that already damages our human relationships (we are 'driven by the demon into solitary places').

(l) Thus, we continue to break the second commandment as well, and we remain unable to love others properly.[44]

(m) This plight throws us ever more onto the impersonal created order, such that our addictive substance abuse (see above) deepens.

(n) However, wanting to keep up appearances and hide the truth of this predicament even from ourselves, we boastfully project an outward image of conformity to a distorted version of God's law (see above).

(o) In reality, though, this distortion of God's law is embedded within an inversion of God's law: the negation of love for God and neighbour (see above).

(p) Thus, Jesus calls the Pharisees not sons of 'God' or of 'Abraham', but sons of 'the devil' himself (and the Pharisees thought the same of Jesus!). The Pharisees were not righteous, even by comparison with those who were demon-possessed, but were part of the *very cause* of demon-possession.[45]

And so, by sovereignly allowing us to fall into this terrible trap, and also through the Holy Spirit and the Scriptures, God finally gets through to us that our problem goes deeper than lawlessness. Moreover, we eventually come to see true lawfulness as involving somehow being delivered from our self-arrogating, self-righteous autonomy-drive away from God and into loving communion with God, and as involving somehow being delivered from our sinful self-serving use of others and into genuine loving relationship with others. Only then do we realize that law doesn't *get* us 'right relating' with God and neighbour, but rather that law (at least centrally) *is* 'right relating' with God and neighbour.

The problem, though, is that we also find that we are still alienated from God and, to a large extent, from our neighbour – and that, in the case of our relationship with God, we are unable to do anything about it. By ourselves, we are still 'under law' in the sense of our being under its stimulation of 'sin and death' in us and in the sense of our being under its 'condemnation', its sentence of 'death' for our 'sin' – such that Paul calls Mosaic law, 'the law of sin and death'. We realize the truth of Isaiah's words, 'your iniquities have separated you from your God.' We realize that, 'There is only One who is good.'[46] We realize that, unless God intervenes, we are lost forever.

Jesus' Life, Death and Resurrection Ministry as Satisfaction of God's Law

Fortunately, 'when the time had fully come, God sent his Son, born of a woman, born under law, to redeem those under law, that we might receive the full rights of sons'.[47] But *how* does God's Son – namely Jesus Christ – redeem us from being 'under law'? An example from life will help us at this point, where we will use letters in brackets to flag up certain points or criteria as we proceed – as follows.

Thus, if I break into my neighbour's house, do damage, steal a lot of money and spend it all such that I have nothing left, then (a) justice – or my justification (i.e. my being made right again by law through due process) – will demand certain procedures.

I will have to (b) attend a court meeting, and submit to a legal penalty. That legal penalty, ideally, will include: (c) reparation to my neighbour for damages and loss. But, since I have also (d) broken a prior covenant – as a British citizen – to uphold the law, the legal penalty will also involve a punishment intended (e) to help reform me back to being law-abiding; and (f) to satisfy the neighbour's – and also the state's – honour through a state-regulated forfeit.

This legal process, ideally, will (g) appease or propitiate the neighbour's anger. Since the neighbour is under British law, it would be illegal, and also anarchic, for the neighbour to be propitiated by taking the law into his own hands. So he is *necessarily* propitiated (h) *through* the law as one who is himself (i) *under* law.

Reparation, however, causes a complication as I have no money. How will the neighbour be compensated for damages and loss? Fortunately, my rich brother comes and covers all such costs. This does not hinder justice, but secures it, since the point of the reparation is to restore what was lost to the neighbour. I can still be reformed in other ways. Thus, my brother (j) legally becomes my penal substitute; and in any event, there is good legal precedence for this, for how else could reparation be made in such a case?

Then, something amazing happens: the neighbour says that, so long as I am reformed, he is happy for (k) my brother (l) to face the forfeit that restores his honour in my stead: so long as there *is* a forfeit, his honour and his displeasure at the offence will be satisfied. The state is also satisfied, because there is (m) a legal precedent for this second aspect of penal substitution, because (n) its displeasure at law-breaking is still duly recognized by the forfeit, and because I will still be reformed. In addition, my brother offers to be involved in my reform, and his offer is accepted and applauded by both state and neighbour.

And so, in due course, I am then (o) duly released, under legal supervision, into (p) a kind of probation overseen by my brother in which I am to be reformed. My brother then brings the matter (q) to my father, who (r) instructs my brother to send (s) a professional counsellor to me to bring about my reform.

Now then, this situation would be complicated much further, of course, if not only I but (t) *all of humankind* had committed the offence, and if (u) the property that we had damaged was *all humankind, the earth and even the heavens*. To make reparation, the penal substitute would (v) have to *be God*, for *only God* could re-create humankind, the earth and the heavens. (w) No legalism on humankind's part could do that! (NB Damage to the heavens includes air pollution and space junk, yes, but perhaps also results from our involvement in the reciprocal seductions operating between fallen angels, demons and ourselves – cf. 1 Cor. 10:20–22; 11:10; Jude 6–7; 2 Pet. 2:4–6; cf. Gen. 6:1–4, Jewish apocalyptic, and our often-unwitting worship of idols or demons).

Moreover, what could the forfeit be for damaging all humankind, the earth and the heavens? Most legal systems would (x) sanction the forfeit of death for such cosmic genocide! But, if we are part of the property we destroy, then how could there be both reparation (involving our re-creation and reform) and forfeit (our death)?

The only way forward would be for our penal substitute (y) to submit to the forfeit according to legal precedent, as we have said. But now, our penal substitute is God, and so cannot be killed. Moreover, the legal precedent says that our penal substitute has to be (z) a human being who fulfils certain criteria. So now, the penal substitute has to be *both divine* (in order to make reparation) *and human* (in order to fulfil these criteria and in order to die)! But even then, how can the penal substitute both submit to the death-forfeit and make reparation by re-creating humankind, the earth and the heavens? He would (aa) have to *both die and then be raised!* (The forfeit of death – being the propitiatory restoration of honour that is preconditional for the possibility of the acceptability of reparation, and for even approaching God's throne at all – has to happen first, prior to reparation, and thus necessitates the resurrection).

Moreover, if (bb) the offended party is God himself, then how does one meet with God in court? One would have to go into the heavens and be utterly holy in order to even approach God! (cc) No legalist could do that. And how could any forfeit, even death, be sufficient to restore the honour due to God? The forfeit would have to be (dd) perfect, of infinite value.

And, in addition, if God is both the offended party and the penal substitute, then how can God appease God? He would have to be (ee) *more than one Person!* Indeed, since reparation includes our reform, and since our penal substitute hands us over to a counsellor to ensure that our reform happens, then the counsellor would (ff) also have to be divine, for our reform (gg) involves our re-creation. So now God is (hh) *three Persons!*

Furthermore, God being God, through which law could God be appeased or propitiated? Certainly not British law! Even the law would have to be (ii) God's law, and (jj) the state would thus have to be God's too. Only then could God be (kk) 'under law' so as to be appeased through law.

A final complication arises if we defendants had, by falling into law-breaking, (ll) fallen under the power of the mob – in our case, a demonic mob (who seduced us, but also whom we seduced and courted favour with in our idolatry, such that – somehow – we perhaps also became involved in their damaging of the heavens). In order to secure due process (mm) the demonic mob would have to be opposed, disarmed and destroyed so as to avoid deadly reprisals.

But, of course – and here's the rub: since human beings actually *have* broken God's law and brought destruction to themselves, to the earth, and even to an extent to the heavens – (and have therein fallen into the hands of a demonic mob) – then we actually are faced with impending death and judgement in God's court on God's terms by God's law. Fortunately, we also really *have* been offered a redemption-scenario in which a divine–human penal substitute, namely Jesus Christ, pays the/our forfeit by his death and, through his resurrection and post-resurrection actions, secures our re-creation, reform and deliverance from condemnation and wrath and from demonic powers as part of his making reparation to God on our behalf.

And we had better accept this offer – for it is our only hope. 'The armies of heaven' will soon be on their way.[48] And so we'd better 'ask for terms of peace', for the next time Jesus Christ appears, it will not be in 'weakness', but it will be 'with power and great glory' to 'judge' all of humankind.[49] Whatever the positive aspects of judgement may be – and Anthony C. Thiselton rightly speaks of them – with both D.A. Carson and Thiselton we cannot ignore the fact that Jesus Christ also 'treads the winepress of the fury of the wrath of God Almighty'[50] – and 'No-one can hold back his hand', for 'He does as he pleases with the powers of heaven and the peoples of the earth'.[51] 'The angels will come and separate the wicked from the righteous and throw them into the fiery furnace, where there will be weeping and gnashing of teeth.'[52]

Fortunately, Jesus Christ does indeed offer us 'rescue' 'from the coming wrath',[53] and does so through fulfilling kinds of criteria that are similar to those that we have just outlined in our example above using the letters '(a) to (mm)'. We may present this complex point under a series of headings, as follows.

God the Trinity and Jesus' divine nature

Thus, Jesus espouses a Trinitarian God of three Persons – the Father, the Son, and the Holy Spirit – and is identified as the Son. Jesus also identifies the Holy Spirit as our divine Counsellor. Jesus, then, is thus divine, perfect, sinless and of infinite worth or value;[54] and criteria similar to '(v)', '(dd)', '(ee)', '(ff)' and '(hh)' above are thus fulfilled.

Jesus' human nature and legal qualification as our penal substitute

Jesus is also human.[55] And, as a human, Jesus was born in God's nation, ancient Israel, under God's law as it was revealed to that nation through Moses[56] – and Jesus respectfully submitted to that law.[57] That same law both prefiguratively sanctioned – in its sacrificial cultus – the death sentence as the forfeit for human sin,[58] and prophetically sanctioned legal criteria and precedents for a human penal substitute to suffer that death penalty as an atoning sacrifice on all of humankind's behalf.[59]

That same law stipulated that this substitute was also to be divine, a king,[60] a kinsman, and one who both *offers* the sacrifice for sin as a holy and sinless high priest,[61] and who *is* the sacrifice for sin as 'a lamb without blemish or defect' (i.e. perfect, valuable),[62] and who also thereby meets with God in a most holy place to mediate on behalf of sinners, so that God will not destroy us but will rather dwell with us.[63] Jesus is thus our lawful penal substitute,[64] fulfilling criteria similar to '(i)', '(k)', '(x)', '(z)', '(jj)' and '(kk)' above.

Jesus' life: his earthly mission and our human predicament

Jesus' earthly mission presupposes that all humankind has offended God and has been involved (collectively) in the destruction and/or damaging of God's property – namely, ourselves, the earth, and even the heavens. Jesus thus proclaims that all humankind is guilty of sin before God.[65]

Jesus' earthly mission also presupposes that human legalism is woefully inadequate when it comes to our justification. Legalism cannot restore our communion with God, for God can only be approached in heaven by those who are without sin, whereas we are slaves to sin and to demons, and cannot offer a sufficient propitiatory sacrifice to God for our sin.[66] And legalism cannot restore humankind, the earth and the heavens back to God, for such reparations involve us, the earth and the heavens being re-created and reformed.[67]

Therefore, Jesus proclaims that *he* has to secure our justification, and that in order to appropriate that justification, we have to ally ourselves with Jesus and trust that he will indeed then justify us.[68]

And so, criteria similar to '(s)', '(t)', '(u)', '(w)', '(cc)', '(gg)' and '(ll)' above are fulfilled.

Jesus' death: the legal forfeit that procures our justification

Jesus himself then pays the legal forfeit for human sin, on our behalf, in our stead, as a penal substitute, according to legal precedent. The legal forfeit that Jesus pays, or submits to, is death by crucifixion.[69]

In paying this legal forfeit, Jesus therein offers himself as a perfect sacrifice to God. This sacrifice is of infinite worth, and thus propitiates and proclaims divine righteous anger at law-breaking. Being of infinite value, Jesus' sacrifice properly offers to God the honour due to God.[70] Thus, Jesus has 'deliberate disregard', or 'scorn', for the false evaluation of 'disgrace' or 'shame' that people at the time attributed to his sacrifice on account of their false human 'honour–shame' criteria.[71] Jesus' sacrifice thus proceeds through and under God's law, and thus Jesus honours, fulfils and satisfies God's law by submitting to its requirements.[72]

Jesus thereby justifies Christians, securing our freedom from having to carry out the duties involved in our own justification, duties that we could never have carried out.[73] Jesus also thereby opposes the demonic powers who, via their oppressive regime (see above), try to enforce a false 'self-justification by law' principle.[74]

And so, criteria similar to '(f)', '(g)', '(h)', '(l)', '(m)', '(n)', '(o)', '(y)', '(ii)', '(kk)', and to some of '(mm)' above are fulfilled.

Jesus' resurrection: establishing the new covenant with believers

Jesus is resurrected, ascends to heaven, and meets with the Father in heaven. He can approach the Father because he is divine, perfect, holy, sinless and blameless. In this meeting, Jesus sets aside the prior covenant between God and humankind, since it failed to establish our lawfulness, and establishes a new covenant through which believers' law-keeping will be achieved.[75]

Thus, the old covenant of the Levitical priesthood and the Mosaic law (the Mosaic law was outwardly applied and outwardly written on stone) is replaced by the new covenant of Jesus Christ's priesthood and of Jesus Christ's law of the Spirit of life (Jesus Christ's law is inwardly and outwardly applied and inwardly written on our hearts). Those who ally themselves with Jesus by trusting in him and in his redeeming actions are then brought into the context of this new covenant with God.[76]

In this new covenant context Christians are:

(i) Eternally justified already in relation to propitiation, eternally forgiven, in a reconciled relationship of eternal peace with God, and guaranteed or promised full eternal justification in relation to reparation as well;[77]

(ii) Sanctified, or made holy in the sense of being reconsecrated to God;[78]

(iii) God's redeemed and reclaimed property, his slaves under his protection and care, and yet also his friends, his adopted sons and daughters, and heirs – in some cases heirs to thrones;[79]

(iv) Given the indwelling Holy Spirit (sent by the Father through Jesus), by whom we are cleansed or washed through an event of rebirth, renewal or re-creation;[80]

(v) Initiated by the Holy Spirit into a process of reform (see below);[81]

(vi) Initiated by the Holy Spirit into God's people, or into Christ's body, the church, in which the Holy Spirit dwells;[82]

(vii) Thereby given and/or promised eternal redemption, eternal salvation, eternal life and eternal glory.[83]

Thus, Jesus also disarms the demonic powers in that his people are now delivered or rescued from the oppressive regime explained above – and particularly from the false 'self-justification by law' principle (though, under certain conditions of discipline, some Christians may temporarily be handed back to Satan again).[84]

And so, criteria similar to '(a)', '(b)', '(d)', '(p)', '(q)', '(r)', '(aa)', '(bb)' and to much of '(mm)' above are fulfilled or accounted for.

Jesus' exaltation: his enthroned redemptive mission

Sitting at the Father's right hand in heaven, Jesus oversees and, through the Holy Spirit's ministry, brings about believers' reform, sanctification or purification towards holiness as Christ-like-ness – where the latter involves lawfulness or righteousness, the perfecting of our faith – and thus towards glory, both individually, and, collectively as the church. Thus, Jesus builds both Christian and church, completing this process after our death and through our resurrection.[85]

During this process, Jesus continues to act as our high priest: mediating between us and the Father; helping us in our weakness; and calling us to imitate how he lived on earth.[86] During this same process, the Holy Spirit acts as our Counsellor: leading us progressively into the way of truth and into assurance of peace with God – primarily, though not exclusively, through formative and transformative speech-actions through the biblical texts – speech-actions that, again, build both Christian and church.[87]

This same process, therefore, depends ultimately not on us, but on Jesus and the Holy Spirit (who, through it, also progressively destroy the demonic powers and authorities through the destruction of the work of those demonic powers and authorities, which was to oppose and to attempt to destroy Jesus and his creation and redemption of humanity).[88] Nevertheless, our efforts are integral to this same process, as we go about doing 'good works, which God prepared in advance for us to do'[89] in the church and in the world – particularly those good works that manifest the fruit and the gifts of the Holy Spirit.[90] More than this, however: Jesus oversees and – through the Holy Spirit – brings about a broader process as well: the re-creation of the earth and the heavens. Once these two interrelated processes are complete, Jesus hands the whole – i.e. the new creation, the kingdom – back to the Father, to be reconciled with the Father. Within this kingdom, we receive our inheritance or reward.[91]

And so, in this way justice is completed, since God then receives back not only the honour due to him, but also the property of his that we damaged or destroyed. Thus, our justification is achieved by Jesus in this latter, second, sense also, since Jesus therein makes reparation to God on our behalf, in our stead, as a penal substitute, and according to legal precedent.[92]

And so, criteria similar to '(a)', '(c)', '(e)', '(j)', and to the rest of '(mm)' above are fulfilled.

This account of how Jesus – in and through his life, death, resurrection and heavenly redeeming ministry – satisfies God's law on believers' behalf is, due to space considerations, only a necessarily brief sketch of *some* of the biblical doctrines that have to do with this matter. The Bible says much more than what we have said here about Jesus' life and saving work! Four further points may be noted now, though, as follows.

Four Further Points Related to Jesus' Satisfaction of God's Law

Thus, first, some have argued that divine justice would demand the restoration of all humankind, since reparation could not be full otherwise. However, conceivably, God could accept some other compensation in lieu of the restoration of all humankind, as long as that compensation came from Jesus, our penal substitute. Our argument above, therefore, does not necessarily support 'universalism'.

Second, the folly of legalism now becomes clearer. To justify ourselves before God we would – by ourselves – have to:

(a) Become sinless;
(b) Appease God's offended honour by offering to God a perfect sacrifice of infinite worth;
(c) Ascend to heaven in order to meet with God and set up a new covenant;
(d) Assume divine identity, attributes and authority ourselves;
(e) Destroy demonic powers;
(f) Re-create humanity, the earth and the heavens; and
(g) Hand the whole lot back to God!

Therefore, what folly legalism is. And that is aside from our points above about how legalism falsely defines God's law as non-relational rules, serves and boasts about self-righteousness, leads to demonic oppression, and violates the first two commandments. Thus, only Jesus fulfils God's law, and so only Jesus can procure our justification. We simply have to trust him to do this – and even this trust is a gift.

Third, the preceding point demands the conclusion that Jesus' penal substitution on our behalf and in our stead not only remains central to the gospel message – it was utterly unavoidable given that God had decided to justify believers. Legalistic attempts at self-justification are so futile, so misguided and so unrelated to what is actually required by God's law in relation to our justification, that Jesus' penal substitution in our stead and on our behalf remains the *only* possible way for us to be justified before God in accordance with God's law.

Fourth, some have rejected the biblical doctrine that says that 'God's anger is propitiated through Jesus' crucifixion as our penal substitute under God's law' as though this doctrine presupposed a barbaric view of God. Such a rejection, however, confuses sinful anger with righteous anger. Sinful anger reacts when sin is *thwarted*, whereas righteous anger reacts when sin is *perpetrated* (whether actively or passively).[93]

In full-blown sinful anger, the sinful human self narcissistically and falsely deifies the self as so exclusively and centrally important, so righteous and so infinitely worthy that even tiny offences against the self are met with utterly disproportionate, harsh, vengeful and destructive rage. Such rage is also reflected in today's Lamech-style, explosive, tabloid ethics of brutality – in what S. Hall, a few years ago, called 'the new brutalism'.[94] Sinful anger focuses only on the self, or on a corporate self (e.g. a family, party, faction, corporation or tribe), and is either individualistic, or is corporately tribal or feudal. 'Taking sides' and 'winning' are what matter to sinful anger. Thus, to Lamech-style sinners, it seems absurd if a penal substitute pays a penalty on behalf of another, since Lamech-style sinners want revenge, and desire neither mercy nor restored community, despite the fact that restored community reflects restored lawfulness.

Righteous anger, by contrast – especially in the case of God, who alone actually is divine, exclusively and centrally important, righteous and infinitely worthy – is proportionate,[95] and does not focus only on the offended self or corporate self, but also focuses on the other as well. Thus, righteous anger seeks justice in a fuller sense: it seeks propitiation, yes; but it also seeks the offender's restoration and reform unto righteousness, so that right relating or love or paradigmatically positive lawfulness is restored. Righteous anger seeks peace and restored relationships, and is thus neither individualistic nor corporately tribal or feudal but, rather, is concerned about biblical law and, therefore, about community.

To propitiate God's anger, then, is not barbarism, but loving, since that anger, in part, is due to God's *love* for the ones destroyed by sin. To appease God's anger is primarily to restore to God what was lost to God, namely God's communion with us – God's dwelling with us – which is precisely what the risen Christ does indeed restore to God. To the righteous, therefore, it is not at all unjust if a penal substitute faces a legal penalty through which that penal substitute makes reparation, serves honour, and thus secures appeasement on another's behalf. On the contrary, since justice restores lawfulness, which is God-centred loving community, then unless a way can be found to restore such community, justice cannot be attained.

Righteous anger, of course, does not at all dismiss all notions of punishment of the guilty themselves. Paul says that 'the one in authority' 'is an agent of [God's] wrath to bring punishment on the wrongdoer'. Nevertheless, Paul also says that 'the one in authority' is 'God's servant to do you good'. Even when Paul hands a Corinthian sinner 'over to Satan' it is 'so that the sinful nature may be destroyed and his spirit saved on the day of the Lord'. Not that such a sinner is handed over to Satan *until* the day of the Lord. Far from it! After a time, the Corinthians 'ought to forgive', 'comfort' and 'reaffirm [their] love for him'. Thus, Paul is very careful 'not to put it too severely', 'so that Satan might not outwit us. For we are not unaware of his schemes' – i.e. 'we are not unaware of' Satan's demonic schemes, schemes that are aimed at the destruction of biblically lawful community. For Paul, to make this point is not a matter of saying that divine anger is never destructive, but is rather a matter of saying that the priority of divine anger is restorative, which is why Scripture speaks of divine wrath that *saves* (cf. Isa. 63:5).[96]

Sinful anger, though, breeds a Lamech-style culture of pseudo-justice that seeks to destroy or permanently exclude even repentant sinners so as to banish all possibility of true justice – of restored biblically lawful God-centred community. Such cultures thus exalt themselves above God and above God's law. But Jesus' brother, James, rebukes such attitudes saying, 'Who are you to judge your neighbour? . . . There is only one Lawgiver and Judge.' Such cultures, though, follow Satan, not God, desiring to 'call fire down from heaven to destroy'. But Jesus himself rebukes such attitudes saying, 'You do not know what kind of spirit you are of.' Such cultures, though, even attack those who forgive, who then become targets of rage themselves. But even the great patience of Jesus and of his brother, James, runs out at this point: 'If you do not forgive men their sins, your Father will not forgive your sins.' And, 'Judgment without mercy will be shown to anyone who has not been merciful.'[97]

Mercy, then, is paramount in biblical lawfulness, but is anathema to a Lamech-style tabloid culture of vengeful pseudo-justice. Conversely, though, and by implication, this means that tabloid, Lamech-style pseudo-justice (cf. 'the new brutalism' of 'chav culture') is anathema to God. Scripture is at its harshest when it is confronting Lamech-style harshness. Thus, there remains a right-eous anger that is anger against sinful anger and against unforgiveness – and against other such self-deifying sins that refuse to restore love as far as is possible. But if sinful anger is propitiated through anarchic vengeance, righteous anger (even at its harshest) is still propitiated through and/or under law. Indeed, it is precisely because of the dangers of sinful anger that all propitiation in our societies must follow the propitiation secured by Jesus in the sense of being through and/or under law.[98]

Justified by Grace, by Faith, apart from Law, but still under Christ's Law of Love

The inescapable implication of the above discussion taken as a whole is that, 'no-one is justified before God by the law'. That is to say, 'no-one will be declared righteous in his [i.e. God's] sight by observing the law'.[99]

Indeed, our being justified before God could never have been something that we achieved by any law, or by any means at all for that matter. As we have already said, our justification involves a priest who is both divine and human, who lives a sinless life under God's law, who offers to God a perfect sacrifice of his sinless self that is of infinite value, who dies and is resurrected, who enters heaven to meet with God, who establishes a new covenant, who has divine authority and power, who defeats demonic powers, who re-creates humankind, the heavens and the earth, and who presents the whole re-creation back to God as reparation. Only Jesus could ever be and/or do all of these things.

That is, the justification that I as a Christian am given by God was procured under law by Christ. Thus, I receive justification 'freely' 'by . . . grace' and 'by faith' – a 'faith' that is itself a 'gift of God'. Even when my sin or 'trespass' was (and/or is) excited and augmented through my response to God's revelation of the 'law', 'grace' simply 'increased [and/or increases] all the more'. Nevertheless, God gives me justification by this grace through a costly sacrifice that – in Jesus' life and death – was a matter of being 'under law', such that I am justified through 'faith in his blood'.[100] Christ was under Mosaic law on our behalf, Christ satisfied Mosaic law on our behalf, and Christ then cancelled Mosaic law on our behalf, so that we are not under Mosaic law ourselves.

And yet, as Christians, we are still 'under Christ's law of the Spirit of life' such that 'we uphold the law', even if we are not 'under the Mosaic law of sin and death',[101] so that we do not uphold Mosaic law – unless any of the latter is reaffirmed under the new covenant, which it is (e.g. we keep a form of the Sabbath still, but in a non-legalistic way).

That is, we are *not* under one law, but we *are* under another law; and, *we* do not justify ourselves by either of these two laws, but rather *Jesus* justifies us by both of them. This takes some explaining – as follows.

Thus, when the people of Israel were under the 'first covenant', they had 'the Levitical priesthood', the 'law' of Moses, and divine 'promises'. Jesus, though, 'was designated by God to be a high priest in the order of Melchizedek'. And, 'When there is a change of the priesthood, there must also be a change of the law.' Moreover, 'The covenant of which he [Jesus] is mediator is superior to the old one, and it is founded on better promises.'[102]

And so, on the one hand, we have the old covenant, the old priesthood, the old law, and the old promises. On the other hand, we have the new covenant, the new priesthood, the new law, and the new promises. Thus, we are not 'under law' when it comes to the old law, but we are 'under law' when it comes to the new law. Thus Paul says, 'I . . . am not under law', but 'am under Christ's law'. Paul also says, 'the law of the Spirit of life set me free from the law of sin and death.'[103] So, human distortions of God's law to one side, there are two manifestations or outworkings of God's true law in the Scriptures.

Now then, obedience to God's law is ultimately about imitating God's nature, for 'God is love', and 'love is the fulfilment of the law'. Our love is not wholly different from God's love for Jesus says, 'Love each other as I have loved you', and John writes, 'since God so loved us, we also ought to love one another . . . if we love one another, God lives in us and his love is made complete in us.'[104]

Nevertheless, God's ultimate 'perfect law' of love, which our love is to imitate,[105] outworks through two different covenants (old and new), two different priesthoods (the Levitical, and that of Jesus), two different laws (the Mosaic 'law of sin and death', and 'Christ's law of the Spirit of life'), and two different sets of promises (good, and better).

Thus, and to profer an analogy, parents may love their children with unchanging love, but through different sets of instructions, delivered in different ways, at different stages of their children's development. Their love adapts to its changing objects. Similarly, God has the same unchanging love for us, but God – at an earlier stage in our develop-ment – revealed his law in an outward way, in order to expose our lawlessness and legalism *to* us. This process made us ready for our next stage of development, wherein God revealed his law to us in an inward way also (as well as outwardly), in order to eliminate our lawlessness and legalism *from* us. Not only nations go through this process (i.e. Israel), but individuals too (e.g. Paul).

All this means that, as Christians, we uphold a law that says, 'Justification is not by our fulfilment of law but by Christ's fulfil-ment of law'. And yet, the law we uphold still says, 'Be perfect, therefore, as your heavenly Father is perfect'.[106] Hence, as Chris-tians, we are to aim for perfect lawfulness in the context of freedom from condemnation when we fail to achieve perfect lawfulness. When we fail to achieve perfect lawfulness, we do not fret about loss of justification or loss of salvation, but always have the space to keep trying. That is, we are not 'law-keepers first and saved eventually', but are 'saved first and law-keepers progressively' (even though such progress can be erratic).

Moreover, this 'aiming at perfection' is, centrally, a matter of learning to love or to relate rightly, and of removing distor-tions from our loving or from our relating, first to God, then to neighbour. Our aiming at perfection is not primarily a matter of conforming to systems of non-relational rules, even if such rules can also apply to us in our varying life-situations.

Thus, it is the flesh and the demons who say that we have to 'obey God's law *in order* to be at peace with God', for by telling us this lie the flesh and the demons:

- Subtly tie God's law to a regime of terror, rather than to a sanctuary of grace, when in fact: 'there is now no condem-nation for those who are in Christ Jesus'; it is those who are 'forgiven' much who 'love much'; and 'There is no fear in love' for 'perfect love drives out fear';[107] and . . .
- Subtly presuppose a law defined *pre*-relationally as 'rules', or even *anti*-relationally as rules that promote boasting and

elitism,[108] when in fact God's law is defined relationally as love that is not elitist but inclusive.[109]

That is, as a Christian, I am given and promised justification already, such that I have 'peace with God' already – before I do any acts of lawfulness or righteousness, or 'apart from law' or 'works', or rather before I do any acts of loving or right relating. If it seems otherwise, then I have already fallen under a false teaching that panders to fleshly self-righteousness, or even possibly under a demonic oppressor who 'masquerades as an angel of light'.[110]

And so, 'In Christ . . . the only thing that counts is faith expressing itself through love'.[111] That is,

- If I am a Christian, then I simply trust that Jesus has both given me and promised me justification already – depending upon which aspect of my justification is in view. My justification comes through Christ taking my punishment for my sins – and through Christ restoring me (and what I have damaged or destroyed) completely to God as reparation – on my behalf, in my stead. The punishment (i.e. the cross) is over; the full restoration (including my ultimate resurrection) is still future, but has already begun, is promised, is guaranteed on oath, and is utterly unstoppable. And . . .
- If I am a Christian, then I also learn to love God and neighbour, and to remove distortions from my love for them.

If I refuse to become a Christian, then I am not justified before God, but have rejected his offer of legal representation through Jesus, and will potentially remain eternally separated from God and from his blessings ('Whoever does not have, even what he has will be taken from him'[112]). Whilst these days many reject the notion of a hell of eternal torment in favour of universal salvation or in favour of the view that those who reject Jesus, are simply destroyed or annihilated, scholars remain divided over the question of hell, and so by far the safest course of action is to turn to Christ for salvation. Why risk the possibility of suffering eternal torment for the sake of destructive patterns of shameful fleshly lawlessness or of deluded fleshly legalistic self-righteousness?

As a Christian, though, I simply trust that the whole 'justification' problem has been, is being, and will be dealt with by Jesus, and I get on with the art and science of right relating – which is what love is – first to God, then to neighbour. To this we now turn, for this is central to lawfulness, biblically speaking.

The Heart of God's Law: Love for God as Genuine Worship

Jesus says, 'Love the Lord your God with all your heart and with all your soul and with all your mind and with all your strength' and 'Love your neighbour as yourself', where 'All the Law and the Prophets hang on these two commandments'. And, whilst John says that loving one another – especially in the church but also outside it – is a major part of loving God, he also says that our love for God cannot be reduced to our love for each other.[113]

Thus, love for God includes worship, for 'the Father seeks' 'worshippers' who 'worship in spirit and in truth'. In such worship we:

(a) Have union with Jesus Christ;
(b) Have communion with Jesus Christ, with God the Father, and with the Holy Spirit, through Jesus Christ's mediation, in the Spirit;
(c) 'Glory in [God's] holy name';
(d) 'Give thanks in all circumstances';
(e) 'Remember the wonders [God] has done';
(f) Shun 'unbelief regarding the promise[s] of God'; and
(g) 'drink' from God's 'Spirit'.[114]

These points do not exhaust what could be said about true worship (which involves our love for others too), but form its core.

True worship, then, is possible only if we become Christians, for Christians alone have *union with Christ*. One cannot both worship God the Father and reject his Son, Jesus Christ. To become a Christian one 'calls on the name of the Lord', confesses verbally that 'Jesus is Lord', and chooses to 'believe . . . that God raised him from the dead'. Then, 'you will be saved.'[115]

True worship, though, also involves *communion with Christ*, and *with the Father*, and *with the Holy Spirit* also. The Holy Spirit enables us – as God's reconciled servants, friends, and adopted sons and daughters – to choose to actually relate with the Father, through the Son, in the Holy Spirit. Thus, we are to 'remain' in 'connection with' Jesus, and are thereby to be 'filled with the Spirit', so that we can 'worship God acceptably with reverence and awe'.[116] Even Christians, then, have to choose to commune with God.

True worship, certainly, has a *mystical* aspect. We worship One whose 'greatness no-one can fathom'. We can 'come to know him', but only partially, at least in this life, and even in the next. Paul also speaks of the 'profound mystery' of Christ's relationship with the church where, for Paul, the 'one flesh' relationship of marriage is analogous to that same 'profound mystery'. For Paul, moreover, Christ is 'the Head, from whom the whole body [i.e. the church], supported and held together by its ligaments and sinews, grows as God causes it to grow'.[117]

True worship, though, also has a *linguistic* aspect. To 'glory in' God's 'holy name'[118] means to glory in who God is – not only in his attributes, but also in his great historical deeds. Knowledge of these attributes and deeds is communicated to us by biblical language, such that we have historical-linguistic knowledge of the true God. Worship that marginalizes biblical language, therefore, is counterfeit – it is a 'worship of worship *itself*', or a 'celebration of celebration *itself*', that suppresses the historical-linguistic knowledge of the true God – the knowledge of the true God that leads to thanksgiving.

Indeed, in marginalizing biblical language such counterfeit worship also suppresses true mystical worship, for it suppresses the Holy Spirit's formational and transformational biblical speech-action – the biblical speech-action by which Jesus builds or forms Christians and the church. Such counterfeit worship also therein suppresses the biblical criteria by which we 'test the spirits', such that the demonic inspiration behind counterfeit worship goes undetected.[119]

Furthermore, such counterfeit worship also suppresses the biblical criteria by which we interpret so-called prophetic pictures. Anthony C. Thiselton rightly argues that such pictures are open to any and every interpretation unless it is a biblical framework that we interpret them *through* (even St Peter didn't know what spirit he was of at times).[120]

Counterfeit worship, moreover, remains wilfully ignorant of even 'the elementary truths of God's word', particularly 'the elementary teachings about Christ', or Christology. By contrast, in true worship, whilst we must 'keep hold of' these truths and teachings, we are also commanded to move beyond them. In true worship, it is even unacceptable to keep on repeating 'the basics' in such a way as to prohibit advancement unto maturity.[121]

True worship, then, retains its linguistic aspect, and involves: the proclamation and celebration of God's attributes and great deeds in history, the anticipation of the fulfilment of God's great promises in and at the end of history, the formational and trans-formational activation of the biblical texts as speech-acts by the Holy Spirit, the biblical interpreting and testing of spirits and of prophetic pictures, and a kind of adherence to the basics that perpetually moves beyond the basics. For loving God involves listening to God, and therein involves being formed and matured by God's biblical speech-acts.[122]

Counterfeit worship, though, in worshipping a 'god' divorced from his own character, actions and promises – from both his past and his future, from his formative speech-actions, from his reve-lation of criteria for testing spirits and prophecies, and from his moving us on into maturity – does not worship or love the God of the Bible at all, but worships and loves a mute idol, a mere social construct, a mere psychological impression. Counterfeit worship, then, is often about hedonism, showing-off and narcissistic self-affirmation, and is no better than paganism.

Counterfeit worship, moreover, emerges from church regimes that insist on speaking only 'the basics' so as to maintain their power-bases through a propaganda that keeps people infantile. If church leaders fail to promote the kind of worship culture that gave them *their* wisdom and maturity, it must be because they wish to be seen as 'the wise ones' in a kind of weekly theatre that, in fact, actu-ally suppresses growth unto wisdom and maturity for *everybody else*.

True worship, though, and finally, brings empowerment and sanctification. Paul links the notions of baptism 'by' the Spirit and 'drinking' from the Spirit to becoming part of the church, to thankfulness, to living a holy or sanctified life marked by the fruit of the Spirit, to using the gifts of the Spirit within the church, and also to mission outside the church (which, similarly, employs the gifts of the Spirit).[123]

Thus, love for God, which involves true worship, inevitably overflows into love for others and into obedience to God more broadly.[124] God empowers those who love him to mature so as to obey him, where this obedience involves our relating rightly in love for others (cf. the fruit of the Spirit), in callings that align with our gifts (i.e. the gifts of the Spirit), both in the church and in the world.

We have already written about communion with God in this book, and so now we may turn to that aspect of biblical lawfulness – or of love for God – that is love for others. In all that follows, intercessory prayer remains of paramount importance in our loving of others – but our focus has now shifted to our relating to human persons.

The Social Outworking of God's Law: Lawfulness as Love for Others

The heart of God's law concerns a love for God that can no more be reduced to love for others than theology can be reduced to sociology. And yet, it remains true that a major aspect of love for God is indeed love for others (cf. Gal. 5:14). We may consider a biblical view of this love for others under several sub-headings, as follows.

Love as biblically wise relating to others

Thus, to begin with, we should note that in Romans 12:1–2 Paul writes, 'offer your bodies as living sacrifices, holy and pleasing to God – this is your spiritual act of worship. Do not conform any longer to the pattern of this world, but be transformed by the renewing of your mind. Then you will be able to test and approve what God's will is – his good, pleasing and perfect will.' Paul also writes in this context, 'think of yourself with sober judgment', as part of 'one body', the church, in which 'members do not all have the same function', but have 'different gifts' that are all to be used to serve others.[125]

Bearing Paul's points in mind we also read, in Jesus' Parable of the Good Samaritan, that a 'priest' and a 'Levite' leave an injured, fellow-Jewish countryman by the roadside. By contrast, the Good Samaritan helps the injured Jew, despite the racial tensions that exist between their two peoples. Thus, Jesus urges that the command to 'Love your neighbour as yourself' concerns merciful right relating to all people, not just to God's people.[126]

And so worship, love for God, or biblical lawfulness, extends to embrace love for others that, (a), involves renewal of the mind so as, (b), to leave behind worldly patterns and, (c), mature into sanctified active embodied service, (d), especially (but not solely) according to the use of our gifts, (e), both in and outside the church, (f), especially in response to the discernment of God's merciful will with respect to, (g), others' observable needs.

Therefore Paul prays, 'that your love may abound more and more in knowledge and depth of insight, so that you may be able to discern what is best'.[127] Without knowledge and depth of insight, mature love is impossible, since mature love is discerning, and is thus as inseparable from astute observation and wise interpretation as it is from merciful, redemptive action.

Persons have unique identities, histories, likes, dislikes, abilities, gifts, vocations, callings, situations, responsibilities, weaknesses, sins, problems and predicaments. Loving a person, therefore, involves discerning what is best for them, given who they are, and who they are created to become, under God. It may be that such discernment dictates that we are not to be involved with a particular person – our own uniqueness has to be taken into account as well. But, in either case, discernment is essential. If I am not to be involved with a particular individual, then even this non-involvement will presuppose a loving decision that discerns what is best for the other and, indeed, for myself.

Love, then, involves lots of discernment regarding particular and unique scenarios. Love, or biblical lawfulness, is right relating guided by wise interpretation which, in turn, involves a combination of open questions, reflective listening, and silence – so that the other can speak and thus be known. Love always moves on into *appropriate action*.[128] But, as a precondition for the possibility of appropriate action, *love involves interpretation or hermeneutics*. Overall, love, or biblical lawfulness, is *very wise relating*.

Need to expand this bit, [illegible] option for poor

Of course, love can also have a *corporate* object. Thus, showing love to the poor is part of what it means to be a Christian. Thinking of international relations we could ask, with J. Moltmann, whether or not the West has always acted in a loving way towards the poor of Africa.[129] But, whether love between individuals or between continents is in view, mature love demands or necessarily involves great wisdom and insight.

Biblically wise relating versus anti-intellectualism

Love, then, is not helped by the contemporary Western anti-intellectual hedonism that 'bins' thought as 'merely academic'. And yet, under the spell of such sub-Christian culture, even some church leaders no longer wish to develop their biblical devotions or theology, as Thiselton rightly argues.[130] But this means that their 'loving' necessarily becomes subtly abusive, since 'love' without wisdom can have the same effect as hate.

That is: a right engagement with the Scriptures is a necessary precondition for the possibility of mature love, for it is through the Bible (as well as through others) that God shapes us into wise relaters. Paul makes it clear: renewal of right relating only comes through a process that involves a biblical renewal of the mind, for love does not suppress truth but rejoices with it.[131] Jesus makes this even clearer: sanctity or holiness is love or right relating; sanctity comes through the Father's word of truth; and the Spirit of truth leads us into the word and way of truth.[132] Even the future is biblical for, 'the Scriptures must be fulfilled'.[133] To think unbiblically at all, therefore, is to be under a spell of unrealism about the future. The Holy Spirit, though, through his and our engagement with the Scriptures, reprograms us for life in the real world (which is not the so-called corporate world, since the latter is lost in its own self-seeking, narcissistic rhetoric of boasting self-advertisement), and so breaks our spells of delusion along the way.[134]

Many in the church today, however, habitually marginalize the Bible through which God seeks to train them 'in righteousness', to equip them 'for every good work', to judge their hearts' 'thoughts and attitudes', and to feed them 'solid food' by which they can train 'themselves to distinguish good from evil'.[135] But how, then, will such folks love others maturely if they are untrained in righteousness, unequipped for good works, un-refereed in their thoughts and attitudes, and undiscerning in relation to good and evil? Such folks are positively dangerous – and yet some of them lead churches.

Indeed, as sinners, we are all dangerous, unless God's Spirit uses the Scriptures to highlight and to purge us of our sinful patterns of relating. And so, being transformed by God's Spirit, through the Scriptures, so as to be able to relate to God and to others wisely, maturely and with discernment, is at the heart of biblical lawfulness as love for God and neighbour. Love presupposes wisdom, and wisdom presupposes being transformed by the Scriptures wielded by the Spirit. The Scriptures are the Spirit's primary tool for making us lawful or loving – though relationships with key others also play a part in this process.

In saying this, we are not at all suppressing the mystical aspect of the Spirit's work by which 'streams of living water . . . flow from within'. Indeed, when the woman at the well asks Jesus for living water he responds by telling her about her relational life! He uses *language* to interpret her *relationally*. Yes, infants are given just milk. But very soon, they progress to 'solid food' and to language.[136] The point is not simply to be comforted and succoured mystically (although this happens), but to be transformed unto Christ-like right relating linguistically (i.e. through the Spirit's use of biblical language).[137] When our mystical relationship with Jesus Christ gets uncomfortable and 'linguistic', therefore, we should not sulk like infants who refuse to grow up, but should ask how we can relate more wisely to others linguistically and extra-linguistically (i.e. in both words and actions).

At the heart of biblical lawfulness, then, is a communion with God in which God's Spirit transforms our relating, and does so through his use of the Scriptures to renew our minds through speech-actions that expose and reshape our thoughts and attitudes, and therefore our relational actions.

With the best will in the world, therefore, 'love' without biblical wisdom remains unaware of the subtle sin-patterns that distort such 'love'. Biblical wisdom, though, functions as a referee, pointing out foul play when it occurs, and exposing our self-deceptive tendencies regarding the purity of our relational motives and actions.

[handwritten annotations: "LGBT = doctrine led → love is universal → cannot chose a favourite outcast"; "one set of beliefs about one issue"]

Thus, we must repudiate the postmodern emphasis on 'play' through which we refuse to form and referee our relating by and according to biblical wisdom and criteria. Conversely, we must repudiate the modern emphasis on 'system' by and according to which we reduce Christianity to a 'referees' meeting', or to a 'doctrine test' that negates right relating in the service of the so-called knowledge of puffed-up elitism. Doctrine, then, must serve love: 'system' is to be *re-relationalized*. Being made holy involves being transformed away from distorted patterns of relating and into right relating that is formed, directed and refereed by biblical wisdom that is worked into us by the Holy Spirit (and by key others in our lives).[138]

And right relating, or love, as we have seen, is 'redemptive caring actions for the other (whether individual or corporate) based upon biblically wise interpretations of the other and of ourselves, in the context of appropriate boundaries'.[139]

Repudiating sinful manipulative strategies

This issue of appropriate boundaries is important because, as we have already noted, love involves turning from worldly patterns and towards Spirit-sanctified relating.[140] Worldly patterns include: 'sexual immorality, impurity and debauchery; idolatry and witchcraft; hatred, discord, jealousy, fits of rage, selfish ambition, dissensions, factions and envy; drunkenness, orgies, and the like'. These worldly patterns distort or negate love, and the Holy Spirit in us opposes these – and other – sinful traits. By contrast, Spirit-sanctified relating or 'love' presupposes and/or involves: 'joy', 'peace', 'self-control', 'patience, kindness, goodness, faithfulness' and 'gentleness'. These – and other – sanctified relational traits characterize love, and are formed and directed by the Holy Spirit.[141]

Notably, though, even relational discernment and relational skills can be used to serve sinful ends rather than loving ends. Sin, often born of anxiety, uses skill sets corruptly in order to manipulate the other into enacting pre-defined role-performances that purloin the other from submission to Christ's lordship and into secondment to performing an instrumentalized function within one's own relationship to oneself in a coveted future.

That is: our sin, in its anxious craving for a corrupt kind of comfort, tries to manipulate and control the other into submitting to performing a present or future role in relation to us that we have previously imagined. Thus, manipulation seeks to impose a role-performance and a social contract onto the other that the other might not agree to if he or she could see properly what was going on. Indeed, manipulation often seeks to behave as though a certain agreed understanding or social contract was already in place, when in fact it isn't. Or, manipulation might seek consent to one set of relational parameters, but then subtly introduce another set of relational parameters over which there has been no consent (or at least no responsible consent).

Moreover, manipulation uses all manner of dirty tricks: threat of tears, or of vulnerability, induces false guilt that indirectly rebukes or intimidates the other into submission. Threat of anger, or of volatility, induces fear that terrorizes the other into submission. Promise of reward can tempt, bribe or seduce the other into submission. Accusation with respect to distorted 'law' can confuse or persuade the other into submission, partly by inducing fear of guilt. Threat of abandonment can coerce the other into submission by appealing to their dread of loneliness and grief.

Furthermore, manipulation adopts all manner of theatrical roles. Transactional analysis usefully distinguishes between healthy adult-to-adult relating and unhealthy adult-to-child relating *amongst adults*. A manipulator can act out the role of 'critical parent' in order to bully or intimidate another adult into submission as though the latter was a 'rebellious child'. Or, a manipulator can act out the role of 'nurture parent' in order to cajole or bribe another adult into submission as though the latter was a 'compliant child'. Such dynamics can even operate within the mind of an individual such that, for example, he or she experiences an inner 'critical parent' that terrorizes an inner 'compliant child'.[142]

Alternative manipulative theatrical roles include playing the spiritual advisor, the expert, the probation officer, the teacher, the counsellor, the rescuer, and so on. Conversely, such theatrics presuppose that the other also plays a role – whether it is that of the disciple, the fresher, the offender, the pupil, the patient or the victim, and so on. A tool known as 'the drama triangle' is useful in that it distinguishes between the stereotypical roles of 'persecutor' (sometimes an absent third party), 'rescuer' and 'victim'.

The drama triangle thus helps us to expose unloving manipulative strategies.[143]

And, of course, we have already noted how it is not God but the flesh and the demons that and/or who oppress, bully and manipulate us into submission. Those who use manipulation to control others, then, are not following God, but Satan. Like 'Satan', who 'masquerades as an angel of light',[144] a manipulative person refuses to speak plainly about what is going on in their relating. And so, for example, some misuse the 'sanctity of marriage' principle in order to perpetuate not a loving marriage, but an unacknowledged regime of abuse.

Love, though, frees the other from non-agreed patterns of relating, from one's own pathology of needs and desires. If somebody offers to help me in some way, and I accept, then that is often (if not always) all right. If I ask somebody to help me, and they agree to do so, then that is often (if not always) all right as well. But if I coerce or manipulate somebody into helping me, then that is not love. Love cannot serve the sinful nature since, 'Those who belong to Christ Jesus have crucified the sinful nature with its passions and desires'.[145]

Trinitarian inclusiveness that confers freedoms

Admittedly, psychosocial models such as transactional analysis and the drama triangle are not taken directly from Scripture. And yet, they sit well with biblical, Trinitarian thinking. In the Trinity, the unique Persons of the Father, the Son and the Holy Spirit respect one another, and do not manipulate one another: Jesus is not a victim of abuse by the Father but says, 'I lay down my life . . . of my own accord'.[146]

Moreover, the Father, the Son and the Holy Spirit neither simply close ranks against us sinners nor play the 'victim' nor call us merely 'persecutors', but rather reach out so as to redeem, affirm and include us in relationship. This is not manipulative 'rescuing' since it is we who benefit. God could compensate himself without us, as we have said, but instead prefers to redeem us. Thus, God is not an elitist clique indulging in only a counterfeit intimacy characterized by strategically deployed, spoken, shared negatives about excluded third parties, but a community that enjoys a genuine intimacy that shares celebrated positive things about one another and about outsiders whom it seeks to include in relationship (on the point about 'counterfeit intimacy', see Chapter 9, Endnote 96).

Now, of course, genuine Trinitarian love, which shares positive things about absent others whom it seeks to bring back from exiled alienation and into inclusion in relationship, cannot take the form of possessive or manipulative 'evangelism'. One cannot coerce or manipulate people into a mode-of-being that fundamentally contradicts coercion and manipulation.

Rather, genuine love relates closely to *freedom*. Thus:

(a) Love is not 'freedom as negation of full humanness' – i.e. love is not the worldly 'freedom to sin'. Such 'freedom' is destructive, as we have seen. Love is not lawless licentiousness, but presupposes deliverance from such counterfeit 'freedom', for love 'is not rude' and 'does not delight in evil'. Worldly 'freedom' is really slavery falsely marketed, for 'everyone who sins is a slave to sin'.[147] One cannot love others properly if one is trapped in patterns of sin for, as we have said, love sets the other free from one's own felt needs and desires, especially when these are sinful.

(b) Love even frees the other from one's own *legitimate* needs and desires, since these are met on the grounds of grace, and not on the grounds of merit. Even where a contract, such as a marriage covenant, is in place, love still refuses to control the other – even if it also refuses to be controlled and retains the right to cite and invoke 'breach of contract'. Love thus releases the other and, in this sense, is submissive.[148]

(c) Love promotes others in their unique identities and service(s) for God – and, in doing so, love is freedom. That is: one becomes oneself (and thus one becomes free) when – under Christ's Lordship and in, and as an overflow from, one's union and communion with Christ – one uses one's gifts to serve others' true unique identities. One becomes oneself as one – as part of one's union and communion with Christ – uses one's gifts to creatively promote others in their otherness – subject to appropriate boundaries (on which, see above).

Love sets people free because they never belong to us, but always belong to God. Slavery has been abolished: 'do not become slaves of men.' If slaves 'can gain' their 'freedom', then they should 'do so'.[149] We do not have 'rights' over others, but must submit to what God wants for them. We have no 'right' to relate intimately with others at all unless they freely, responsibly and appropriately sanction it with God's permission. The other is God's business, not ours: God must permit us to be involved with the other; and they, under God, must also freely permit us to be involved in their lives.

Moreover, I am God's property too. The Christian, who is already God's property by creation, has also been redeemed or purchased by God from slavery to sin, demons, death and destructive judgement. We each belong to God, and so all others have to relinquish ownership of us, as they have no innate 'right' to assume lordship over our lives.

Admittedly, we are commanded by God to submit to governing authorities, to people such as bosses at work, and even to each other. In Christ, we do not have a Nietzschean individualistic freedom from responsibilities towards others. And yet, it is *God* who says what our responsibilities towards others are. Most Western governments these days would sanction resistance in relation to an authoritarian or totalitarian regime that refused to confer freedoms upon its citizens. And submission to a boss at work should be part of an agreed contract. Bosses who use their position to manipulate employees into non-contractual actions are thus guilty of power abuse.

Helping others into the freedom of right relating

Love also promotes *the other's* 'love for God and neighbour', and therein desires that the other attains freedom – from being turned in on himself or on herself – through his or her becoming properly worshipful and properly socialized.

People rightly withdraw in order to protect themselves from sinful relationships. In a fallen world, self-protective boundaries are essential. Nevertheless, since we often do not know how to deactivate such boundaries, then such boundaries can also starve us of healthy relationships. Trapped in such relational starvation, we then often anaesthetize ourselves with sub-relational stimuli – for example, the fantasy worlds of TV serializations – and so patterns of addictive self-anaesthesia develop.[150] These patterns reinforce withdrawal, and so on, down a deadly whirlpool into introversion.

As withdrawal advances, persons become more and more disengaged or detached from social reality, and so are less and less able to think truly about themselves – for philosophy has shown that true self-understanding is 'only' possible through reading 'the signs' that we put out into the world through our *social* actions.[151]

Even when we begin to come out of withdrawal, we initially bring our 'turned-in on ourselves' problem with us, and therefore we tend to relate to others in a manner that reduces them to a function within our relationship to ourselves, as we noted above. We thus often bring into relationship our addictive self-anaesthe-tizing tendencies, sometimes moving from addictive self-anaes-thesia through *sub*-relational stimuli to addictive self-anaesthesia through *relational* stimuli.

Love for the other, therefore, tackles such tendencies when permitted to do so, and thus helps the other to grow back into right relating, first to God, then to neighbour – and thus into freedom. Thus love, as 'the perfect law', 'gives freedom'.[152] Love, therefore, and within appropriate boundaries, seeks to heal others by helping them to refine how they relate to God and neighbour. Love asks: 'What is it that this person needs to learn next about healthy relating to God and neighbour?'

Helping a withdrawn person to grow into right relating to God and neighbour brings them back to life, back to truer perspectives, back to freedom from addictive self-anaesthetizing patterns, and back to the freedom of being themselves that comes through them doing what they are designed to do – which is: to relate well to God and to others, in accordance with their unique identities and gifts. This way of helping others into right relating need not at all be patronizing, but may be part of an interaction in which one's own relating is also refined – for 'as iron sharpens iron, so one . . . [person] sharpens another'.[153]

Such redemptive action into others' lives – within appropriate boundaries – is a large part of what our holiness is. To a large extent, holiness is love – or right relating to God and others. And since God redeems fallen people, then love for people co-operates with God by learning to love others redemptively. Holiness is thus inseparable from consecration – within appropriate boundaries –

to the redemptive loving of others through the use of our gifts (i.e. our gifts of the Spirit).

Such holiness is not possible for the individualist or for the isolationist, since such holiness is fundamentally relational in character. Holiness and love, therefore, are not opposites, but are coincident. Therefore, legalism that marginalizes right redemptive relating is biblically illegal and unholy, and presupposes a misunderstanding of God's law and of holiness. To be holy, 'Each one should use whatever gift he [or she] has received to serve others, faithfully administering God's [redemptive] grace in its various forms'.[154]

The Advancement of God's Law: Lawfulness and Human Laws

Moving on, then just as our love for others is a major aspect of our love for God, then so our relationship to the human laws that pertain to various levels of government (and to other human authorities) is to constitute a major aspect of our love for others. Thus, love as biblical lawfulness is to be the paradigm according to which God's law advances in its shaping of, in our negotiations with, and in our submission to, human laws. We may consider a biblical view of this advancement of God's law under three sub-headings, as follows.

Submission, testimony and refinement

And so, to begin with, we noted earlier that Paul writes, 'Everyone must submit himself to the governing authorities.' This is perhaps a surprising command, coming from Paul, because Paul was forever *not* submitting to 'governing authorities.' He endured 'beatings', 'imprisonments', 'five times . . . the forty lashes minus one', and other perils – including flight as a 'wanted man'. So how can Paul say, 'he who rebels against the authority is rebelling against what God has instituted',[155] since then either Paul, too, is presumably a rebel, or the authority is presumably disobedient to God and not what Paul says it is?

In part, the answer to this question is that the authorities often do the right thing in God's eyes. They are 'God's servant to do you good' if you 'do right', and they are 'God's servant', an agent of wrath to bring punishment on the wrongdoer'. Thus, Paul was not iconoclastic, anarchic or anti-authority. He suffered only as a 'servant of Christ'. Peter adds that one should resist human authorities only when they prohibit one from being 'a Christian' who does 'good'. In such circumstances, one 'should . . . continue to do good', 'according to God's will'.[156]

Rebellion against authorities, then, is permitted only when they oppose Christianity itself, good deeds or anointed apostles. And even then, 'God's will' must be taken into account. This is because it is quite possible for it to be God's will for us to endure or forbear an oppressive regime – particularly, (a), when we are commanded to choose our battles according to our callings or, (b), when we ourselves are under God's discipline.

Thus, (a), an oppressive and/or authoritarian regime might wrongly threaten destruction either as a disproportionately harsh punishment for genuinely wrong action or as a punishment for apparently right action. In either case, though, it is not necessarily always right to charge into battle against the regime and into a supposedly sanctioned martyrdom.

Thus, Moses ran away into the desert in order to avoid probably disproportionate reprisals when, arguably, Moses *had* actually sinned by killing the Egyptian who was beating an Israelite. Moses' time for engaging with the oppressive authorities was later, when he had God's anointing to do so. And when 'Jesus' brothers' wanted Jesus 'to become a public figure', and to 'show' himself 'to the world', Jesus' response was, 'The right time for me has not yet come'. Even for Jesus, then, the time for engaging with oppressive authorities was often later than others wanted, for the time for Jesus' engagement with oppressive authorities was when he had the Father's anointing to do so. For the zealot, though, 'any time is right' – for the zealot does not submit to God's leading, since he cannot wait to assume authority over God and to take matters into his own hands. And so he dies – not at all as a righteous martyr, but as one who has 'offered unauthorised fire before the LORD'.[157]

Sometimes active rebellion against authoritarian regimes is right. Sometimes hiding from such authoritarian regimes is right. One's calling, or God's specific will for one's life, and

especially God's anointing pertaining to the particular season at
hand, must decide. Of course, if one hides or withdraws from
oppressive regimes, then Satan will likely accuse one of 'not
being willing to lose one's life for Christ' or of 'being a Jonah'.
But these are almost always false accusations – demonic temptations designed to block a future ministry. That is, there are
particular 'good works' that 'God' has 'prepared in advance for
us to do'. Therefore, it is best if we get on and do these *particular*
good works instead of submitting to any false impulses towards
martyrdom, even if 'This calls for patient endurance and faithfulness on the part of the saints'.[158]

And so, (b), sometimes it is actually wrong to rebel against
oppressive authorities even when it seems right. When Israel
sinned they were commanded to submit to oppressive Babylonian
authorities. God ordained it that Israel should experience oppressive masters for a season in order to teach Israel the difference
between submission to the true God and submission to idols.[159]
Thus, it is not wise to presume to be an apostolic challenger of
authorities when one is in exile under divine discipline oneself.
There is no point in our riding into battle against our enemies if
the Lord is no longer with us in the battle. The options in such
instances are either patient endurance coupled with repentance
and waiting on God for deliverance – or an unnecessary, self-righteous self-destruction.

These considerations, though – considerations that caution us
against overhasty rebellion against human authorities – do not
seem to fully explain Paul's complete silence about any kind of
sanctioned rebellion against human authorities in Romans 13:1–7.
Are there other reasons not to challenge human authorities –
reasons that we have thus far missed?

Well, clearly there are times when Paul challenges worldly
governments as we have seen. But he does not seem to command
such challenges as though they were a matter of general obedience
to God. Paul even writes, 'What business is it of mine to judge
those outside the church? Are you not to judge those inside? God
will judge those outside.'[160]

We may turn again to Anthony C. Thiselton to help us with the
complexities here. Thus, Thiselton writes, 'it is not for the church
to try to impose its corporate house rules upon' 'those outside' the

[handwritten left margin: Gandhi – civil disobedience as love]

[handwritten marginal marks: X, ?]

[handwritten bottom: But we've been taught that now (see earl.er)]

church, for 'they have God as their judge'.[161] But Thiselton is quick
to add that:

> This does not imply that the church should keep silent about what
> God has ordained for the welfare of humanity. But it places its impo-
> sition of 'rules of conduct' for the internal affairs of the church and
> the external affairs of the world on a different footing. Against the
> laissez-faire, consumerist culture of today, Paul asserts that to become
> part of the Christian community is explicitly to place oneself under
> the discipline of a Christian lifestyle.[162]

That is, the church is to espouse the discipline of a Christian lifestyle for Christians; and the church is to impose certain 'rules of
conduct' for its internal affairs. But the church is not to impose
these outworkings of Christ's law on the world outside the church.
The church should only *testify* to what God 'has ordained for the
welfare of humanity' to those outside the church. cf . Ghandi

That is, Christians are not to impose Christian 'law' or 'rules'
upon the world by a will-to-power, but are to testify to the world
concerning Christian 'law' or 'rules'. Conversely, Christians are
to submit to Christian 'law' or 'rules' themselves, whilst still
refusing to impose the same on the world. As Jesus says: 'Do not
resist an evil person', for the way of the cross is not that of the will-
to-power. Nevertheless, the way of the cross is consistent with a
testimony in favour of the will-to-love – a testimony that exposes
the will-to-power as sin.[163]

That is, the authoritarian traditionalist submits to every human
law slavishly, but thereby falls into idolatry, for all human laws
are subject to refinement according to our growing understanding
of biblical law. Conversely, the anarchic iconoclast rages against
every human authority and law, but thereby either falls into an
opposing authoritarianism of the idolatrously exalted self or falls
into an opposing authoritarianism of a different – often 'tribal' or
'protest-group' – kind.

Thus, the demonstrations in Britain during 2011–12 outside St
Paul's Cathedral in London were in a sense anti-establishment.
And yet, at least one clergyman in St Paul's viewed the demonstrations as being authoritarian in that they imposed upon the cathedral a mode of complaint that was alien to the cathedral – leaving

the cathedral no room to complain in its own non-authoritarian way. Indeed, such was the authoritarianism of the demonstrators that even some of their sympathizers could not be told that they were being authoritarian!

And so, only prophetic tradition-refinement avoids the authoritarian pitfalls of traditionalism and iconoclasm. The prophetic tradition-refiner seeks to accommodate to what is good about human authority and law, but also seeks as far as is humanly possible to work with others within the 'system' – through proper channels of complaint and protest if necessary – so as to improve it.

Paul, then, would never ordinarily encourage rebellion against human authorities. Such rebellion is the last resort of long-oppressed peoples, not the 'right' of self-righteous iconoclasts. The way forward, then, is ordinarily a matter of submission to human authorities – of testimony and of co-operation in order to bring about reforms from within.

Qualified respect for human judgements

Another reason why Paul does not encourage rebellion against human authorities relates to his mixed view of human conscience and judgements. Paul writes, 'I care very little if I am judged by you [Corinthians] or by any human court; indeed, I do not even judge myself. My conscience is clear, but that does not make me innocent. It is the Lord who judges me. Therefore judge nothing before the appointed time; wait till the Lord comes.'[164]

Thiselton argues that, here, Paul contrasts future divine infallible judgement with present human fallible judgement. For Paul, Thiselton argues, human 'conscience' is as fallible as human 'public opinion' when both are compared with divine judgement.[165] Drawing on 'C.A. Pierce's analysis of conscience', Thiselton writes:

Pierce rightly argues that the sense of remorse or pain consequent on infringing the standards set internally by the conscience can never in Pauline thought be absolute, for *a person's conscience derives its criteria and standards from the character and moral mind-set of the moral agent.*

Hence it is like the pointer on a dial which registers *wrong* or *clear depending on how the mechanism has been set*. Thus a person's conscience may be oversensitive and overreact, or undersensitive and underreact. Thus Paul can place no trust in the relativity of human conscience *as over against the absolute verdict of God*, although conscience has value as a *relative* indicator of self-approval or self-disapproval'.[166]

For Paul, then, a clear conscience is no guarantee of innocence because conscience is not exempted from human fallenness. That is, conscience can be illegitimately clear.

Conversely, we implied earlier that, when one was under the bondage of fleshly legalism, one's conscience could be illegitimately burdened by demonic or fleshly oppressive demands for immediate, total obedience to the whole of a distorted, de-relationalized version of 'God's law' as a supposed precondition for 'justification' – as though the latter were by law, works, or merit. Such demands should be resisted, as we argued earlier. That is, again, conscience can also be illegitimately burdened.

Thus, whilst Paul's additional point about the fallibility of 'any human court' might seem to encourage rebellion against human authorities, Paul is also saying that his own judgement about the fallibility of human courts in any given instance is itself also fallible, which cautions us against any such rebellion. There is a lesson in humility here for us today: the occasional violent riots or so-called protests in London and elsewhere that purport to be over matters of conscience and that damage others' property indiscriminately are – at best – criminal actions flowing from a self-arrogated, distorted conscience that unbiblically refuses to admit its own fallibility.

Nevertheless, both conscience and law-courts may also bear true testimony against us to the extent that God's law really is written on our hearts and into our human laws. Thus Paul says, 'it is necessary to submit to the authorities, not only because of possible punishment *but also because of conscience*.'[167]

That is, and against what I have heard some evangelicals say, we cannot just cite 'Paul on the fallibility of conscience and courts' and 'fleshly legalism' in order to justify 'refusal to submit to authorities' in legal matters. Rather, we are to affirm authorities and courts wherever possible. It is the practice of *denying people access to justice* that the Bible forbids, not the practice of *justice itself!*[168]

One passage that is often abused in order to shun human courts illegitimately is 1 Corinthians 6:1–8, where Paul comments on lawsuits between believers. Thiselton explains, however, that:

(a) Paul had 'trivial' or 'small claims' 'cases' in view – cases that could legitimately be settled 'out of court', just as they can in Britain today;

(b) Paul had corrupt 'local' courts in view, not the major 'criminal courts of the Roman government' where one could still find 'justice';

(c) Paul did not have genuine quests for justice in view, but the bad witness of the manipulative use of corrupt 'local' courts – i.e. by rich materialistic Christians who were using their wealth to assert their 'rights' against poor Christians in a manner that contradicted the Christian principle of Christlike 'sacrificial service of others'.[169]

Thus, Paul was not advocating a kind of pseudo-Christian separatism that distrusted law-courts *per se.*

Therefore, we should have qualified respect for human conscience and for human courts – that is, for human judgements. Conscience and courts very often judge us rightly. Conversely, therefore, where conscience seems to contradict the judgement of a legal authority then the problem is as likely to be with our conscience as it is with the legal authority – for both are human. This means that our default response to such a scenario is to be submission to the legal authority whilst we interrogate conscience, in case the latter is wrong. If the legal authority does eventually prove to be wrong, then testimony through proper channels – rather than us trying to impose our convictions on the legal authority through an authoritarian will-to-power – is the Christlike way ahead.

Confusion can arise when both fleshly/demonic legalistic demands and right legal compunctions coexist in relation to different aspects of the same case. Thus, one could rightly process a matter legally, but one could then also be caught in a demonic trap of fleshly legalism, especially if one were handed over to

int this fleshy legalism?

Satan for the sin that constituted the legal infringement in the first instance. In such a case, the thing to do is to interrogate the whole matter biblically, following right legal compunctions, but resisting wrong legalistic compulsions (though, when one is actually handed over to Satan, there are limits to the extent to which this may be possible, for the enemy is then permitted a certain amount of destructive authority). Then – after one has followed any outstanding right legal compunctions – one should proceed as we directed earlier in relation to fleshly legalism (see above).

Resonance, witness, love and wisdom

But how does Paul's command that 'Everyone must submit himself to the governing authorities' square with his assertion that 'love is the fulfilment of the law'?[170]

Well, first, Christians should obey both the positive lawful paradigm of love for God and neighbour and the negative lawful prohibitions that Jesus, Paul and others reiterate in the New Testament. Such prohibitions include the commands, 'Do not commit adultery', 'Do not murder', 'Do not steal', and 'Do not covet' (and so on). National and international laws also tend to reiterate many such prohibitions (adultery and coveting aside) alongside more paradigmatic positive requirements consistent with love, and so there is often no conflict, but rather there is often resonance, between Christ's law and many state laws. Therefore, we should obey such state laws. After all, we are still 'under Christ's law'.[171]

Second, love seeks to respect others by honouring legal, vocational and other social contracts and expectations. Paul writes: 'we are taking pains to do what is right, not only in the eyes of the Lord but also in the eyes of men.'[172] After A. Schweitzer, Thiselton aligns with Paul's point that we Christians belong to two overlapping eras – that of the kingdom and that of the present age. Thus, we witness to those who still belong only to the present age. Paul writes: 'To those under the law I become like one under the law . . . so as to win those under the law' and, 'Though I am free and belong to no man, I make myself a slave to everyone, to win as many as possible.'[173] That is, love accommodates itself as far as is possible to legal – and other social and cultural – restrictions, so as not to destroy redemptive relationships.

Third, love, and not fleshly legalism, should determine the *way* in which we obey national and international laws. If we cannot justify ourselves even through Spirit-led true obedience to God's true law, then certainly we cannot justify ourselves through demonically demanded distorted obedience to distorted law. And human laws *are* distorted as we saw earlier, which is why Christ's law judges human law.[174] Therefore, genuine lawfulness under Christ's law accommodates itself to national and international laws in the mode of love, discerning how society actually practises its law and how government would have one 'be lawful' in each and every instance under consideration – 'so that we may not offend them'.[175] Certainly, if an authority does not demand fleshly legalistic observance of some of its laws, then Christ will not demand such fleshly legalistic observance of those same laws either, for Jesus said to the woman caught in adultery: 'Has no-one condemned you? . . . Then neither do I condemn you.'[176] And when God sent Moses back to Egypt it was certainly not in order to ensure that Moses would face murder charges.[177] Biblically, forgiveness is lawful because forgiveness often creates lawfulness; conversely, 'he who has been forgiven little loves little.'[178]

Fourth, after Paul reiterates the commands, 'Do not commit adultery', 'Do not murder', 'Do not steal', and 'Do not covet', he also says, 'Love does no harm to its neighbour.'[179] Thus, there are both 'rights and wrongs' and 'good and bad outcomes' to consider in true, biblical, relational lawfulness. Here, philosophy aligns with Paul, and stresses both 'Deontological' or 'Formalistic' ethics ('obligation' to 'right' 'principles') and 'Axiological' or 'Teleological' ethics ('obligation' to 'good' 'valued' 'goals').[180] Overstressing deontological or formalistic 'rights and wrongs', or doing what is 'right' regardless of the consequences, can bring harm to one's neighbour. We have called this de-relationalized, system-based distortion of law 'fleshly legalism'. Conversely, overstressing axiological or teleological 'good and bad outcomes' – regardless of which 'rights and wrongs' have to be shelved, relativized, swept under the carpet, or covered up – can seem to protect others or oneself in the short term, but may also lead to even greater harm being done to others or to oneself in the long term 'when the truth comes out'. We may call this relationally distorted, non-refereed, relativistic, system-negating distortion of law socio-pragmatic[181] – or neo-pragmatic – consequentialism. Love, or true biblical lawfulness, however, avoids both harmful legalism and harmful cover-ups. This is sometimes a very difficult tightrope to walk and can demand great wisdom in any given case under consideration. Yet again, therefore, being steeped in and formed through the Holy Spirit's use of the Scriptures in order to reshape and renew our minds and lives in accordance with biblical wisdom proves to be the precondition for the possibility of our practice of biblical lawfulness as love.

of difference in relation to the interpretation of certain biblical texts. And yet, these days, one could still easily imagine a Christian within almost any church speaking in such a way in order to rebuff a legitimate confrontation over a blatantly obvious issue – for example, adultery.

Our point is that, these days, both 'intellectuals' and 'non-intellectuals' frequently church-hop to churches where popular relativism is sufficiently embraced, or where the teaching is sufficiently vague and nebulous, in order to persistently avoid awkward confrontations of their own unfaced personal and relational failings. That is, because of relativistic self-evasion, deep personal and relational flaws can go unchecked or unconfronted for years or even decades.

Distorted Theological Persuasions as a Cause of Church-Hopping

Clearly, then, distorted theological persuasions in the church can also cause church-hopping. It is just a bit too convenient to blame church-hopping only on individuals' relational problems or only on individuals' cultural sinfulness – genuine though these issues are.

Indeed, in my view, the main causes of church-hopping are distorted theological persuasions that result in distorted church structures, in distorted styles of worship, in distorted pastoral practices and in distorted witness. Indeed, such distortions become inevitable when churches marginalize biblical theology since, then, such churches inevitably end up propagating non-biblical systems of thinking and behaviour – either covertly or (even) overtly.

People can feel theological distortions

Thus, often, people leave churches because they intuitively sense that some kind of 'alien' or 'dodgy' theology has been covertly directing actual church practices. They know that their church leaders pay 'lip-service' to the Bible but their adverse experience of church makes them suspect that something else – something

Part Two

Relating Faith: Church

4.

Church Distorted by Modernity

The Parable of the Talents[1] implies that we Christians will be judged in relation to whether or not we use our spiritual gifts (i.e. our gifts of the Spirit) wisely. Admittedly, the word translated as 'talent' refers to a unit of money, and not to a spiritual gift. Nevertheless, the parable clearly suggests that we each have a personal responsibility to steward wisely that which we have been given, which includes our spiritual gifts.

Naturally, though, when God judges us in relation to this matter he will not only take into account what we have achieved – or what we have attempted to achieve – through using our spiritual gifts. Rather, God will also take other factors into account as well.

Thus, first, if the church suppresses individuals' ministries, or promotes a kind of pseudo-Christianity that does not involve the kind of discipleship-training through which individuals can learn to discover and use their spiritual gifts, then God will judge such individuals to be less culpable for failings related to using, or to attempting to use, their spiritual gifts. For when Jesus was rejected, even *he* struggled to exercise a ministry: 'He could not do any miracles there, except lay his hands on a few sick people and heal them.'[2] How much more will *we* struggle to be fruitful if we find that we too are rejected?

Second, there are also questions that concern maturity, call and season. Somebody with a teaching gift may not be mature enough to teach adequately yet. Or, somebody with a healing gift may not yet have realized that they have this gift, or may not yet have received a call to use it. Alternatively, somebody who is under God's discipline may have to step back from using their gifts in certain ways for a season, as might somebody who has just been bereaved or taken ill.

Since we can't do much about this second set of issues except continue to grow as Christians, then we may focus on the first set of issues, as follows.

How the Church Blocks Right Relating, Gifts and Ministries

Thus, in my view, the church too often blocks individuals from using their spiritual gifts because it has not adequately guarded itself against certain aspects of Western thinking.

The theologian Leonardo Boff links the Western philosophical legacy of Platonism to the problem of overly hierarchical church-leadership structures, and argues that a more biblical (i.e. non-Platonic) view of God as the Holy Trinity will help us to address this problem. Another theologian, Colin E. Gunton, links the same Platonic legacy to ensuing problems in the history of theology that have to do with how to relate the unity or oneness of God to the three Persons of God. Additionally, Gunton and Boff both link the question of the character of God to the question of the nature of God's creation, and both thinkers come to important conclusions to do with how the unity or oneness of God's creation relates to the diversity or many-sided character of God's creation. Here, drawing on Boff's and Gunton's arguments, we may provisionally conclude that since, in 'Platonized' Western thinking, God was viewed as *one* 'substance' or Spirit from which/whom *three* Persons emanated then, in Western thought and culture, and notably in modernity (see below), this viewpoint led to human persons being subordinated beneath and conformed to 'systems'. Such 'systems' included political systems of government, economic systems, systems of church structure or church leadership, systems of industrialization, scientific and/or technological systems, and so on. In such 'Platonized' 'modern' Western thinking and culture, therefore, the uniqueness of human persons, and also relationships between persons, were under-emphasized.[3]

Biblically, however, God is three unique Persons who are eternally interrelating in one relationship. Thus, divine 'oneness' is not primarily a 'fixed substance' or 'system' but a dynamic love relationship. Biblically, then, divine unique Persons and divine relationship are both prioritized, and are not subjugated beneath 'divine substance' or 'system'. This biblical teaching – when applied to human persons who, after all, are to reflect the divine image – reinstates important emphases on unique human persons and on good human relating, whether in cultural, political, industrial or church-related (or any other) contexts of life.[4]

Modernity, though, tends to reduce persons to 'cogs' in the economic or industrial machine, and thereby tends to suppress persons' unique identities and relationships, and so alienates them.[5] J. Habermas talks about 'system' becoming separated from 'life-world'.[6] That is, if people are treated as mere 'units' of economic production,[7] or as 'assets' to be traded by the privileged few, then people's unique identities and gifts – their lives or life-worlds – can be suppressed beneath the conveyor-belt 'always-the-sameness' of industrial processes streamlined for maximum economic efficiency – i.e. beneath 'system'. People forced into such a 'boundless etcetera' of over-regulated patterns then experience ill effects in their relationships.[8] That is, if financial 'system' is allowed to drive everything, then people – including even very well-paid people – can be reduced to near-slavery and can thus be deprived of valuable relational and/or family-time as they are forced into tightly controlled corridors of individuality-suppressing, repetitive and non-creative behaviour during very long workdays, often for years on end.

That is, the unbiblical subordination of unique persons' life-worlds – i.e. their unique identities, gifts, and relationships – beneath 'systems' oppresses millions of people. The real needs and gifts of relational and unique persons are flattened beneath the systematized demands of distorted industrialized socio-economic cultures. Uniquely gifted persons and their relationships are treated as 'expendables', and people often become slaves to the 'dehumanizing' 'collectives' of certain socialisms or to the 'homogenizing', market-driven forces of certain capitalisms.[9]

Admittedly, Scripture says that our work is also potentially a source of blessing, and is not only a cursed outworking of human fallenness.[10] Moreover, when faced with the curse, many make noble, unavoidable and sometimes terrible sacrifices in their work-lives in order to provide for others. We would not wish to devalue their efforts. Nevertheless, the harrowing dystopian predictions of films such as *1984, Brave New World,* or *Gattaca* warn us of the consequences of subjecting uniquely gifted persons and relationships to oppressive 'systems'. Political calls for 'noble sacrifices', 'hard work' and for 'getting up early in the morning' can help perpetuate great evils as well as great goods.

In *Gattaca*, for example, genetically 'impure' individuals are expendable. Retina scans and dust-collection devices sift for genetically below-par DNA in order to stop those with a genetically deficient make-up from taking part in society. Such persons are ferreted out and excluded from the socio-economic 'system'. In *Gattaca*, persons are only worth preserving if their genetics serve the system's requirements.

And it is not just in extreme cases – such as in Nazi Germany before and during World War II – that 'systems' crush those not meeting their 'required criteria'. Western history is littered with examples analogous to *Gattaca*. And we are not just talking about communism either. Colin E. Gunton actually *compares* authoritarian, communist-bloc 'collectives' with an American 'homogeneity' in which, under the guise of 'freedom', many millions are conformed to media-promoted and market-driven, stereotypical, social behaviours.[11] After all, 'all good Americans like football or baseball', don't they?

It is against this kind of cultural backdrop, then, that Western churches often suppress people's gifts and ministries. Indeed, Western churches often become 'systems' that demand conformity in ways that suppress both right relating and personal uniqueness, gifts and ministries.

And so, for example, we have said that 'love sums up the law and the prophets';[12] but in some ultra-Reformed churches, you'd think that the Scriptures said, 'doctrinal system sums up the law and the prophets.' If *Gattaca* scans for faulty DNA, 'Reformaca' scans for faulty doctrine. Any who confess to, or who accidentally betray, their faulty doctrine are marginalized at the expense of their being valued or loved as persons. In Reformaca, Sunday lunch at the Reverend's house is an uncomfortable experience. Every clipped utterance or social nicety is first inwardly scanned for 'soundness' before being tentatively proffered in the fear of being corrected. Huge relationally erroneous camels are swallowed whole, whilst doctrinal gnats are dissected *ad absurdum* under often-inquisitorial conditions.

Similarly, the conservative evangelical church – which we may here dub 'Evangelica' – often acts as though 'behavioural system sums up the law and the prophets'. Any who accidentally betray weakness are shunted down a hierarchy that subjugates unique persons (and their unique gifts and ministries) and real relationships beneath a politics of projected 'conformity to system'. In Evangelica, one 'looks good' as a 'helper of the weak'; but one is sure *never* to project the image of *being* 'the weak one who needs help'.[13] The problem, though, is that such hierarchies overrule the Spirit's promotion of 'right relating' and of unique individuals and their unique giftings and unique ministries and, instead, turn doctrine into a non-relational 'system' that is applied by church leaders and congregants non-relationally or competitively. Thus neutered, 'application' then becomes a tool we use for self-promotion, rather than the Spirit's wielding of us – through our employment of our spiritual gifts – to build up others through right relationships. Thus, love is subordinated to 'application system', and not the reverse. And 'application system' then becomes an oppressive total activism that is mislabelled as 'keenness' or as 'no compromise'. However, right relating (which involves the promotion of unique persons and their unique gifts and ministries), and therefore the true gospel, are therein banished by systems of 'application' in that the latter *leave no time* for actual right relating or, in plain English, for true Christianity!

And so, given that these (and other correlative) problematic scenarios have become commonplace in the church, then we need to redefine what we mean by 'church leadership' in order to make church leadership subject to prior concerns about right relating, unique persons, and persons' unique gifts and ministries. The emphasis should not be on conforming people to a prior system, but on developing unique persons' different characters, gifts and ministries in the context of healthy relationships. A church body will then emerge that is organized differently in each instance of church – i.e. organized differently according to *which* unique individuals, giftings, ministries and relationships are present in *each particular instance* of church.[14]

Sin, in the framework of this more biblical kind of church, is not 'lack of conformity to a system', but 'bad or distorted relating'. For if 'love sums up the law and the prophets' then sin is absent or distorted love – first towards God, second towards neighbour. To preach against sin, therefore, is to preach against wrong patterns of relating – first towards God, second towards neighbour. But if this is what preaching against sin amounts to, then why do we never hear sermons with titles like, say, 'Three ways we wrongly manipulate others'? — Political / personal Q?

In *biblical* Christianity, then, psychosocial models such as 'transactional analysis' become relevant, as we have already noted. That is, earlier, in Chapter 3, we indicated that transactional analysis, in speaking about relationships between adults, distinguishes between unhealthy 'parent-to-child' relational dynamics and healthy 'adult-to-adult' relational dynamics. One adult might play a 'critical parent' role in distorted relationship with another adult who plays a 'rebellious child' role. Or, one adult might play a 'nurture parent' role in distorted relationship with another adult who plays a 'compliant child' role. Transactional analysis highlights numerous distorted relational dynamics, and thus aligns with the Bible's emphasis on treating unique adult persons as adults, with dignity and respect – which means *not* infantilizing them. That is, transactional analysis fleshes out biblical emphases on 'right relating', or on 'love', which 'sums up the law and the prophets'.[15]

Another psychosocial model that we noted in Chapter 3, known as the 'drama triangle', usefully highlights some of the distorted role-plays that are deployed in manipulative relating – namely, 'persecutors', 'victims' and 'rescuers'. Thus, for example, a manipulative person may play the 'victim' whenever they are confronted, being never willing to take responsibility for or to repent of their manipulative traits. Another manipulative person, when confronted, may turn the confrontation around by playing a 'rescuer' who then identifies the confronter as the 'victim' of a third party. Such rescuers respond to confrontation with retorts like, 'What's wrong, friend? You don't seem yourself today', and therein they adopt a 'nurture parent' role (cf. transactional analysis) as one who 'rescues' (cf. the drama triangle); they choose never to be the one helped or confronted.[16]

Biblical Christianity, then, promotes *both* unique individual persons and their use of their unique spiritual gifts in unique ministries *and* right relating – from the immediate interpersonal level all the way up to the international level – for 'love sums up the law and the prophets'. Biblical Christianity, therefore, will be very interested in psychosocial models that are of use in highlighting and confronting 'bad relating'. Such psychosocial models are not authoritative or canonical, of course – but they *do* enable us to see certain biblical emphases that *are* authoritative and canonical with fresh eyes.

Biblical church leadership, then, is not to 'lord it over' or infantilize members of the congregation by playing the role of 'critical parent' (cf. the glowering, inquisitorial, overcoated, doctrine-testing preacher of Reformaca), or of 'nurture parent' (cf. the 'caring-but-patronizing-buddy' pastor of 'Charismatica'), or of 'the rescuer who never themselves needs rescuing' (cf. the power-suited, application-formulaic, strength-exuder of Evangelica). Rather, *biblical* church leadership is to lift up unique others in their unique giftings and ministries, and is to promote right relating, in part by repudiating distorted relational power dynamics at the leadership level. Biblical church leadership is the antithesis of a non-relational emphasis on 'conformity-to-system' that suppresses right relating, unique individuality and individuals' unique gifts and ministries.

The thing to watch out for, then, is a de-relationalized distortion of Christianity that, unfortunately, is extremely prevalent in the Western church – even dominant.

Moreover, sometimes, 'every-member ministry' *rhetoric* masks overly hierarchical 'one-man-wonder ministry', 'clergy-versus-laity' or 'leadership-versus-non-leadership' styles of *practice*. That is, the 'every-member ministry' label often becomes a mere rhetorical device that is used to perpetuate a scenario in which congregants do not exercise their spiritual gifts so much as only their right and proper willingness to serve in other ways.

Additionally, Anthony C. Thiselton observes that, in today's 'postmodern' church, some preachers 'ape chat-show hosts' and seek the 'effusions' 'of ready-made applause' that accompany *audience-affirming content*.[17] In such 'local-celebrity-leader' church cultures, ministers can 'hug the limelight' patronizingly whilst suppressing all other high-profile spiritual gifts – typically teaching, prophecy, counselling and healing. Those with such gifts are then assigned only to functions related to the practicalities of running church (e.g. making the coffee). Such practicalities are unavoidable, of course. But it is wrong if people with gifts of teaching, prophecy, counselling and healing are not also assigned to functions related to their spiritual gifts. Biblically, church unity flows not only out of our sharing of practical tasks, but also out of our using our spiritual gifts.[18]

Sometimes, though, congregation-members who challenge systemically oppressive and/or 'local-celebrity-leader' church cultures face further, superimposed, abusive relational dynamics. They are told 'not to be proud', or that 'the practicalities of running church are not lesser roles'. That is, celebrity-seeking leaders project their own sin onto those whose ministries they are suppressing. Their *own* sin is marketed as the *challengers'* problem. Further insult is only added to injury when those who are thereby marginalized and alienated are also then labelled as being part of the '96 per cent' who 'refuse to contribute'!

Now, of course, many do indeed refuse to contribute. Some are indeed individualists who refuse to build church. But one church leader who understands these issues recently said to me: 'I have a feeling that up to 40 per cent of Christians are currently alienated from traditional church attendance and are looking for other modes of living out their Christian faith.' Are we then to call the whole 40 per cent 'individualists'?

Individualism, then, is not the main issue here. Christians are often alienated from the church because the church is often not biblical, but has remained, or has become, distorted by the legacies of other world-views – legacies that undermine the relational and unique-person-promoting character of biblical Christianity. Ironically, psychosocial models then serve prophetically so as to call the church back to biblical emphases both on right relating and on promoting unique persons and their unique gifts and ministries.

I'm afraid this situation is serious. The Bible does not say that only leaders have gifts of teaching, prophecy, counselling and healing. The Bible does not say that all leaders have such gifts, or that leaders have the most mature expressions of such gifts. Therefore, when people's unique identities, gifts and ministries are manipulatively subsumed beneath other role functions to do with the practicalities of church-running (though the two spheres do overlap), then leadership-level institutional sin is occurring – the sin of 'Diotrephes, who loves to be first'.[19]

That is, a distorted Platonized Christianity coupled with modern and postmodern emphases on 'systems' of institutional power and on local celebrity leads to the death of valuable ministries within congregations. Overly hierarchical limelight-hugging and patronizing control subsume gifts such as teaching, prophecy, counselling and healing beneath institutional roles such as 'clergy', 'leadership' or 'pastor'. Non-leaders with certain gifts are then marginalized to a non-place or non-role in the church. Indeed, it is undeniable that, in many churches, even wisdom about how to *find* one's gifts is systematically suppressed so that power bases are not threatened by people becoming dangerously mature. But aren't we taught that those who 'love the place of honour' and who 'love' 'to have men call them "Rabbi"' 'will be punished most severely'?[20]

That is, if Boff, Gunton and Thiselton are right, then unaddressed ideological problems in the Western Church have engendered unbiblical hierarchies that suppress right relating and the ministries of all but the ordained, and that *train* congregants into coming to church without *any* expectation of doing ministries of various kinds.

We said earlier on that infantilization sometimes accompanied this situation, making this situation even more vulnerable to charges that it had to do with issues related to power. If infantilization were indeed a reality, we might also expect to see:

(a) 'Sunday-school culture for tots' becoming the culture of the whole church;
(b) Evangelistic strategies that infantilize non-Christians in order to make sure that only those who 'can be controlled' enter churches;
(c) The systematic removal of the maturity-forming power of the Scriptures from preaching – leaving only the endlessly repeated domesticated-familiar, falsely marketed, in direct disobedience to Hebrews 6:1–3, as 'the importance of not forgetting "the basics"' and as 'right pitching';

(d) The alienation of intellectuals who might expose this situation, particularly prophets, teachers and theologians.

Oh dear. I'm afraid that this is often precisely what we see.

Caveats in Defence of Church Leaders

Admittedly, it is hardly just the fault of church leaders that people
are not using their spiritual gifts. Initially, we highlighted personal
responsibility in relation to Christian development and growth.
Jesus said, 'the worries of this life, the deceitfulness of wealth and
the desires for other things come in and choke the word, making
it unfruitful.'[21] Lives are easily controlled by patterns of relieving
anxiety (e.g. avoiding facing issues); by seeking a middle-class
lifestyle; and by wanting something such as local celebrity, world
travel, a marriage partner, social status, a family, a certain kind of
career, a better car, and so on (the list is endless). Such preoccupa-
tions, such agendas, can easily displace and perpetually defer the
decision to grow in Christian discipleship.

Moreover, Thiselton warns against over-easy generalizations.[22]
It is all too easy to shoot from the hip about problems in the church
and to assign churches to an overneat pigeonholing system of
errors. Nevertheless, Thiselton does allow for a general axis of
interpretation.[23] And, having experienced numerous churches and
church-related cultures, it seems to me that certain general trends
of common cultural distortion do indeed seem to emerge after-
the-fact in many Western churches. I am not at all saying that this
or that cultural distortion can be equated with any given church.
Rather, with Boff, Gunton and Thiselton, I am only identifying
cultural distortions that *affect* churches, and am not identifying
individual churches themselves.

Finally, I am not anti-hierarchy or anti-authority, for hierarchy
and authority originate in heaven.[24] In heaven, though, honour
comes through lifting up the other, not through self-promotion.
As the Bible puts it, 'whoever exalts himself will be humbled,
and whoever humbles himself will be exalted.'[25] Since Jesus
'humbled himself . . . God exalted him to the highest place',
where this was 'to the glory of God the Father'.[26] Thus, *even the*

Father is glorified through lifting up the other, and not through self-promotion.

So, church leaders who want exaltation, take heart! There is a biblical way for this to happen: humble yourselves into right relating, and lift others up both into right relating and into their unique identities, callings, giftings and ministries.

5.

Church Distorted by Postmodernity

In the preceding chapter, we drew on the thinking of Leonardo Boff, Colin E. Gunton and Anthony C. Thiselton in order to highlight how Western ideological problems – which originated in antiquity but which persist into (and develop throughout) modernity and postmodernity – had adversely affected the Church. We indicated how unique persons, their unique gifts and ministries, and 'right relating' – which are key emphases in genuine, biblical Christianity – had often been suppressed beneath the unbiblical conforming of people to various non-relational or even abusive hierarchical systems.

In our appeal to Anthony C. Thiselton, however, we also indicated how postmodern churches potentially added a further dimension to this problem – namely, the *localization* of previously broader systemic oppressions. Postmodern church leaders potentially succumbed to temptations to become local celebrities who preached local-audience-affirming messages that stripped preaching of its transcendental, biblical content and formative capacity so as to secure and extend their local-hero status by seeking local-audience applause.

If modernity is characterized by monolithic oppressive systems of power built around colossal institutions, postmodernity is characterized by fragmented – or by competing localized – oppressive systems of power built around celebrity personalities. Naturally, superimposed 'modern' and 'postmodern' trends coexist in our Western cultures, including in our Western church cultures. Nevertheless, we may now focus a little more on what Thiselton says about the postmodern side of this problem – as follows.

'Corinthian' and Postmodern Cultural Sins in Churches Today

Thus, in part through his article, '1 Corinthians', Thiselton draws parallels between the problems St Paul finds in Corinthian church culture and the problems that Thiselton and others find in 'today's' 'postmodern' church culture.[1] That Thiselton draws such parallels at all, though, suggests that he is pointing to something much more ancient – namely, human sinfulness itself.[2]

The Bible, of course, says that human sinfulness involves us trying to 'be like God' in a wrong way.[3] Naturally, since we are created to be God's imagers, then we are in some ways like God already. Furthermore, during the processes of redemption, the Holy Spirit in us seeks to transform us into Christ's likeness in certain respects, so that we eventually become much more like God than we currently are in our fallen human condition.[4] But Scripture also says that, as sinners, we want to be served, exalted and even worshipped – that we want a kind of satanically reconfigured version of God's position and status.[5]

Naturally, many non-Christians find such teachings absurd. But humanity's quest for individual- or family-scale 'designer realities', or for a 'middle-class' affluent ideal, is very often an idolatry that both centres on ourselves and denies God's ownership of our lives.[6] That is, this quest often colludes with Western modernity's humanistic and materialistic utopianism. In other words, and putting it in J. Moltmann's terms, in pursuing the middle-class affluent ideal – in our attempt to manipulate our own advancement towards our own designer futures – we exploit millions of poorer people, cause humanitarian and ecological disasters, and build 'fortresses of wealth . . . in a sea of mass misery'[7] – in effect serving ourselves so as to exalt ourselves. It is in this horrific context that middle-class discourse boasts about 'products' purchased (e.g. a new conservatory), 'pleasures' indulged in (e.g. a trip to Malaga), and 'performances' achieved (e.g. a promotion from our bosses at work). Therefore, Scripture says that such 'sinful' 'boasting' 'comes not from the Father but from the world'.[8]

Naturally, of course, we boast in order to win others' adulation, acceptance or approval which, in turn, makes certain key others more likely to give us preferential treatment so that we can advance in society.[9] This sociological motivation, though, accompanies a psychological motivation: to achieve a kind of 'proof' – in the face of our insecurities – that our own adulation, acceptance, or approval of ourselves (or, rather, of our self-ascribed personas) has a basis in reality.

Winning others' adulation, then, bolsters our own self-adulation, and thereby engenders a pleasing sense of our own supposed ascendancy towards our being our own 'gods'. Similarly, 'advancement in society' also serves to 'prove' the value of our self-ascribed and outwardly projected personas[10] – a 'proof' that, inwardly, we can reference so as to help us to find self-acceptance in the face of our insecurities.

Thus, sin's aim is not just self-adulation. Rather, sin's aim is to prove self-adulation valid by performing to win others' adulation. It is not enough for pop-stars to give themselves adulation privately. They require public adulation from others as 'proof' that their private self-adulation isn't delusional.

Of course, though, it is precisely because private self-adulation is delusional that public adulation is required, in the face of insecurities, in order to reinforce the spell that says 'self-adulation is justified'. The lie that we should serve and worship ourselves is unstable, unrealistic, escapist, humanistic and utopian. Thus, we try to creatively alter public realities in order to preserve the illusion that our self-worship is supposedly 'grounded in fact'.

And so Thiselton, in his article '1 Corinthians', argues that Corinthian culture, like our own 'celebrity-seeking', 'postmodern' culture, was characterized by people who performed in order to win others' adulation so as to advance socially and bolster their own self-adulation. A structure may be imposed upon Thiselton's points – as follows.

(a) Corinthian and postmodern sin, in the church, asserts personal rights to autonomous freedom in order to:
   (i)   reject God's ownership of one's life;
   (ii) live to please others so as to:
       (ii.i)   gain their adulation;
       (ii.ii) bolster one's own self-adulation.
(b) Corinthian and postmodern sin, in the church, achieves '(a) (ii)' by:

(i) understanding local consumer-values and honour–shame criteria;

(ii) putting on show-casing 'theatrical' performances that are tailored to whatever impresses key others according to such values and criteria;

(iii) developing competitive skills and strengths in order to so perform;

(iv) through such performances winning the competitive game of pleasing, manipulating and exploiting contacts, associates, or 'patrons' who will confer:

  (iv.i) positive attention, honour, prestige and reputation;

  (iv.ii) status, position, power and influence;

  (iv.iii) other contacts, associates, or 'patrons' who will confer the same.

(c) Corinthian and postmodern sin, in the church, is characterized by:

(i) vanity, or pretentious, over-inflated, prematurely triumphalistic self-ascriptions related to status and capacities or skills;

(ii) self-centred, self-absorbed obsession with the empty art-form of ambitious self-sufficiency;

(iii) a kind of gluttonous addiction to '(a)', '(b)', and '(c) (i)–(ii)'.

(d) Corinthian and postmodern sin, in the church, creates a culture that is:

(i) self-centred and faction-centred;

(ii) characterized by unspiritual jealousy, strife, and fragmentation – all of which undermine the unity of the Spirit.

Thus, for Thiselton, it is not only church leaders who are affected by such sins, but the whole fellowship – even though church leaders can spearhead these sins.[11]

Corinthian and Postmodern Cultural Sins versus True Christian Spirituality

Next, Thiselton argues that Paul contrasts such sins with true Christian spirituality.[12] Again, a structure may be imposed upon what Thiselton says. That is, first, Thiselton says that, according to Paul, true Christian spirituality:

(a) is a work in progress – we haven't 'already arrived';
(b) is Christ-centred, not human-centred:
   (i)   worshipping and serving God, not the 'rights' of an 'autonomous free self';
   (ii) following transcendental biblical theology and criteria, not the 'local' theology and criteria of patrons, consumers, or 'celebrity';
   (iii) proclaiming the Gospel of Jesus Christ, not a message about oneself, one's faction, or one's patron;
   (iv) using the Holy Spirit's gifts to promote Jesus Christ, not to aggrandize oneself, one's faction, or one's patron;
(c) is Christ-shaped or cruciform, and is not a way of chasing image, status, or power:
   (i)   adopting the image of a purchased slave – just a messenger or labourer (not a professional, clever social-climber) who will be judged by God (not by humankind);
   (ii) accepting the sober status of a 'nothing' lifted up by Jesus Christ – just a subordinate helper with only a shared ministry – not the pretentious 'status' conferred by the 'puffed up' to the 'puffed up';
   (iii) using the Holy Spirit's gifts to serve others' best interests and to build church community, not to empower oneself or some exclusive faction or patron (cf. how 'tongues' at Corinth made those not speaking in tongues feel 'excluded').[13]

Second, Thiselton's 'Pauline' contrasts between the sins of Corinthian/'postmodern' church cultures and true Christian spirituality[14] may thus be tabulated as shown in Table 1.

Table 1. Corinthian/Postmodern Church Culture versus True Christian Spirituality

Human-centredness	Christ-centredness
Serves the rights of a free automomous self	→ Worships and serves God
Evaluates the self by local human criteria i.e. consumer-values embodied in celebrity	Evaluates the self by universal divinely revealed criteria, i.e. a biblical view of holiness
Proclaims a message about human celebrity: one's own glory, and that of one's patron or faction	Proclaims a gospel message about Christ crucified and risen
Uses the Spirit's gifts to aggrandize self or one's patron or faction	Uses the Spirit's gifts to promote Christ as Lord
Image-chasing self-centredness	**Cruciformity, not 'image'**
Chases a consumer-desirable image through skilled 'theatrical' performance tailored to win positive evaluation from consumers (e.g. professional, clever social-climber)	Adopts the image of a purchased slave who will be judged by God and who will be viewed as a shameful spectacle by the world
Recruits consumers' allegiance and support by manipulation	Risks rejection and persecution through consumers' reaction to effrontery
Status-chasing self-centredness	**Cruciformity, not 'status'**
Receives status from patrons and consumers and thus receives others' praise and becomes 'puffed-up', like a 'local hero' or a 'celebrity' patron	Accepts a sober status given by Christ – who lifts up 'nothings' – to become a subordinate helper with a shared ministry
Uses others' praise to bolster unstable self-adulation and self-attributed status	Retains a sober view of the self as a lifted-up 'nothing' to whom Christ gave status
Power-chasing self-centredness	**Cruciformity, not 'power'**
Uses the Spirit's gifts to empower oneself, or to establish the exclusive church-defining superiority of one's faction or patron	Uses the Spirit's gifts to serve others' best interests and to build church-community
Receives praise, power and further contacts from patrons and consumers	Empowers others at the expense of one's own power
Vanity	**Humility**
Addictive self-centred vanity in action	Liberating Christ-centred humility in action

Fragmentation of the church	Building of the church
Causes community-fragmentation through jealousy and strife	Builds church community as diversity in unity (after the Trinitarian image of God)

Drawing on Thiselton, then, Table 1 exposes sins within 'today's' 'postmodern' churches – which is alarming.[15] Moreover, others align with Thiselton's analysis. Thiselton's analysis, therefore, cannot simply be rejected as though Thiselton had somehow succumbed to alarmism.

Thus, P. Ward, following D.F. Wells, analyses 'transconfessionalism' within today's broader, postmodern, evangelical church as a 'move' 'away from *doctrine* [and] towards *strategy* and *organizational power*'. Ward argues that a simultaneous swing towards 'the charismatic' – which, in Thiselton's estimate, overemphasizes *'present' 'experience' of the 'Spirit'* – 'has merely . . . emphasize[d] these developments considerably whilst complicating the organizational picture'.[16]

That is, increasingly charismatic, postmodern evangelicals are more concerned with *'local'* 'strategy and organizational power' and with immediate 'present' 'experience' of the 'Spirit' than they are with historical *'transcendental'* biblical doctrine and/or 'criteria'. This situation generates a post-doctrinal – and sometimes even a pluralistically multi-doctrinal – church culture.[17]

That is, evangelicalism today – and indeed, we would suggest, even the broader church today – is deserting the biblical criteria and doctrine by which its practices and experiences can be identified *as* 'Christian' and regulated so as to *remain* 'Christian'. By implication, the church is instead increasingly regulated and shaped by *the state* and *its laws* only, when we should be regulated and shaped *both* by biblical doctrine and criteria (including biblical lawfulness) *and* by state laws, *and* in different ways (see Chapter 3 on biblical lawfulness above).

That is, these days, evangelicalism – and even the broader church – is being conformed largely to the culture of the state – to today's Zeitgeist – and is losing the positive shape of biblical Christianity.

Moreover, it is precisely the postmodern antipathy towards historical transcendental biblical-theological doctrine and criteria, and the postmodern love for local theology and for local-celebrity culture, that feeds the church's refusal to address its older distortions as well, including its Platonic and 'modern' distortions (see Chapter 4 above).

Now, of course, theologians have registered Nietzsche's and Heidegger's complaints that traditional orthodox – including much conservative evangelical – 'Christianity is Platonism for the People'.[18] And theologians have exposed traditional British liberal Christianity's affinities with a more 'modern' neo-Kantian legacy (which affects both positivist and existentialist tendencies in traditional theological liberalism).[19] And theologians have exposed contemporary Christian liberalism's – and much contemporary popular charismatic and (post-)evangelical Christianity's – more postmodern or neo-pragmatic shape.[20] But such statements as these are double-Dutch to folks in popular church circles today – which is precisely my point! We *should* understand how non-biblical philosophies continue to distort (and even sometimes to define) the church!

But today's postmodern shift from 'confessionalism' to 'transconfessionalism' – from concern for historical transcendental biblical doctrine and criteria to concern for 'local-hero' status bolstered by 'present' 'experience' of a 'gagged' 'Spirit' – does not help us to understand or to address such distortions, but merely hides them from us, perpetuates them, and allows them to get worse.[21]

That is, today's postmodern church has become unconcerned about heresy. A pseudo-Christianity defined by local-heroism – by the narcissistic pursuit of 'experience', 'power', 'prestige', 'applause' and celebrity within the 'local' context – threatens to displace biblically shaped Christianity.[22] According to Thiselton, even 'ordinands' can't wait to *stop* studying biblical theology and 'get out there'.[23]

The implications are terrifying: we could very soon end up with – and in some cases have already ended up with – a church that refuses to be confronted by the Bible or by the true prophet.

The concerning ways in which unbiblical ideologies distort the shape of today's Western church cultures are worth exploring in more detail. To this task we now turn.

6

Distorted Church as the Main Cause of Church-Hopping

Why do Christians so easily hop between churches? Is church-hopping related to the cultural prioritizing of consumer choice? Or is something more sinister going on? Is church-hopping related to commitment phobia? Or is it more to do with what people are being asked to commit *to*? Is church-hopping a theological issue? Or does it stem from broken relationships? Well, my suspicion is that church-hopping relates to:

(a) relational problems;
(b) cultural sinfulness;
(c) distorted theological persuasions;
(d) distorted church structures;
(e) distorted styles of worship;
(f) distorted pastoral practices;
(g) distorted witness;
(h) horizons of expectation; and even,
(i) consecration to God – as follows.

Relational Problems as a Cause of Church-Hopping

Thus, relational problems are a cause of church-hopping – though these relational problems are not all caused by sin by any means.

Relational pre-emptive manoeuvring

Thus, wise, relational, pre-emptive manoeuvring can precipitate a 'no fault' church-hop, as when one minister leaves a church and another arrives. The new leader's authority could be undermined if church members continued to attribute authority to the former leader. Such a scenario could even cause a church split and all manner of relational breakdowns, and so it is often best for the former leader to move to a different church. There must, surely, be other scenarios, too, in which the pre-emptive evasion of relational problems could rightly precipitate a 'no-fault' church-hop.

Relational breakdown

Serious relational breakdown – for example, a broken marriage – can also precipitate a 'no fault' church-hop. In order to recover from the trauma of a broken marriage, the two parties concerned may need to attend different churches. It would be unmerciful and counter-productive to expect the two parties to keep seeing each other every week – to keep experiencing painful triggering of hurts and reminders of loss.

Certainly, hard-line 'Reformed' stigmatization of divorcees is wholly inconsistent with God's love, which seeks to restore and to rebuild. Broken relationships have enough pain of their own without the judgemental impositions of a rule-based religion with its de-relationalized (i.e. without relational wisdom) pseudo-biblical ethic and 'pastoral' practice.

Of course, divorce remains a serious matter, and some divorces are conducted sinfully and merit confrontation. However divorces, and serious relational breakdowns more broadly, are so complexly variable that very different superimpositions of biblical considerations and pastoral sensitivities are required in each particular case. Such an approach to pastoring, though, is quite beyond a hard-line 'Reformed' framework that, even today, still hasn't separated biblical Christianity from ancient Western philosophy.

Jesus says, 'Stop judging by mere appearances, and make a right judgment' and his brother says, 'judgment without mercy will be shown to anyone who has not been merciful.'[1]

Relational sin

Serious relational sin, though, can indeed precipitate a church-hop. In these cases, the church-hop itself is not necessarily sinful, but is often a necessary response to sin. Thus, for example, a married man may have committed adultery with a single woman from the same church that he and his wife attend. Even if there was repentance and forgiveness on all sides, just 'being around one another' could still perpetuate the 'world' of the sin, reminding all concerned of it and keeping the matter alive so as to cause anxiety, pain or perhaps covetousness and further temptation.

Thus, new agreed boundaries would need to be set up in order to allow healing, encourage objectivity and prevent wrong attachments recurring. Ordinarily, this boundary-setting process would necessitate a church-hop, either by the couple or by the single person, in order to shut down the sinful reality of the adultery. Forgiveness and reconciliation would not likely consist of a recommencement of the original closeness between the three persons, but would restore only the right 'kingdom relational dynamic' between them, which would involve that level of distance that facilitated both maintained holiness and the respective consecrations of each to their callings and vocations under God.

Now, of course, relational sins can be committed by institutions as well as by individuals, which is a scenario that sometimes gives individuals just cause for church-hopping. Naturally, the abusive relational dynamics that are operative within cults would make a 'church'-hop essential. And yet, mainstream churches also sometimes sin against individuals in a manner that necessitates church-hops, as we shall see later on.

Relational dissonance

Serious relational dissonance can also precipitate a necessary church-hop. Somebody may not be able to cope with the ongoing – but not deliberately sinful – behaviour of another person within their fellowship. We all grew up in a fallen world, and each one of us manifests both distorted fallen relational behaviours and certain sensitivities to certain distorted fallen relational behaviours in others. Our faults can trigger others' sensitivities; and their faults can trigger our sensitivities. Further, we may feel this kind of problem, but may not yet always understand it.

Jesus says, 'I have much more to say to you, more than you can now bear. But when he, the Spirit of truth, comes, he will guide you into all truth.' That is, we cannot hear the whole truth straightaway, but are gradually re-educated by the Holy Spirit. Eventually, 'we regard no-one from a worldly point of view'. Initially, though, we view even ourselves falsely.[2]

Therefore, it takes rightly-timed 'prophesying' for 'the secrets of [the] heart' to 'be laid bare' so instantaneously as to produce 'worship'. Normally, the Spirit re-educates us gradually. Then, eventually, we come to realize both how others' sins have damaged us and how our sins have damaged others. We also come to realize that God is not just an ego-extension who wants what we want or who 'smiles' on us whatever we do. Rather, our coming 'to will and to act according to' God's 'good purpose' is a process that we 'continue to work out' – a matter of 'fear and trembling'.[3]

And so, when a person's particular distorted fallen relational behaviours are beyond what we can yet handle, we may feel discomfort, withdraw from them, and set boundaries in relation to them. But, we may not yet understand the other's distorted fallen relational behaviours. We may even eventually realize that it was our own fallen relational distortions causing the problem, not the other person's – and that we projected our issues onto the other, as a way of denying the reality of our own faults.

Alternatively, neither I nor the other person may yet be able to face, understand, come to terms with or do anything about the fallen relational distortions or injury activations that are occurring between us. And even if one person can understand and deal with a certain problem, it may not be right to confront, or to proffer analyses of, the other person, since it may not be the Holy Spirit's will for them to face or to deal with that particular issue *yet*.

Sometimes, then, a problem involving relational dissonance is as yet insurmountable, and a church-hop may be the best option for a person. At other times, relational dissonance can be surmountable and should be addressed without church-hopping.

Relational difference

Significant relational difference can also precipitate a necessary church-hop. When Christians move to a different town or city, then they will commonly try out different churches. This is not necessarily consumerism, for certain kinds of person really do fit better into certain kinds of church.

People need empathy – to be around those who can understand and accept them where they are at now. This is consistent with right desires to grow as a Christian through good-quality relationships. Good-quality relationship, however, is not just 'one kind of thing'. Single mums might benefit from being around other friendly single mums. Students will likely benefit from a church with a developed student ministry. Self-designated homosexuals will likely suffer needlessly in churches that relate abusively to them. People go where the love is, because love is right and love is attractive. Love combines acceptance with holding each other to our best for Christ.

Now, of course, in churches where an emphasis on right doctrine *displaces* right relating, then love – the heart of *genuine* Christianity – will be comparatively absent. Mere *systemic* biblical exegesis generates not *relational* wisdom, but merely a huge calculus of propositions that allows some – quite unchallenged – to replace the complexities of right relating with singular oversimplistic sinful anti-relational dispositions such as patronizing sternness, elitist superiority, political correctness, authoritarian enthusiasm, interrogative domination and other relational evils.

When people encounter such counterfeit Christianity upon moving to a new city, therefore, then church-hopping can become an entirely biblical course of action for such folks. In such circumstances, church-hopping has nothing to do with avoiding right confrontation, but merely avoids oppressive authoritarian regimes that are bereft of relational wisdom. It is not only individuals who sin. Whoever said that putting a group of sinners together created something 'above criticism' simply because it is an institution? If institutions were above criticism then why did Jesus say of the temple stones in Jerusalem, 'every one will be thrown down'?[4]

And so, somebody who is looking for a new church will often encounter different flavours of institution that are more or less conducive for right relationship for them in their particular place in their life and personal development – in their relational difference. Again, this process is not a matter of consumerism, but is rather a matter of respecting the particularities that pertain to persons and to institutions. And sometimes, additionally, institutions are sinful, as we argued earlier and as we will see later on.

Cultural Sinfulness as a Cause of Church-Hopping

Of course, though, individuals' cultural sinfulness can certainly cause church-hopping as well. Three sins that we may highlight in this respect are: narcissistic self-promotion, materialistic self-diversion and relativistic self-evasion.

Narcissistic self-promotion

Thus, in his criticism of neo-pragmatic 'postmodern' culture, theologian Anthony C. Thiselton speaks of a narcissistic 'socially constructed value-system based on "recognition" and virtual realities created by rhetoric, consumerism, peer-group competition, and self-promotion'.[5] That is, Thiselton closely relates 'the "virtual reality" of postmodern construction' to 'the obsessive desire for a self-perception and status defined by how peer-groups "recognize" themselves or others'.[6]

That is, and as we indicated in our previous chapter, neo-pragmatic, Corinthian-style 'Christianity', according to Thiselton, becomes a mere 'vehicle of self-affirmation, peer-group self-promotion, or triumphalism' that espouses 'a notion of "God" that amounts to a projection of human desires and interests'.[7] Neo-pragmatic pastors thus 'ape chat-show hosts' and design their sermons in such a way as to create 'pragmatic rhetorical effect' and win '*local*' 'audience applause'. With 'Every effusion . . . greeted with a storm of ready-made applause', however, '[t]he result is vanity and empty self-sufficiency'.[8]

Thus, we can easily imagine how somebody could become disappointed that their right role under God, currently, did not generate the attention or peer-group applause that they desired. Such a person could then try to manufacture other roles for themselves

that hugged more limelight. If they still couldn't perform to win
the peer-group applause that they wanted in a particular church,
then they might decide to 'hop' to another church. Very often,
narcissistic desires for self-promotion, when thwarted or objected
to, lead to church-hopping. A pastor may not win the applause he
seeks, even when he alters his sermon content in order to please his
local audience; an attractive female personality may not win the
peer-group recognition she desires when she speaks from the front,
sings in the worship group, or wears provocative clothing; a charismatic male personality who doesn't quite feel affirmed enough
may speak more loudly, become more exhibitionistic, adopt more
pretension, accept more flattery – or church-hop – and so on.

In such cases, narcissistic self-promotion has been given the
highest priority, and the serving of others according to what is best
for those others has been de-prioritized. Consequently, 'strutting'
happens, but proper gift development and genuine ministry do
not. And when such narcissistic behaviours fail to win sufficient
addictively craved applause, church-hopping often happens.

Materialistic self-diversion

Moving on, then we may note that the famous theologian, Jürgen
Moltmann, links Western modernity's humanistic self-sufficiency to an international-scale, godless and materialistic theft
and exploitation of the world's resources that actually creates the
suffering of the Third World.[9]

That is, Western materialism rests on a disastrously sinful
footing. Western wealth-oriented lifestyles, which serve money
rather than God, cannot simply be self-deceptively labelled as
'good, old-fashioned, hard-working weeks' punctuated by 'letting
off steam at the weekends'. Western materialism is not at all innocent, but is grounded in modernity's apostasy, and in modernity's
profligate greedy purloining and re-routing of the resources that
God intended for *all* to enjoy.

That is, Western materialism is grounded in stealing. Moreover,
behind Western materialism there is also modernity's apostate
diversion of people away from service to God and into enslavement to the service of the affluent image of the middle-class
dream. Indeed, in the slave trades of the past (and present), in

*if it is wrong to challenge the state
(conscience) surely the same applies
to modernity.*

today's far-Eastern sweat shops, and even in the long hours of well-paid but in-all-but-by-name-enslaved contemporary 'professionals', 'enslavement' for the middle-class dream has been, and still is, quite factual.

Thus, commonly, Christian families driven by enslavement to a materialistic middle-class lifestyle, and thus to paradigms and structures of status-seeking behaviour that render them too busy for ministry, relocate or church-hop to what *they* would call 'less fundamentalist' or 'more moderate' churches where others who are also committed to similar affluent life aims similarly hide from real Christianity. Such churches endlessly repeat neutered domesticated doctrinal structures in sermons that are guaranteed never to touch earth or offend. Such churches are less likely to challenge, and are more likely to facilitate and reaffirm, a middle-class lifestyle – perhaps calling it 'upstanding', and perhaps calling the persons trapped therein 'pillars of the community'.

In fact, however, whilst appearing dynamic, such a lifestyle actually amounts to a kind of apostate profligate paralysis – to an inability to move forwards when it comes to being transformed and reoriented towards serving divine, kingdom, biblical or gospel interests. These interests – the 'interests... of Jesus Christ'[10] – are thus displaced and peripheralized by the interests of materialistic self-diversion.

Not that I am condemning wealth. Not at all! It is poverty that is wrong. Rather I am saying that if we genuinely serve God first, and wealth still comes, then all well and good. Such wealth may even sometimes be counted as blessing. But then we will also have stable church commitments and visible ministries (unless the church blocks us).

Relativistic self-evasion

Relativistic self-evasion, which is 'always learning but never able to acknowledge the truth',[11] also causes church-hopping. Relativistic self-evasion has both older and newer manifestations, and more and less intellectual manifestations.

Thus, older-style liberal intellectuals, particularly those who like to project artistically savvy intellectual personas, can tend to substitute intellectual questioning for tough sanctification-related questions about various personal and relational matters to do with growth, such that they perpetually defer the latter. Relational and personal questions are out; metaphysical and other more-or-less profound questions – e.g. concerning 'the accessibility of truth', 'ethically ambiguous matters', 'philosophical conundrums', 'the nuances of the arts', 'the etiquettes of culturedness' and so on – are in.

In this relativistic self-evasion, an intellectual sleight-of-hand occurs. What is assumed to be the complete relativity or unanswerability of questions about profound or subtle realities is transformed into an evasive assumption about the supposed complete relativity or unanswerability of questions about painful personal issues and relational behaviour. Etiquettes of sophisticated self-cultivation (German: *Bildung*) then displace what should be a more primary focus on relational and personal sanctification.[12]

When young intellectual Christians rightly become dissatisfied – either with what Anthony C. Thiselton would call dumbed-down, narcissistic, charismatic church cultures or with what Thiselton would call the endlessly neutered and familiar 'cosy trivializing illustrations' of materialism-affirming evangelical church cultures 'in which the Gospel is toned down to the lowest level of memorable harmlessness' – then they often church-hop to so-called liberal churches.[13]

Thus, either these young intellectual Christians then mistakenly conflate older-style, liberal intellectual church culture with truly Christian or biblical intellectual maturity; or, more commonly these days, they then mistakenly conflate newer-style, often still charismatic – but also vaguely intellectual – 'post-evangelicalism', 'liberal evangelicalism' or 'Green-Belt Christianity' with truly Christian or biblical intellectual maturity.

Older-style, liberal intellectual church culture, however, is influenced by a paradigm that is shaped in part by neo-Kantianism – i.e. by existentialism and/or by positivism. By contrast, truly Christian or biblical intellectual maturity is *not* shaped by neo-Kantianism-influenced existentialism or by neo-Kantianism-influenced positivism.[14] And post-evangelicalism, liberal evangelicalism and/or Green-Belt Christianity are strongly influenced by neo-pragmatism. But, by contrast, truly Christian or biblical intellectual maturity is *not at all* neo-pragmatic.[15]

Therefore, whichever way they turn, our church-hopping young intellectual Christians end up in deeply unbiblical waters. The problem, though, is that truly Christian or biblical intellectual maturity so rarely manifests itself in churches, that such young intellectual Christians really have nowhere else to go. We could almost exonerate such folks from all blame were it not for the fact that, of course, God will not primarily ask us for our views on the arts and social sciences on Judgement Day, but will focus more primarily on truths about how we related towards others in our everyday lives. True Christianity does not buy into overextended postmodern notions of the supposed relativity of all truth-statements in order to avoid awkward questions about ourselves and about how we are relating.

Relativistic self-evaders, however, will church-hop in order to avoid such questions, and so are not innocent. There are even theological colleges that are set up in order to satisfy such folks. Thus, just a few years ago, purportedly, one such theological college set an exercise in which ordinands were asked to construct reasons why a certain adulterous relationship between a Reverend and a married woman in his congregation could be 'both justified and kept secret'. Neo-pragmatic ethical relativism (i.e. 'almost anything goes') and neo-pragmatic epistemological relativism (i.e. 'there is almost no stable truth') had so completely taken over the college that, purportedly, only three persons in the college still believed the Bible to be God's word!

Naturally, there is also an anti-intellectual form of relativistic self-evasion that is common in more popular Western culture. Neo-pragmatic relativistic premises, when adopted implicitly through behavioural mimicry of cultural habits but not understood, are commonly deployed in order to justify individualistic – or interest group-based – ethical autonomy or ethical independence, and in order to avoid truthful challenges from others.

That is, when faced with a difficult or unwelcome criticism, a Christian these days, following popular culture, will often answer: 'Oh, you see it your way, we believe differently'; or, 'But the Spirit told me such and such'; or sometimes, 'The Spirit told me that the Bible said such and such.'

Now, of course, differences really do exist between the belief systems of different communities; and there are genuine points

of difference in relation to the interpretation of certain biblical
texts. And yet, these days, one could still easily imagine a Christian within almost any church speaking in such a way in order to
rebuff a legitimate confrontation over a blatantly obvious issue –
for example, adultery.

Our point is that, these days, both 'intellectuals' and 'non-
intellectuals' frequently church-hop to churches where popular
relativism is sufficiently embraced, or where the teaching is
sufficiently vague and nebulous, in order to persistently avoid
awkward confrontations of their own unfaced personal and relational failings. That is, because of relativistic self-evasion, deep
personal and relational flaws can go unchecked or unconfronted
for years or even decades.

Distorted Theological Persuasions as a Cause of Church-Hopping

Clearly, then, distorted theological persuasions in the church can
also cause church-hopping. It is just a bit too convenient to blame
church-hopping only on individuals' relational problems or only
on individuals' cultural sinfulness – genuine though these issues
are.

Indeed, in my view, the main causes of church-hopping are
distorted theological persuasions that result in distorted church
structures, in distorted styles of worship, in distorted pastoral
practices and in distorted witness. Indeed, such distortions
become inevitable when churches marginalize biblical theology
since, then, such churches inevitably end up propagating non-
biblical systems of thinking and behaviour – either covertly or
(even) overtly.

People can feel theological distortions

Thus, often, people leave churches because they intuitively sense
that some kind of 'alien' or 'dodgy' theology has been covertly
directing actual church practices. They know that their church
leaders pay 'lip-service' to the Bible; but their adverse experience
of church makes them suspect that something else – something

unbiblical – is going on. They may not be able to analyse the issues at hand, but they can certainly feel them.

When such persons try to flag up such issues, however, they are often stonewalled – which only deepens their suspicions. Their attempts at straightforward communication are often met with a subtle counter-force – a hindrance, a perpetual deferral, a silence, a wading-through-treacle effect, an effect that makes them feel like Kafka's 'Josef K' being passed from pillar to post; and so their efforts to communicate stall. Flattery, certainly, meets no such resistance. But anything remotely critical is blocked.

Thus impeded, those with their suspicions may eventually leave the church to join the other 40 per cent of often-healthy Christians who have already done so.

But what *are* the theological distortions that such persons can feel but can't necessarily analyse, that hinder their attempts at communication and that make them resort to church-hopping? What are the theological distortions that, moreover, make British folks in general see God and Christianity as increasingly irrelevant?

Platonic or traditional theological distortions

Well, to begin with, and simplifying matters somewhat, there are largely 'orthodox' or 'traditional' (including 'Reformed' and 'conservative evangelical') theological distortions that are related to the ancient and modern legacy of Western thinking, and especially to Platonism and to logical positivism. These distortions lead to the overemphasizing of cognitive or propositional language at the expense of relationship.[16]

Now, of course, the opposite error of suppressing propositions or doctrinal content is also to be avoided. And yet, the Bible should not be reduced to propositions or to doctrinal content because, as noted already, this erroneous practice suppresses the multiple, varied, relational speech-actions that God performs towards us through the Scriptures. The result of this erroneous practice, notably, is both that immediate relationship with God is suppressed and that biblical relational wisdom is lost, which leaves only a 'de-relationalized' calculus of doctrinal propositions – i.e. doctrinal propositions that are abstracted both from relational dynamics and from relational wisdom. The problem with this situation, of course, is that it is not de-relationalized doctrine – but rather 'love' – that 'sums up the law and the prophets', as we have seen.[17]

And yet, much orthodox, traditional, Reformed and conservative evangelical biblical exegesis asks systemic questions of the biblical texts such as, for example, 'What eternal "truths" can I get from this passage?', but not questions pertaining to relational wisdom such as, for example, 'What does this passage say "manipulation" looks like?'

But this erroneous practice then leaves sermons emptied of the relational wisdom that people need in order to enable them to address life's concrete relational and personal problems. This wisdom is then found amongst only a few counsellors, whilst sermons become reduced to getting doctrinal propositions 'correct' and to 'applying' 'correct' doctrine.[18] Emphases on 'right doctrine' thus *displace* right relating.

Now, of course, doctrinal content and application are both utterly essential. But it is *doctrinal content divorced from relational wisdom* that we are sometimes trying to apply! So, we end up with rule-based religion. Real biblical Christianity, though, is a relational religion that preaches that 'righteousness' is 'the art and science of loving' and that 'sin' is 'distortions in the patterns of love', first towards God, second towards neighbour.

People are always getting into relational scrapes. Therefore, if we preached the true gospel, which recentres love for God and neighbour (not as 'doctrines' only but as incisive wisdom on relational practices) in criticism of orthodox, traditional, Reformed and conservative evangelical rule-based religion (which is still rather Platonic), then both Christians and the world would be more interested.

Orthodox or traditional Christianity (including Reformed Christianity and conservative evangelicalism), however, often suffers from the theological irrelevance of *abstracted (i.e. de-relationalized) doctrine applied* – or from the theological irrelevance of doctrine divested of its relational aspects and then applied non-relationally as rules.

Later, we will again distinguish between two strands of this distortion – a more doctrine-focussed 'Reformed' strand, and a more application-focussed 'evangelical' strand.

Charismatic theological distortions

Still simplifying matters somewhat, then there are also 'char-ismatic' theological distortions that react against, but that do not adequately address, the orthodox, traditional, Reformed or conservative evangelical theological distortions. Charismatic Christianity does not tend to transpose abstracted biblical cogni-tive language and/or doctrine back into a relational key. Rather, charismatic Christianity tends to pay lip-service to the conserva-tive abstract calculus, but then tends to simplify it to the level of a few slogans that are then – additionally – put to jingles played by a rock band. The emphasis is thus shifted covertly from abstract truth to immediate experience.[19]

The problem, though, is that this emphasis on 'immediate experience' tends to bypass the Holy Spirit's speech through the Scriptures and proceed straight to experience of the Holy Spirit, or rather to experience of a 'gagged' Spirit (to use D.A. Carson's phrase).[20] Never was such a healthy emphasis on listening to God's Spirit combined with such an utter refusal to engage prop-erly with the Spirit's biblical speech-acts.

True Christian experience, though, emerges from right relating with God and neighbour, which is inseparable from the Spirit's use of biblical language in order to form and transform us towards right relating with God and neighbour, which is Christlike.

Charismatic Christianity, then, often manifests the influences of unbiblical philosophies – especially neo-Kantianism-influenced existentialism, and, neo-pragmatism:[21] the propositional content 'doesn't matter so much, so long as God moves', or so long as I 'move on', 'step out', 'break through', or 'receive'. If one asks what one is 'receiving' or 'breaking through' *to*, however, then the answer is often vague, such as 'whatever God has for you' or 'the river of blessing'. Thus, metaphors are up-anchored from their proper explanatory biblical matrices and are given to worshippers to fill entirely with their own content.[22]

Thus, in charismatic Christianity, biblical and systematic theology is routinely suppressed, whilst massive experiences of blessing or of healing are sometimes promised on the basis of cartoon-like surrogate theologies and brute assertions to do with 'realizing one's identity in Christ'.

Of course, though, whilst God does indeed bless and heal, such divine favour cannot be causally or manipulatively invoked through asserted fervour marketed as 'faith'. God's actions are beyond our control. Moreover, much of our healing comes through repenting of bad relational patterns, and through being retrained into good relational patterns. Charismatic Christianity, though, often neglects these emphases and tends to indulge in what Thiselton calls 'over-realized eschatology' – i.e. in making false promises concerning 'breaking through' to a quasi-eschatological 'freedom from suffering' that we do not yet have.[23]

Charismatic Christianity, then, often suffers from the theological irrelevance of *abstracted (i.e. de-relationalized) experience asserted* – or from the theological irrelevance of experience divested of its relational and linguistic aspects, invested with eschatological presumption (to use Moltmann's language), and then fervently asserted and theatrically show-cased. This charismatic strand of Christianity is also linked to certain forms of neo-pragmatic – or newer-style liberal – evangelicalism (see below).

Older-style liberal theological distortions

Again simplifying matters somewhat, then there are also older-style (or mid-twentieth-century) 'liberal' or 'high church' theological distortions. These distortions also react against but, again, do not adequately address, what we have called the orthodox, traditional, Reformed, or conservative evangelical theological distortions. Older-style liberalism does not tend to transpose abstracted biblical cognitive language and/or doctrine back into a relational key. Rather, as in much charismaticism, such language and/or doctrine is again held at a respectful distance, but this time as part of a focus on experiences of God's transcendence rather than on experiences of God's immanence. High arches, candles and symbols replace low ceilings, strip-lights and flags.

Again, though (early- or) mid-twentieth-century often-unbiblical Germanic philosophy lurks behind the scenes. Admittedly, in older-style liberalism, such philosophy is recognized more consciously, through a greater awareness of theologians such as Bultmann and Tillich (who said much of profound value).[24] Unlike in much charismaticism, there is a healthy respect for the intellect, for difficult questions, and for unknowns that cannot simply be transposed into cheery certainties.[25] And yet, as Thiselton and others have demonstrated, philosophy has come on a long way since Bultmann, Tillich and their successors[26] – and has shown that the Bible is far too sophisticated to be seen as merely a 'primitive expression of early Christian faith'. Christian tradition cannot 'move beyond Scripture' if hermeneutical (i.e. interpretative) philosophy shows that Christian tradition has never yet actually completely arrived *at* Scripture.

Older-style liberalism, though, on the basis of its out-of-date hermeneutical philosophy, and as we noted above, tends to replace biblical relational wisdom pertinent to sanctification or to relational holiness with something akin to *Bildung* (i.e. 'the German tradition of self-cultivation'), which has more to do with refinement through (in this case, dated) knowledge of the arts and social sciences.[27] Now, of course, it is good to discuss the works of William Blake and others, but not at the expense of rigorous self-criticism of one's own distorted patterns of relating. Artistic, socio-scientific and other understanding must be subordinated to biblical-relational repentance and refinement. We cannot run from uncomfortable home truths by invoking metaphysical uncertainties, ethical conundrums and aesthetic subtleties forever. Again, on Judgement Day, surely, God will ask us how we related to people, not how much Chaucer we learned (valuable though such learning is).

Much 'high church' liberalism, then, suffers from the theological irrelevance of *abstracted (i.e. de-relationalized) self-cultivation* (cf. *Bildung*) – i.e. from the theological irrelevance of emphases on self-cultivation that suppress the biblical formation that makes our relating holy.

Post-evangelical theological distortions

Simplifying matters considerably, then the most recent and increasingly pervasive theological distortion in the church is what one Reverend friend of mine would call the liberal evangelical or post-evangelical theological distortion, or what I – following Anthony C. Thiselton – would call the neo-pragmatic theological distortion,[28] which is a new kind of shape-shifting fundamentalism.

At the non-intellectual end of things, this distortion often leads to almost imperceptible changes in what is otherwise very like 'normal charismatic' church culture – on which, see above. It is just that the unwittingly adopted philosophical premises behind the charismatic culture have been up-dated from Germanic, neo-Kantianism-influenced existentialism to American neo-pragmatism. Of course, non-intellectual charismatics do not think in such terms, but this change has happened nonetheless.

And, of course, we should not overlook more 'intellectual' neo-pragmatic Christianity, which often looks like a blend between the older liberalism, contemporary evangelicalism, and (sometimes 'Celtic-style') charismaticism. The result of this blend can be a kind of 'Green-Belt-style' carnival that is both more-or-less-superficially multiculturally inclusive, and yet also post-doctrinally – or multi-doctrinally – pluralist. Neo-pragmatism both markets itself as the champion of multicultural difference, and yet also tends to slip into what D.A. Carson calls 'philosophical pluralism'.[29] In philosophical pluralism, all views are declared 'equally valid' – which looks inclusive and multicultural; and yet, at the same time, all views are effectively declared 'equally non-valid' as well: no community is allowed any basis in truth from which to challenge other communities – even though neo-pragmatists (in theory at least) allow challenge on pragmatic or consensus-related grounds.[30]

Having said this, and as we argue in our longer chapter on modernity and postmodernity below, there are actually strong unacknowledged dogmas behind neo-pragmatism. One of these dogmas is a selective adherence to the post-structuralist view that there is supposedly no legitimate stable truth or language. We say 'selective' because, actually, certain 'allowed rhetorics' to do with environmental sustainability, liberal democracy, economic expansion, naturalistic humanistic utopianism and technological progressivism (see later) – or to do with whatever those in power want – do effectively become expediently 'fixed truths and fixed speech' in neo-pragmatism. Neo-pragmatists only apply the 'no stable truth, no stable language' rule to the perspectives of those who oppose their stance. That is, neo-pragmatism asserts itself in an authoritarian manner along the lines of desired fixed propagandas, and relativizes all challenges (in practice, if not always in theory).

In its Christian outworking, a neo-pragmatic foundation often undergirds a pseudo-Barthian (i.e. supposedly after Karl Barth) 'biblical' or 'neo-orthodox' fundamentalism and so can seem 'very sound and biblical'.[31] Karl Barth, though, is famous for two reasons, and not just one. On the one hand, he was the greatest theologian of the last century, and a brilliant biblical thinker.[32] On the other hand, however, he was famously criticized for being biblical within a non-biblical, philosophical framework related to Neo-Kantianism.[33] In some Christian neo-orthodoxies, this non-biblical, philosophical framework has, these days, been replaced by another non-biblical, philosophical framework, namely neo-pragmatism.[34]

And so, 'neo-pragmatic Barthianism' can seem biblical, but it asserts a 'biblical' viewpoint in a non-biblical, authoritarian manner. And yet, at the same time, since neo-pragmatism relativizes all viewpoints that oppose its corporate self or community, then it is easy for Barthian biblical theology itself to be pragmatically replaced by culturally postmodern rhetorics – or by whatever expediently fixed rhetorics the community's leadership prefers. Authoritarianism never submits to truth, but only to what those with the authority want, which can change arbitrarily.[35] So, 'neo-pragmatic Barthianism' easily morphs into 'neo-pragmatic multiculturalism', 'neo-pragmatic Buddhism', or 'neo-pragmatic whatever-you-like-ism'. Neo-pragmatism (like the demons themselves) is a shape-shifter: since (supposedly) belief is not anchored in accessible testable truth, then its only anchorage (in neo-pragmatism) becomes desire and power. 'Neo-pragmatic Barthianism', then, may look 'biblical', but it is ephemeral and self-exalting – it is a mere Bible-instrumentalizing, consumer choice of the community and of its leaders in particular.[36]

The problem with neo-pragmatic religion, therefore, Thiselton argues, is that it makes the community – and especially the community's leaders – the arbiters of what counts as 'true' within the community.[37] A leader *may* exalt Karl Barth, but he or she could also exalt a much less biblical figure, or anybody he or she likes. Since the leader's desire decides matters, then the community becomes an ego-extension of a personality, or of a clique of back-slapping nepotists – and thus becomes a self-imperializing tribe (we shall argue later that neo-pragmatists unsuccessfully resist this charge).[38]

Thus, neo-pragmatism inevitably descends into manipulative power abuse disguised by various masks of 'rightness' – whether such 'rightness' is 'biblical', 'pluralist', 'multicultural', 'environmental', 'artistic-protest-related', 'liberal democratic', 'feminist', and so on.[39] It often depends on whom the mask-wearer is trying to placate or impress. Thus, in neo-pragmatism, a shape-shifting chameleon-style expedient semblance, artifice or imposture of 'politeness' and 'right relating' masks elitist authoritarian absolutism, but is exposed by its relationally ephemeral character – by its lack of follow-through on promises, or by its pseudo-relational trans-temporal unfaithfulness. That is, and to build on Thiselton's analysis, we may deduce that neo-pragmatic pastors would tend to be exposed by their aped theatrics of 'right relating' through which they failed to follow up on promises. Anybody who complained about any of this would become like Kafka's 'Josef K' – passed from pillar to post in a sea of neo-pragmatic communicative unfaithfulness.[40] Thus, dealing with neo-pragmatic pastors would become like dealing with corporations who regarded themselves – and to use Christopher Norris's language – as 'beyond good and evil'.[41]

Much neo-pragmatic church, then, suffers from the theological irrelevance of *abstracted (i.e. de-relationalized) politically expedient-rhetoric* – i.e. from the theological irrelevance of emphases on political power and on nepotistic leadership cliques that suppress 'faithful relating that lifts up the other – over time'.

Now, of course, I agree that many who would call themselves liberal evangelical, post-evangelical or even neo-pragmatic Barthians are not at all this bad! Many are people of the highest moral calibre, I'm sure. And yet, it is not the people I am criticizing – it is the distorted theological and philosophical influences – and how they could (and sometimes do) outwork – that I am criticizing. It takes time for bad yeast to work through good dough – though, of course, 'God alone' 'is good'.[42]

Marginalization of biblical-relational Christianity

The problem, then, and moving on, is that these four or five kinds of distorted theological persuasion, which greatly affect the Western church today, all marginalize a biblical theology of right relating. In our view, this problem is a major cause of both Christian church-hopping and non-believers in the West seeing the Church as increasingly irrelevant.

But people's lives are relational. Their families are relational. Their workplaces are often relational. Their music is often about relationships. Their media are obsessed with relationships. And in many ways rightly so! For God created people to be relational, and wishes to redeem people from wrong relating and into right relating – for love sums up the law and the prophets, and sin is negated or distorted loving.

But why, then, do we almost never hear biblically based sermons with titles like: 'Three right ways of relating versus three wrong ways of relating'; or 'The relational fall-out from fornication'; or 'The distorted relational traits of the manipulator'; or 'What love means in practice'; or 'Kinds of bad relating that masquerade as love'; and so on?

If the entire flavour of the church was relational then Christians would stay involved, and non-believers would become interested. As it is, though, it is surely *God* who is closing non-relational churches down – simply because such churches have become distorted in their actual implicit theological persuasions, and in ways that undermine right relating as it is biblically defined. Surely, it is *Jesus himself* who is saying, 'Leave them; they are blind guides.'[43]

Again, Christian folks may not always be able to analyse these problems, but they can certainly feel them. No wonder they keep church-hopping. No wonder 40 per cent of real Christians are alienated from the church. They keep looking for their Master's voice, and can't abide listening to strangers.[44] Sometimes, it is the church-hoppers who are the true sheep, for the church sins in that it often shuns both proper biblical relational formation and those who help provide proper biblical relational formation.

This pervasive sin is far more serious than the obvious sin of the odd fallen priest. It is this pervasive sin, and not the odd obvious sin, that keeps the true gospel from literally millions upon millions of people. Those who condemn the whole church unfairly because of one tabloid exposé know that they are being unfair. Individuals mess up, regardless of persuasion. This is nothing new to the worldly, who mess up just the same.

But what the world takes more serious objection to in its more sober moments is distorted ideology and its effects – and rightly so! Christians too easily take cheap shots at great philosophers like Nietzsche and Heidegger for confusing biblical-relational Christianity with Platonism when,[45] all along, it was (and still is) *the church* that conflated biblical-relational Christianity with Platonism and with other philosophical strands. Nietzsche and Heidegger were (often) accurately describing the church, if not true biblical-relational Christianity. The confusion was our fault, not theirs!

Thus, it is often from the standpoint of a distorted non-biblical ideology that Christians say things such as: 'Oh dear, that "post-modernity" thing is a bit dangerous'; or, 'That Dan Brown's a bit of a problem.' So, surely, Jesus says, 'first take the plank out of your own eye', 'Stop judging by mere appearances, and make a right judgment' and 'You are Israel's teacher . . . and you do not understand these things?'[46]

And so, as Christians, we should not abandon cultural studies. Rather, we need such studies to help *us* to understand how *we* have distorted biblical-relational Christianity! That is, we need to ask: what kinds of distorted theological persuasion are actually implicitly or covertly (or even overtly) operative in our church structures, in our styles of worship, in our pastoral ministries and in our witness to the world? To these we now turn.

Distorted Church Structures as a Cause of Church-Hopping

Distortions of theological persuasion give rise to distortions of church structure. The latter also cause church-hopping, in my view.

Distorted church structures, infantilization and blocked ministries

Here, we will extend our arguments from our earlier chapters in which we highlighted overly hierarchical 'parent–child' church structures and leadership, as follows.

Thus, earlier on, we grounded distorted church hierarchies in the fall, in ancient Greek distortions of biblical Trinitarian thought, and in modernity's oppressive socio-economic, political, cultural, industrial, and even scientific 'systems'. We cited the example of the oppressive, authoritarian, dystopian regime portrayed in the film, *Gattaca*, so as to highlight distorted church hierarchies, structures, or cultures that we dubbed 'Reformaca' and 'Evangelica' – where we also coined the term 'Charismatica'.

In Reformaca unique people, their giftings and ministries, and their relationships, were marginalized and oppressed by 'the doctrine test', a 'system' – sometimes enforced by glowering inquisitorial overcoated Reverends – that strained out doctrinal gnats, but swallowed relational camels. One had to toe the doctrinal line to the letter – or else!

In Evangelica unique people, their giftings and ministries, and their relationships, were marginalized and oppressed by endlessly repeated behavioural formulae of neutered 'applica- tion', a 'system' – sometimes enforced by power-suited strength- projecting 'rescuers who themselves "never-needed-rescuing"' – that replaced right relating with highly competitive wall-to-wall activism. One never confessed an actual sin or weakness, nor desisted from exhausting activities for even a moment, in such settings – or else!

Now, of course, Reformaca and Evangelica are our caricatures of distortions that, in our view, *affect* the church – and are certainly not the whole truth! And yet, these caricatures are more than true enough for us to be worried, and so we may construct some others, as follows.

Thus, in Charismatica (including some less-intellectual mani- festations of liberal evangelicalism), unique people, their giftings and ministries, and their relationships, are marginalized and oppressed by endlessly repeated and insecurely asserted, content- free, super-spiritual theatrical pretensions and infantilizing aped-victimhood, by a 'system' – sometimes enforced by 'the caring-but-patronizing-buddy, nurture-parenting pastor' – that replaces right relating with a culture of perpetuated pleading for mystical succour coupled with bursts of show-cased, overdram- atized pretension that such succour has actually been given. One could never actually grow up as a Christian through an education that involved being formed by biblical language in such settings – or else!

Alternatively, in 'Liberalica', unique people, their giftings and ministries, and their relationships, are marginalized and oppressed by an elitism of competitive *Bildung*-style etiquette, a 'system' – sometimes enforced by Reverend-experts in the Romantic poets and novelists – that replaces right relating with a culture of competitively show-cased nuanced knowledge of the arts, 'right breeding', and theatrically deployed, status-securing, overly dramatized, hypersensitive, hair-trigger blushing embarrassment and exaggerated sharp intakes of breath at the etiquette-breaching gaucherie and ill-bred insensibilities of any who indulge in uneducated assertions, statements of allegiance, displays of feeling, relational divulgences, confessions related to sanctification, colloquialisms, parochialisms, vernacular, and the non-erudite in general. The liberal is 'always intellectually maturer than you' – and Northerners need not apply (that's me out for a start)!

Or, in 'Post-Evangelical Neo-Pragmatica', unique people, their giftings and ministries, and their relationships, are marginalized and oppressed by an elitism of nuanced flattering-but-covertly-nepotistic-and-self-advancing, manicured, truth-deflecting, cliquey rhetoricism, a 'system' – sometimes enforced by skilled slippery manipulators ironically blind to their own abuses – that replaces right relating with a culture of managed initiatives designed to advance leaders' ecclesial careers through the skilled flattery of key others, whilst at the same time 'making all the right public-sphere noises', and yet being known for a lack of faithful follow-through in relation to the expectation-structures created amongst the gullible (read: 'folks with integrity') who are as yet unable to spot the artifice and expedient imposture of faked sincerity. Somehow, and to use C. Norris's language again, the Post-Evangelical Neo-Pragmatics are 'beyond good and evil' *even when the cat is out of the bag* – and one always gets the sense that there is a party somewhere to which one is not invited; so much for bringing 'in the poor, the crippled, the blind and the lame'.[47]

In our view, then, whilst Reformaca, Evangelica, Charismatica, Liberalica and Post-Evangelical Neo-Pragmatica are to an extent caricatures, and not the whole truth, they are still more than true enough and more than real enough for us to be worried.

Moreover, to the extent that these distorted hierarchies are real, which is considerable, then they suppress 'right relating', unique persons, and persons' unique callings, unique giftings and unique ministries beneath conformity to 'systems'. Real biblical-relational Christianity, in which 'love sums up the law and the prophets', is subsumed beneath static – or at least arbitrary – endlessly repetitious cycles of non-relational ritualistic, theatrical, or political habituated conformity.

Western Christianity has been de-relationalized.

In earlier chapters (3–5), and drawing on Thiselton, we argued that a sinful marginalization of doctrinal training amongst some ordinands – resulting in a broad lack of critical awareness – had contributed to this situation. Jesus would exclaim, 'You are Israel's teacher . . . and you do not understand these things?' We also argued, following Thiselton, that postmodern, narcissistic, Corinthian-style, limelight-hugging, applause-seeking, celebrity-seeking local heroism amongst some church leaders had contributed to this same situation.[48] Such deluded, self-sufficient self-promotion was the sin of 'Diotrephes, who loves to be first', the sin of seeking power.[49]

Here, we may extend the additional point that we made through Chapters 3 to 5 in which we argued, in effect, that the double sin of marginalizing doctrinal training and of seeking power was sometimes cloaked or disguised by strategies of infantilization and of blocking certain gifts and killing certain ministries, as follows.

Thus, we suggested that a church culture of infantilization had sometimes developed that hindered and discouraged church members' growth into maturity (cf. the fruit of the Spirit) by turning the razor-sharp relational, partly conceptual, partly critical, person- and church-building, educational and formative power of biblical revelation (cf. the word/sword of the Spirit) into an endless, humdrum, Spirit-quenching, indoctrinating repetition of domesticated, neutered 'basics', or of politically correct rhetorics, in direct disobedience to Hebrews 6:1–3.

But, drawing on Thiselton, if '*education* . . . opens and expands' 'horizons', *indoctrination* or 'propaganda' 'closes and stunts the mind by directing it to pre-packed answers', to the mere 'mechanical' 'repetition' of received systems.[50] Power-seekers, then, love to propagandize – for power is threatened by people becoming dangerously mature. And besides, narcissists *want* to please the anti-intellectual audiences of today – either by spoon-feeding them the bland rhetorics of contemporary postmodern culture, or by spoon-feeding them the content-free 'gospel' of 'harmless nice-ness' – the cartoon-like, home-grown 'local theology' of in-house celebrities that 'their itching ears want to hear'.[51]

The result, though, is a church culture of 'tot-level Sunday-school for adults' that alienates any Christians *or non-Christians* who reject infantilization, and that suppresses any preaching that brings the maturity-forming, disciple-making power of the Scriptures alive. Such church cultures thus deliberately obstruct spiritual development.

But, in order to deny the reality of this sin, such church cultures market their approach as 'right pitching', as 'not forgetting the basics', and as 'an answer to intellectualism and "mere academic knowledge"'. Thus, typical of propagandists, they emphasize the one sin that isn't happening! Today, the prophet does not say, 'Repent of intellectualism', but 'Repent of anti-intellectualism and obey Hebrews 6:1–3!' As Don Carson puts it, 'This is not a gener-ation that thinks; it is a generation which, every time it is threat-ened by thought, turns up the CD player.'[52]

We also argued earlier (in Chapter 4) that, often, church cultures that blocked certain gifts (i.e. the gifts of the Spirit) so as to kill certain ministries had developed in the church. Teachers, prophets, healers, and counsellors especially were often suppressed and marginalized.

To defend this sin against the Spirit, such church cultures either asserted or assumed that these ministries were already covered by the leadership, or mislabelled 'every-member-practical-service' as 'every-member-ministry' (though these two spheres do indeed overlap). Challengers were rebuked and told 'not to be so proud', 'not to want only high-profile roles', 'not to refuse to do practical tasks', or 'not to become part of the uninvolved 96 per cent'.

Of course, though, church leaders did not necessarily have the gifts of teaching, prophecy, healing, and counselling – and / or did not necessarily have the most mature expressions of these gifts. Such rebukes, then, were merely the projected disowning of certain church leaders' own wrong attitudes and tendencies – atti-tudes and tendencies that were falsely marketed by such church leaders as being 'the challengers' problem'.

Thus, whilst such church leaders themselves often had some kind of maturity, they often deliberately fostered church cultures that did not reproduce their own level of maturity in others: they hoarded maturity for themselves so as to preserve power (see Chapters 3 and 4). The systematic suppression of even the wisdom required for folks to *find* their Spirit-given gifts is, we suggested in Chapter 4, an undeniable fact in many churches today: church members, we argued, are *trained* into coming to church without *any* expectation of growing into ministries of various kinds.

That is: people church-hop because of person-oppressing, gift-suppressing, ministry-killing, and de-relationalizing hierarchies, power bases or systems of conformity.

The silencing of true prophets and theologians

The most disturbing aspect of these problematic church cultures, perhaps, is that they cast aside the true prophets, listen to false prophets and have caused God to withdraw blessing.

Jesus said, 'no prophet is accepted in his home town . . . there were many in Israel with leprosy in the time of Elisha the prophet, yet not one of them was cleansed – only Naaman the Syrian.'[53] That is, a national sin of rejecting prophets – a national sin copied by the church – can mean that not a single person from the offending nation or church is healed by God. Divine favour – or disfavour – towards a nation or church is tied to how that nation or church treats the true prophets.

And so will God bless the church if it marginalizes the true prophets and cannot even recognize the true prophets anymore, preferring and favouring instead the false prophecies of home-grown, celebrity-seeking 'local heroes'? I doubt it.

Earlier, we noted Thiselton's true prophecy about the post-modern or neo-pragmatic Western church's narcissistic, 'socially constructed value-system based on "recognition" and virtual realities created by rhetoric, consumerism, peer-group competition, and self-promotion';[54] about its 'obsessive desire for a self-perception and status defined by how peer-groups "recognize" themselves or others';[55] about its 'religion' reduced to 'a vehicle of self-affirmation, peer-group self-promotion, or triumphalism, coupled with a notion of "God" that amounts to a projection of human desires and interests';[56] and about its sermons constructed only to create 'pragmatic rhetorical effect and' win 'audience applause',[57] such that 'Every effusion is greeted with a storm of ready-made applause', resulting in 'vanity and empty self-sufficiency'.[58]

And yet, can we even recognize these comments as prophecy, or understand what this true prophet is saying about us? Have we so perverted even the very notion of 'prophecy' that real prophecy is unrecognizable and mislabelled as 'mere academic knowledge'?

Thiselton exposes our sin here when he writes that, according to Paul the apostle:

> Prophetic speech may include *applied theological teaching, encourage-ment, and exhortation to build the church,* not merely (if at all) ad hoc cries of an expressive, diagnostic, or tactical nature, delivered as 'spontane-ous' mini-messages. The latter debase and trivialize the great tradi-tion of the term in the biblical writings as something altogether more serious, sustained, and reflective.[59]

That is, true prophecy is serious, not trivial; sustained, not a matter of spontaneous mini-messages; and reflective, not a matter of expressive ad hoc cries. Certainly, genuine prophecy does not suppress – but rather includes – biblical teaching.

We, though, have often reinvented prophecy so as to suppress the true prophecy that involves true biblical teaching. Indeed, the church routinely alienates even its internationally renowned theo-logians – as, for example, in the case of Leonardo Boff.[60]

Churches drinking deep from the wells of cultural anti-intellec-tualism routinely mislabel theologians, casting them aside as 'hope-less liberals', 'mere academics in ivory towers', or as having only 'intellectual' or 'academic' knowledge that 'does not relate to life'.

Some church leaders, who confuse their institutional authority with theological authority, thus speak as if only they had, or had courted, 'real-life-experience', or as if only they were 'the most mature teachers'. Perhaps, then, they should try being oppressed or hard-shouldered – just to see if it seems 'real-life enough' for them! No doubt some of their extraordinarily low levels of matur-ity would then be overcome.

Such marginalizing of true prophets and theologians, then, is like saying, 'I fly aeroplanes, so I know everything about aircraft engineering'! But what pilot says, 'I don't need aircraft engineers, because their understanding is "only technical"'? Granted, pilots fly the plane. But only a suicidal pilot who cares nothing for his passengers is unconcerned about his plane's air-worthiness. Without true prophets and theologians, the church crashes and burns on its way to wrong destinations – every single time.

Indeed, this is happening right now in the person-oppressing, gift-suppressing, ministry-killing, and de-relationalizing hier- archies, power bases or systems of conformity that we have highlighted. And this is hardly just my viewpoint. Earlier on, in Chapter 5, we drew on D.F. Wells and P. Ward in order to highlight the evangelical church's degenerative transition from 'confes- sionalism' to 'transconfessionalism', in which distorted philo- sophically neo-pragmatic emphases on 'strategy', 'organizational power' and 'present' 'charismatic' 'experience' of the 'Spirit' are displacing right biblical emphases on 'doctrine'.[61]

The resulting hungry flock: 'the bleating of the lambs'

Unfortunately, moreover, it is not only true prophets, teachers and theologians who are alienated by such abuses of hierar- chical power, by such institutionalized resistance to biblical content and formation. Many, many people – and not just true prophets, teachers and theologians – church-hop or move between churches because they simply can't get the practical theology and the practical wisdom they need these days to help them with the various life crises that come along.

Even as a youngish theologian, I get a constant stream of folks coming to me who are starving for biblical content and formation because the church no longer feeds the flock. The other night I spent about two hours training somebody how to be in relation- ship with God in a way that involves the Holy Spirit's forma- tive activation of biblical speech-acts (see Chapter 1 above). That person had attended church for *thirty years* without having been trained in what to do in order to have such a relationship with God. But it took only *two hours* to train them!

In other words, when you silence the true prophet, the teacher, and the theologian, you don't get 'the silence of the lambs' – you get the bleating of the lambs.

The problem, then, is not so much to do with church hierarchy *per se* but, rather, hinges on *distorted* church structures and hierarchies that presuppose false ideologies and that block truly prophetic, biblical relational theology and its formative outworking.

Genuine church leadership, though, does not 'lord it over' the other but lifts up the other: serving the changing needs of individuals as they grow into their unique personhoods, relationships, giftings and ministries; and forming unique churches with unique every-member ministries that match the unique gift-profiles of their particular members.[62]

And genuine church leadership does not play 'critical parent' or 'nurture parent' to folks who are perpetually rebuked or suckled as though they were infants (even if that's what church members want). Rather, genuine church leadership manages both to exercise leadership and to encourage adult-to-adult relating, free of distorted power dynamics.

Unfortunately, though, many are those who have church-hopped because distorted church structures or hierarchies suppressed their unique individualities, personhoods, giftings, ministries and relationships beneath conformity to an alien ideology, to an unbiblical true-prophecy-and-true-theology-suppressing 'system', to the flock-starving irrelevance of *abstracted (i.e. de-relationalized) repetitious patronization.*

Distorted Styles of Worship as a Cause of Church-Hopping

Distorted theological persuasions also tend to engender distorted worship styles. In Chapter 3, we noted how true worship involved: union with Jesus Christ; communion with Jesus Christ, with God the Father, and with the Holy Spirit, through Jesus Christ's mediation, in the Holy Spirit; glorying in God's holy name; unconditional thanksgiving; remembering God's mighty historical acts; shunning unbelief regarding God's promises; drinking from God's Spirit (which, in line with Jesus' responses to the woman at the well, involved not only mystical succour but also being formed relationally by the Spirit's biblical speech-acts); and empowered sanctity and service for others in the church and the world.

Conversely, we concluded that counterfeit worship stressed only the mystical aspect of worship, and routinely suppressed:

(a) biblical language about God's attributes, historical deeds and promises;
(b) the Spirit's speech-actions through the biblical texts that form and mature the Christian and the church in the biblical wisdom that is necessarily part of wise-relating – or love – towards God and others;
(c) biblical language and criteria by which the church can 'test the spirits' or interpret so-called prophetic pictures.

One could not worship or love the biblical God (as opposed to some idol, unnamed spirit, or subjective impulse), or love one's neighbour, if one did not listen to God through the Bible. Counterfeit worship, in thus subverting love for God and neighbour, narcissistically and hedonistically 'worshipped worship *itself*' and 'celebrated celebration *itself*' – not least so that subtly abusive hierarchies of structural power could therein keep people infantile relative to leaders' weekly 'wise-ones' theatrics.

Distorted 'freedoms' in worship

Clearly, such counterfeit worship is associated with the distorted power structures that we have highlighted using the term, 'Charismatica'. Under existentialist and neo-pragmatic philosophical influences, Charismatica, including charismatic liberal evangelicalism, tends to access biblical texts through an overly prioritized, subjective mystical ecstatic experience of 'the Spirit', and tends to suppress the proper functioning of biblical language by indulging in a hedonistic postmodern spirit – in a biblically un-refereed cultus of post-liturgical 'play'.

Not surprisingly, Liberalica and Post-Evangelical Neo-Pragmatica also tend to marginalize the proper functioning of biblical language – not least during worship.

Thus, under the influences of existentialism and positivism (both of which are related to neo-Kantianism), Liberalica tends

to view cognitive content (including biblical cognitive content
– i.e. concepts, doctrine, promises, historical statements, assertions and/or propositions) as being of entirely human origin.
Thus, Liberalica tends to view the biblical texts as primitive
human expressions of Christian faith when compared with
'modern' 'advanced' concepts[63] – and therein indulges in a 'white
mythology' of modernist 'progress'.[64] At the same time, Liberalica allows that biblical symbolism – falsely up-anchored from its
biblical explanatory matrices on the grounds of malformed hermeneutical theory – can be used in worship in order (supposedly)
to 'mediate' a divine reality that is supposedly wholly beyond –
rather than beyond-but-inclusive-of – the conceptual plane.

Conversely, under the influence of neo-pragmatic philosophy,
Post-Evangelical Neo-Pragmatica can tend to try (unsuccessfully)
to hold together a pseudo-Barthian epistemology of revelation –
in which biblical language is exalted in a fundamentalist manner
that disallows critical questioning – with a Fishian (i.e. after
Stanley Fish) epistemology according to which biblical language
is supposedly inaccessible objectively and assumed to be understood only as community-shaped, Spirit-aided projections *onto*
the biblical texts.

Thus, in Post-Evangelical Neo-Pragmatica, an authoritarianism
of the word is subsumed beneath an authoritarianism of 'what
the Holy Spirit told the church leaders that the word said'. Thus,
despite appeals to Barth, emphases on the authority of the Bible
are in practice subsumed beneath emphases on the authority of
subjective experience, which effectively makes the interpreter
'lord'. In practice, neo-pragmatic church leaders – having thus
asserted lordship over God's word Pharisee-style (see Chapter 3)
– are then 'free' to seek popularity and celebrity by conforming
'God's word' to contemporary, postmodern utopian 'allowed
rhetorics' (on which, see Chapter 9), which leads to some very
odd, very unbiblical, liturgies.

And so, consequently, both Liberalica and Post-Evangelical
Neo-Pragmatica lean towards kinds of counterfeit worship that, in
their marginalizing of the proper functioning of biblical language,
are not entirely dissimilar to the kind of counterfeit worship that
Charismatica leans towards. All three church cultures emphasize
a supposed and purported 'freedom' of expression in relation to

worship. This supposed and purported 'freedom' of expression, however, is grounded in part in an *unacknowledged 'freedom' from the proper functioning of biblical language* (though vestiges of good liturgical practice often persist in older-style liberal settings).

Such 'freedom', though, and as we have already said, easily becomes an 'idolatry of mystical succour *itself*' that suppresses the worship of the biblical God whose attributes, historical deeds and promises should be celebrated and proclaimed, and whose various biblical speech-acts should be allowed to form or build both the Christian and the church.

Thus, Liberalica's high church symbolism, as we argued above, is often abstracted from its biblical explanatory and formative matrices[65] – matrices that do not only function as right explanations of symbols, but also as speech-acts that can be activated by the Holy Spirit – speech-acts that Liberalica suppresses. And Post-Evangelical Neo-Pragmatica, we indicated above, tends to turn state-promoted, postmodern liberal 'allowed rhetorics' (see Chapter 9) into new liturgies that canonize humanistic, utopian propaganda instead of the Scriptures (the latter are considered to be 'offensive' and politically incorrect).

Charismatica's worship jingles are just as bad in that they tend to allow the Holy Spirit to activate – as formative speech-acts – only slogans and teenage-crush lyrics. Thus, the Holy Spirit is allowed to open up only tiny impoverished language-worlds that have few points of relational resonance or connection with our hearts, minds and relational lives. This situation is not helped by an under-developed musical understanding that thinks that the theme tune to *Rainbow* can 'open up' the 'depths of' 'the soul'. The result is a relational claustrophobia that imposes teenage relational crush-dynamics – or even 'tots-at-a-puppet-show' relational dynamics – onto adults who are trying to worship. Thus, Charismatica's jingles deprive adults of genuine adult relational contact with God. And yet, the adults are often then berated (as though they *were* tots) for not 'pushing into worship'![66]

By contrast, the proper *liturgical* use of the Bible in worship does not only involve the proclamation of true Christological (and other biblical) content; it also opens up a myriad of linguistic possibilities for the Holy Spirit to activate as biblical speech-acts in proper self-involving liturgical relationship to us

– so that the Christian and the church can thereby be formed and transformed, or 'built'.

One pastor, known to the present author, brilliantly highlights an additional problem with Charismatica's worship style: the shift from a proclamation of *divine* acts to a proclamation of *human* acts. Thus, celebration of creation, the cross, forgiveness, redemption and promise is replaced by celebration of 'stepping in', 'coming to God', 'shouting praise', 'falling down', and so on.[67] Here, though, we see the narcissistic component of over-realized eschatology: 'Here I am before you, God, in my as-though-fully-redeemed and heavenly state, smiling a sickly smile that is exactly how I would smile if I knew you *now* like I *will* know you in heaven, O Lord.'

True worship, though, is not a theatrical role-performance of self-promoting showmanship embodying grimaces and gesticulations that ape a counterfeit version of the heavenly experience so as to win audience-applause or peer-recognition from supposedly jealous onlookers who have not yet achieved such 'rapture'. Worship has to reflect reality, and in this sense, is not 'free' (to pretend) at all.

Distorted 'forms' in worship

If worship is to reflect reality, though, then it cannot be reduced to alignment with notions of 'form' that we might associate with Reformaca and/or with Evangelica either.

Admittedly, we have argued that Reformaca, Evangelica, Charismatica, Liberalica and Post-Evangelical Neo-Pragmatica are all oppressive systems. We deployed inverted commas when we used the word 'freedom' and its cognates when speaking just now about Charismatica, Liberalica and Post-Evangelical Neo-Pragmatica because, actually, such church cultures promote endlessly repeated, relationally claustrophobic 'forms' of worship every bit as much as Reformaca and Evangelica do. It is just that whereas in Charismatica, Liberalica and Post-Evangelical Neo-Pragmatica biblical language itself is marginalized – in kinds of worship that are 'free' of such supposed 'encumberment' – then, by contrast, in Reformaca and Evangelica, biblical language is kept but is often reduced to its cognitive functions by an overemphasis on abstract systems of de-relationalized scholastic doctrine (in Reformaca) or of de-relationalized activist application (in Evangelica).

True worship, though, is to be properly *liturgical*. It can no more be reduced to cognitive or applied-cognitive language-uses than it can be reduced to pre-cognitive-immanent mysticism or to pre-cognitive-transcendental mysticism. True worship is neither a Reformed cognitive doctrine-test nor a conservative evangelical activistic after-the-fact application of cognitive doctrine. Such aberrations merely self-consciously and self-promotingly purloin and instrumentalize biblical content in order to show-case counterfeit personal piety-levels in ways that suppress the relational-liturgical aspect of worship and that mask the existential and relational realities of the human condition.

That is, true worship embeds correct truth-content *within* loving relational and/or biblical-liturgical, self-involving language-uses towards and from God – loving relational and/or biblical-liturgical, self-involving language-uses that, furthermore, reflect the true existential and relational realities of our 'created, yet fallen, yet being-redeemed-unto-eternal-life' condition. True worship should not tell lies about the human condition any more than it should tell lies about God. True worship does not pretend that people are doctrine-shaped or activism-determined pious automatons, for human beings are not conservative machines.

Rather, true worship in *this* life, whilst being undeniably directed God-ward and focused on God, necessarily involves humans-in-their-current-condition-in-the-fallen-world-praising-the-biblical-God. True worship is a matter of being before God as we really are in the reality we are really in, and involves human persons as they really are, in their real concrete uniqueness and relationships, in the real world, before the real God.

Certainly, true worship is not just a matter of 'form versus freedom'. True worship does not just belong to the emotional, cognitive or behavioural planes, but rather belongs to the broader plane of human life in all its dimensions before God in all his dimensions.

True worship, then, holds together real humanity and real divinity, and is in part the authentic relationship between precisely these two.

Thus, true worship in this life is like true art. Any study of the history of art will show how art has attempted to explore every aspect of reality and truth: God, humanity, creation, form,

beauty, colour, light, darkness, the ideal, the eternal, the existential, rationality, the external world, the internal world, representation, experience, feeling, expression, history, the past, the present
moment, the future, movement, stability, the revolutionary, the
destructive, the family, the male, the female, the young, the old,
the fall, absurdity, the irrational, abstraction, chaos, pain, war, the
tragic, the funny, alienation, inclusion, relationships, celebration,
how things appear now, promise, redemptive hope, transforma-
tion, joy, and so on and so forth.[68]

True worship goes on forever because it progressively and
cumulatively explores and celebrates a Creator whose glories
never end. Even what God has created is a source of endless
complexity, diversity, dynamism, unity and wonder. How much
more so is God himself?

And yet, just as true art acknowledges every aspect of the
real, and seeks to explode harmful delusions, so true worship in
this life does not pretend it is already in the next life. Thiselton's
phrase, 'over-realized eschatology', can be applied just as easily
to Reformaca and Evangelica – which sometimes act as though
their doctrine and/or application were already of eschatological
quality – as it can to Charismatica, which sometimes acts as if its
Christian experience was already of eschatological quality.[69] The
psalmist writes: 'From my youth I have been afflicted and close
to death; I have suffered your terrors and am in despair.'[70] This is
miles away from the pretentiously show-cased 'doctrine', 'application' or 'experience' of such 'over-realized eschatologies'.

Now, of course, in true worship, aspects of the real such as
absurdity or chaos cannot be prioritized above future hope
like they are in art movements such as Dadaism or Surrealism.
Nevertheless, no true worship in this life can deny the full range
– including the darker elements – of human experience, just as
no true art can deny them. True life, true art, true relating, true
liturgy, and true worship converge – for real Christianity in a
fallen world demands 'patient endurance and faithfulness on the
part of the saints'.[71]

And so, if worship is reduced either to 'form' or to 'freedom'
in the ways noted above then it becomes abstracted from a Spirit-led, God-ward, self-involving, biblical-relational, liturgical,
formative and truly-artistic expression of 'the human as it really

is before the real God'. Since this has often in fact happened, then the church suffers from the irrelevance of *abstracted (i.e. de-relationalized) worship expression* – or from the irrelevance of patterns of worship expression that do not relate to true divine identity and relationality or to (the formation of) true human identities and relationships. Therefore, people sometimes church-hop and look for a fuller or 'more real' kind of worship.

Distorted Pastoral Practice as a Cause of Church-Hopping

The distortions of church culture that we have highlighted so far all cause church-hopping – not least because, additionally, they can cause the church to descend into distorted pastoral practices.

Distorted pastoral practice: irrelevant 'abstract salvation'

The following paragraphs summarize some of the concerning pastoral implications that have emerged from our discussion of distorted church cultures so far.

(a) Abstracted *doctrine-applied* brings a lack of ability to interpret pastoral situations wisely, since these situations are largely relational. The theologian Gerhard Ebeling spoke of 'pious words which have no bearing on reality'.[72]

(b) Abstracted *experience* emphases bring a pseudo-pastoral mirage of false hope that says that healing or 'breaking through' can literally be always just around the corner. Such emphases replace biblical solutions to issues with perpetual assertion. Now, of course, we must pray for healing and for reform; and we must wait on God with a right kind of expectation; but we should not do these things at the expense of biblical religion, or at the expense of wrongly defining what redemptive relationship with God involves.

(c) Abstracted *self-cultivation* (cf. *Bildung*) also evades the kinds of biblical wisdom and formation that are required for helping others. A hermeneutically premature ditching of biblical wisdom and formation on the basis of outdated 'neo-Kantian', existentialist, positivist and/or neo-pragmatic philosophy makes way for abstract or near-secular pastoral theologies and practices that prematurely shelve the biblical pastoring and formation that are pertinent to relational sanctification.

(d) Abstracted *politically expedient rhetoric* replaces biblically wise 'right relating' with a politically motivated sophistry of insincere communication that is divorced from relational faithfulness. The result is secretive leadership cliques – internally complicated by their own intrigues – that act out only a semblance, artifice or expedient imposture of 'right relating' towards non-leaders who, when trying to address real issues, face a Kafkaesque 'Josef K' 'bounced from pillar to post' effect – a sheer unwillingness on the part of leaders to communicate honestly and straightforwardly or to follow-through on interpersonal-level promises or pledges. Such leaders are often too busy creating a tribe-level, politically correct, multicultural post-doctrinal carnival of purported 'inclusiveness'.

(e) Abstracted *patronization* suppresses right relating, suppresses unique personhood and giftings, uses infantilization to block maturity, and marginalizes or even kills individuals' ministries. Whole lives of ministry for God are suppressed – sometimes with reference to fictional 'issues' that this or that person from 'God's awkward squad' is 'struggling with'. Meanwhile, limelight-hugging narcissists and ecclesial career-ladder climbers remain blissfully unaware of their own issues, and complain of a 'lack of personnel available for church-based practical tasks'.

(f) Abstracted *expression* blocks biblical-relational-liturgical, worshipful communion with God, and is the other side of the coin to abstracted experience. Through these two distortions, worshipful experience and expression become reduced to 'experience of experience *itself*' and 'expression of expression *itself*' – to a counterfeit 'celebration of celebration *itself*' or 'worship of worship *itself*' – to 'worship' purloined and deployed as show-cased attention-seeking that is abstracted from genuine biblical-relational-liturgical and biblically formative glorying in the Lord, his attributes, deeds and promises.

And so, subtly abusive pastoral practice – marked by (a) to (f) above – suffers from the irrelevance of a proffered *abstract (i.e.*

de-relationalized) salvation – or from the irrelevance of a proffered 'salvation' that does not relate to, but rather suppresses and harms, personal and relational realities.

Distorted pastoral practice: too close to cult dynamics for comfort

It is crucial to note, then, that we are not talking about obvious immorality, cults or fundamentalisms here, but about all-pervasive distortions that affect very large sections of the whole Western church. And yet, having said this, it is also true to say that some of these distortions are in fact co-extensive with cult-type characteristics. R. Howard's study of the infamous 'Nine O'Clock Service' cult in 1980s to 1990s Sheffield superbly analyses cult-type characteristics.[73] We may summarize these characteristics – adding in a few additional observations – in our own paraphrase, as follows:

(a) Secretiveness and information control beyond appropriate confidentialities;
(b) Asymmetries of hierarchical status and privilege;
(c) Different rules for privileged members closer to the centre of power;
(d) Use of social manipulation to undermine people (e.g. putting an older brother in a Bible-study group led by his younger brother);
(e) Creating insecurities and then mislabelling them as something else so as to create 'ministry opportunities';
(f) Parent–child relating, against the principles of transactional analysis;[74]
(g) Requiring assent to unbiblical dogmas;
(h) Arbitrary tests of submissiveness and obedience;
(i) Fraud, indulgence in luxury, or unrepentant immorality at the centre of power;
(j) Complaints about 'having to do everything oneself', and yet lack of delegation of power;
(k) Personality cults, and their sentimentalism, victim-playing and emotivism;
(l) Unwillingness to be confronted coupled with willingness to confront;

(m) Lack of accountability to non-leadership;
(n) Requiring servanthood without modelling servanthood;
(o) Assertions that 'our group is the only group to have the truth';
(p) Assertions that 'our group has the only way to be saved';
(q) Indoctrination where critical questioning is disallowed;
(r) Use of rhetoric about a 'critical spirit' so as to disallow critical questioning;
(s) De-centring of Christ as Lord and God;
(t) Elevation of the cult-leader – e.g. to the status of 'Lord, apostle, or prophet';
(u) Denial of the biblical doctrine and historicity of the cross of Christ and denial of other central biblical doctrines and testimonies;
(v) Exaltation of texts other than the biblical texts in a manner that goes beyond practices that reflect genuine scholarly questions concerning the scope of the biblical canon;
(w) Blocking high-profile ministries of congregation members – notably teachers, prophets, healers and counsellors (cult leaders will tend to steal these roles from those to whom they rightly belong, not least through the use of false testimony and slander disguised as 'legitimate concerns').

When such characteristics shape our church structures, hierarchies or leaderships then Jesus says, 'Leave them; they are blind guides.'[75] Right use of power is never bullying, manipulative, intimidating, patronizing, infantilizing or controlling.

Whilst a good church or institution will strive to abolish such abuses, however, it is sobering to realize that some of the above cult characteristics tend to be present in all church institutions – indeed, in all human institutions. The patterns may be more subtle – but whoever said that mainstream churches were immunized against spiritual abuse?

Distorted pastoral practice: inadequate for complex issues

Thus, for example, the biblical texts may not sanction homosexual practice. But they do not sanction the relational abuse of self-designated homosexuals either. If more 'liberal' churches tend to strip away, from 'relating', the very biblical-relational criteria (including doctrine) by which 'relating' is to be refereed under God – replacing

these criteria with acquiescence to the norms of the cultural Zeitgeist, avoidance of right confrontation, and hermeneutical licence
– then what sins do more 'conservative' churches commit when it
comes to their relating to self-designated homosexuals?

Well, in my view, 'conservative' relational abuses of self-designated homosexuals stem from the replacing of biblical-relational
wisdom with de-relationalized 'biblical' doctrine. Notably, fleshly
legalism then tends to displace right relating despite St Paul's
exposure of fleshly legalism as being a false or erroneous response
to fleshly lawlessness (on fleshly legalism see Chapter 3 above).

The result of this error, first, is a blind, patronizing pseudo-familiarity with the homosexuality issue 'in which it seems as if one
has understood everything' when, in fact, 'understanding has not
genuinely taken place'. Heidegger called such pseudo-familiarity
'ambiguity'.[76] In neo-pragmatic 'conservative' cultures especially,
where one's projected rhetoric about oneself becomes even more
easily confused with 'truth', some could purport to relate well to
self-designated homosexuals without realizing that they were in fact
being abusive. When Jesus confronted such premature pretensions
of 'sightedness', however, he said, 'your guilt remains.'[77]

Second, when de-relationalized 'biblical' doctrine displaces
biblical relational wisdom and right relating, then genuine understanding of unique persons and their unique situations tends to
be subsumed beneath a prior 'netting' of imposed categories,
assumptions, stereotypifications, artificial constructs, closed statements, superficial generalizing explanations or pigeonholes which,
taken together, amount to false testimony. Gadamer called this
premature fusion of horizons 'Method'.[78] When Jesus confronted
such epistemological objectivism he said, 'Stop judging by mere
appearances, and make a right judgment.'[79]

Third, another 'conservative' sin against self-designated homosexuals involves summing up such persons prematurely by using
single words that are strategically designed to impute negative
emotive content and moral defamation. Philosophers call such
stigmatization-by-naming, 'persuasive definition'. However,
Jesus is far from impressed with such relationally delinquent
'phrase-regimes' of self-righteous finger-pointing and intellectual
oversimplification, and warns, 'the tax collectors and the prosti-
tutes are entering the kingdom of God ahead of you.'[80]

Fourth, it is similarly contrary to biblical relational wisdom and to biblical lawfulness or right relating to *a priori* establish discriminating structures of judgement and exclusion or relational deprivation that scapegoat certain kinds of persons as belonging to a 'worse category of sinner'. Such practices directly contradict Jesus' teaching in The Parable of the Pharisee and the Tax Collector – notably where Jesus says, 'everyone who exalts himself will be humbled, and he who humbles himself will be exalted,' for (as Jesus teaches elsewhere) 'No-one is good – except God alone.'[81]

And, fifth, there is the sin of fleshly legalism itself which, like the demons, shows no mercy, but which oppressively demands immediate total conformity to the whole law – or, rather, to a rule-based de-relationalized distortion of the law – as a self-justifying precondition for the possibility of loving relationship when, in fact, biblical lawfulness *is* loving relationship (see Chapter 3 on biblical lawfulness). So Paul says: 'by faith we eagerly await through the Spirit the righteousness for which we hope.' Indeed: 'judgment without mercy will be shown to anyone who has not been merciful.'[82]

And so both 'love' without doctrine and 'doctrine' without love break God's law: neither non-refereed 'play' nor oppressive 'system' constitute true love or right relating. Therefore, both sides of the church's debate about homosexuality strain out ideological gnats and swallow relational camels.

Distorted pastoral practice: divorced from genuine prophetic discourse

Genuinely prophetic discourse, we indicated earlier, presupposes and deploys biblical-relational formative wisdom. Such discourse and wisdom should pervasively salt our preaching, teaching, pastoring and our conversation more broadly – both in and out of church settings.

Notably, genuine prophetic discourse is involved in the pastoral application of biblical-relational formative wisdom to 'promoting unique persons – including their unique gifts and ministries' and to 'promoting right relating – as practised by Jesus'.

Thus, genuine prophetic discourse will be evident when individuals are being pastorally lifted up into their unique personhoods,

gifts and ministries; and when pastoral workshops are training
people out of wrong relating and into right relating.

In genuine prophetic discourse, therefore, sin will be acknowledged and analysed, yes; but such discourse will centre on the
positives of the gospel, mercy, forgiveness and pastoral training
into the twin-goods of 'promoting unique persons – including
their unique gifts and ministries' and 'promoting right relating –
as practised by Jesus'.

Counterfeit pseudo-Christian or pseudo-prophetic discourse,
though, will reflect the five distorted church cultures that are associated with the person-suppressing and right-relationship-sup-
pressing 'systems' that we noted above. That is, counterfeit
pseudo-Christian or pseudo-prophetic discourse will reflect:

(a) the suppression of unique persons (including their unique gifts
     and ministries) and of 'right relating' and/or relationships;
(b) attempts to conform persons to distorted systems through
     infantilizing indoctrination;
(c) leadership that polices these wrong uses of authority;
(d) a theatrics of pretended conformity that disguises a sea of
     'un-dealt-with' personal and relational problems – notably
     those problems that are caused *by* the same church systems
     that claim to offer pastoral solutions *to* those problems.

That is, counterfeit pseudo-Christian or pseudo-prophetic
discourse will be *conflicted*. There will be leadership-policed
infantilizing indoctrination coupled with utterances that show-
case conformity to that indoctrination; and there will be perpetual
disgruntled grumbling – including by pastors themselves –
about perpetually unaddressed and suppressed personal and
relational problems and grievances, notably those caused by the
church.

And never the twain shall meet!

Real Christianity, though, largely *is* a pastoral redemptive
addressing of personal and relational problems and grievances.
Therefore, ironically and shockingly, it is the grumbling side of this
conflicted discourse that is more right: genuinely prophetic Christian discourse seeks to address what the grumbling is about, but
is perpetually overruled and hindered by the leadership-policed

abstracted discourses of distorted pseudo-Christian ideologies – so that you cannot say what you want or need to say!

Above, we said that genuine prophetic discourse centred on certain positive emphases. Nevertheless, we also said that in such discourse, sin would be acknowledged and analysed – as part of building people up, not tearing them down. So then, genuine prophetic discourse still involves appropriate confessional humility and transparency.

These days, though, the creeping sameness of neo-pragmatism has so infiltrated Western churches that a projected propaganda of positivity – a rhetoric of flex-to-current-trend political correctness and self-righteousness – prevails. Unfortunately, such a culture gags at the very thought of a discoursed biblical-relational pastoral wisdom that involves transparency and humility over sins. And remnant pockets of 'Platonized' Christianity are hardly known for their humility either. But this means that pastoral practice is emptied of its 'having begun with self-criticism' relevance and transparency.

One simply has to learn the rhetoric, or leave.

In such scenarios, though, the confessional discourse of biblical-relational sanctification becomes the worst 'sin' of all, since it explodes the *political* 'world' of the rhetoric of pretence. Even good, right and appropriate confession of sin becomes 'illegal' in such an anti-confessional culture.

In this way, the church mimics the world's own sin of 'pretending to be righteous and not sinful'. Having a good reputation biblically speaking, though, is not about exuding self-righteous pretence. St Paul did not do that. Rather, Paul's good reputation came slowly, through a facing of his shameful behaviours – not quickly through a denial of the same. *Politicians* stay in power whilst their sins remain hidden. *Apostles*, though, gained their good reputations by showing the world how to own up to sinfulness and what it means to be sinners who are being redeemed. It was a matter of telling the truth, not of telling lies like the Pharisees did. *We are called to imitate apostles, not politicians.*

These days, then, believers with personal and relational issues do not find in church a refreshing biblical prophetic discourse of humble, transparent, relational wisdom that can perceive the pastoral complexities of their particular cases. Rather, they find something that puts them right off. And so they church-hop, and often rightly so!

Distorted Witness as a Cause of Church-Hopping

Part of the problem, though, is that counterfeit, pseudo-Christian, pseudo-prophetic discourse also puts *non-believers* off the church as well. Instinctively, they know it is rubbish.

1 Corinthians 14:24–5, however, says that outsiders who come into our churches are meant to hear a genuinely prophetic discourse that convicts them of sin in a non-judgemental way. Surely, though, non-believers are convicted of their specific 'secret' sins when realities akin to those sins are honestly represented as part, if neither as the whole nor as the centre, of the public candour of real everyday Christian discourse, preaching, teaching and pastoral conversation (even if such candour or transparency *should* be conditioned by considerations to do with safety, appropriateness and legitimate confidentiality). Non-believers tend to be convicted of their sins when they hear truthful, relationally wise, biblically salted discourse. Normally forced to operate within the claustrophobic discourse-worlds of received, socially conditioned, speech habits, non-believers are often surprised, and not a little defensive, when they first hear language that is wise enough to map onto the hidden 'real' that is their sins.

Such truly prophetic discourse, such a 'language of the real', touches on distorted relational patterns, on right relational patterns, on building others up, on dimensions of healing, on finding personal identity, uniqueness, giftings, ministries and vocations – and so on. More than that, though: it is this truly prophetic discourse, this 'language of the real', this biblical-relational formative wisdom – centred on the gospel of Jesus Christ – that the Holy Spirit activates as speech-acts that impact non-believers. If our preaching, teaching, pastoring and especially our conversation more broadly are not salted by such truly prophetic discourse, then we are quenching the missional Spirit.

Naturally, such discourse is alien to fleshly, legalistic judgementalisms that devalue people unless they conform to de-relationalized systems. Truly prophetic discourse includes analyses of sinful patterns of relating, yes. But, as we noted above, truly prophetic discourse centres on the positives of the gospel of Jesus Christ, mercy, forgiveness, and on the twin-goods of 'promoting unique persons – including their unique gifts and ministries' and 'promoting right relating – as practised by Jesus'.

What non-believers actually experience when they encounter many churches, however, are the distorted non-biblical church cultures and the conflicted pseudo-Christian discourses that we have outlined above. Such church cultures and discourses, though, lack any pastoral or evangelistic power – either to convict non-believers of their specific secret sins or to convince non-believers that they genuinely could be redeemed from their specific secret sins and predicaments.

What non-believers should find in our churches is a discourse that is able to confront because it has the humble, self-critical transparency that is required to make this confrontation non-judgemental, and a discourse that is able to care because it has the framework-sophistication that is required to do so. But what non-believers actually tend to find in our churches is either confrontation without self-criticism, which is judgementalism, or/ and care without sophistication, which can have the same affect as hate. So, non-believers just end up thinking: 'The Christians are even worse than us! We conceal our sins; but the church conceals them even more. We moan about personal and relational problems; but the church moans about such problems even more – and neither sorts them out nor has the wisdom to do so!'

And so, conscientious Christians become too embarrassed to take their unbelieving friends to their churches, and so they end up church-hopping in order to find something that is more presentable to the world. That is, distorted witness is a cause of church-hopping.

Horizons of Expectation and Consecration to God as Causes of Church-Hopping

Church-hopping, then, happens because 'horizons of expectation'[83] are met with disappointment. Clearly, though, this disappointment is often unrelated to consumerism. Even if some individuals are consumerist, there are all-too-often other factors that cause people to church-hop – factors that stem from *the church's* cultural sinfulness. Too often, the holy and the gifted leave the church because their *right* expectations have been dashed.

Naturally, culturally sinful churches, in order to avoid facing their sin, tend to treat such persons (or families) who leave the church as scapegoats who have 'issues', and may misuse their knowledge of such persons' (or families') histories in order to 'justify' such slander.

Now, of course, an empowered person or family may stick around in order to help build a church and address its issues. A disempowered person or family, however, will either leave – obeying the Spirit's requirement that they use their gifts – or disobey the Spirit and conform like automatons. Admittedly, a probation period of forbearance may be warranted as the obedient enquire of God about the way forward. But God will soon move the obedient on from the disobedient church. God doesn't waste talent.

The church, then, should respond to church-hopping with self-criticism, not with finger-pointing. Beginning with self-criticism is biblical, dissolves conflict and suspicion, and avoids a self-righteous, self-deceptive, 'us versus the worldly' dualism.

Unfortunately, though, the church's current mode of self-examination tends to focus on superficialities such as marketing strategies, vocabulary and relevance levels. But this pseudo-self-examination is avoidant corporate narcissism – yet another symptom of the real problems.

The church's real problems, as we have argued, closely relate to inadequate, biblically unlawful, de-relationalized theologies and ideologies that distort its structures, its worship, its pastoral practices and its witness. The church thinks it has sophisticated biblical wisdom, but in reality is all-too-often unbiblical in its implicit ideology and is thus all-too-often incapable of interpreting or helping either its members or the world aright. And the world knows it: it is not only believers' horizons of expectation that are disappointed by the church – it is also those of the world.

False prophets have gotten to us, and we ignore it at our peril.

Unfortunately, then, consecration to God sometimes gives rise to church-hopping. 'If a blind man leads a blind man, both will fall into a pit'[84] – for the sighted may well have left the church by that point.

Are We Being Too Harsh on the Church?

But are we being too harsh on the church? Isn't the church comprised of fallible individuals? Aren't we called to work at our problems? Surely, only consumerists or the childish demand that the church is such-and-such a way, or leave at the first hint of imperfections. Surely, adults attend church to give, and not just to receive. And Jesus commands us to build church, to go on evangelistic missions and to engage in social action. We are baptized by God's Spirit *into* – not 'out of' – the body of Christ. We are God's building, God's field and God's temple!

Granted – but it is bad form to cite some biblical emphases in order to dismiss other biblical emphases. It is never wrong to call the church back to its biblical shape. In fact it borders on the demonic to misuse biblical doctrine in order to avoid a biblical paradigm! That's what Satan did when he tempted Christ!

Unfortunately, though, the shunning of criticism itself – as a mode of discourse – is a common anti-Christian trend in many churches these days. And yet, not all criticism is aimed at destruction. Scripture commands us to begin with self-criticism, and to maintain a policy of beginning with self-criticism.[85] Holiness welcomes criticism, and eagerly explores its content to see if there is an opportunity for growth. Iconoclasm is wrong, yes; but so is traditionalism. We still fall way short of divine perfection, and so the only holy way forward is ongoing tradition-refinement. People who deny this are saying that they are like Christ already, which is delusional self-idolatry.

And so, we need to ask ourselves: what if the theological and ideological distortions noted above really *have* distorted our church structures, our worship, our pastoral practices and our witness? Will God bless us if we do nothing about it? Unlikely.

In my view, even if my account of the church's problems – which draws on Leonardo Boff, Colin E. Gunton and especially on Anthony C. Thiselton (among others) – is only 10 per cent accurate, then we've still got a lot of work to do. Surely, no serious Christian thinker in the world today thinks that we are just talking about marketing strategies, vocabulary or relevance levels when we talk about 'problems with the church'!

Admittedly, again, the problems and issues highlighted above are not at all the whole truth about the church; and indeed we have also had to simplify matters somewhat here. But our description of the church's problems is surely still true enough for us to concern ourselves with solving those problems.

Eight Final Suggestions for Positive Ways Forward

As for solutions, then we may present eight final suggestions for positive ways forward, as follows.

(a) We should keep the orthodox, traditional, Reformed or conservative evangelical emphases on biblical authority and biblical teaching, but we should interpret the Bible all over again, asking relational questions rather than just systemic questions. It is love that sums up the law and the prophets, not a doctrine test against the criterion of de-relationalized content oppressively applied as a precondition for acceptance or justification. It will not do to redefine 'biblical lawfulness' non-relationally, pre-relationally, or even anti-relationally, when biblical lawfulness *is* right relating (see Chapter 3). Right doctrine only becomes truly right when it remains internal to the grammar (or meaning, structure or character) of right relating – for love sums up the law and the prophets.

(b) Moreover, we should keep the conservative evangelical emphasis on active application (though conservative evangelicals do not have the monopoly on this right emphasis). But, we should challenge all oppressive, individualistic, one-man-wonder-ministry, wall-to-wall activisms that seem to have the mode of competitive image-projection rather than of love. The church does not need 'Robo-Vicars' or 'Robo-Pastors' who are too busy to practice right relating. Again, it is love that sums up the law and the prophets, not a dynamism contest designed to impress peers and patrons and aid only the climbing of social or ecclesial hierarchical career ladders. Such activisms actually suppress real Christianity and replace it with false fleshly legalistic religion (see Chapter 3 above). Rejoinders to do with understaffing miss the point here.

(c) We should keep the charismatic emphases on God's imma-nence and on immediate experience of God, but we should interpret all over again what we mean by 'immediate expe-rience of God'. Primarily, if not exclusively, immediate expe-rience of God comes through the Holy Spirit's activation of variable subsets of the myriad of speech-act possibilities that are provided by the biblical texts, and not through confining the Spirit to giving subjective impressions or to deploying the few sentiments or slogans that are present in jingles.

Insisting on mystical experience at the expense of operative biblical language – the *true* 'sword of the Spirit' – is like being a 35-year-old who refuses to imbibe anything other than his mother's milk. God's 'good parenting', however, progresses beyond milk and succour for infants, and towards the meat of relational training that necessarily involves biblical language, biblical education, biblical formation and biblical transfor-mation. And neo-pragmatic charismatic attempts to justify unchallengeable power bases through authoritarian appeals to subjective experiences of the Spirit only compound the problems that already pertain to the infantilizing character of much charismatic Christianity. That is, such attempts add a sinister dimension – namely, the exploitation of infanti-lizing charismatic church culture in order to keep congrega-tion members immature so as to enable leaders to hold onto power.

(d) We should keep liberal, high-church emphases on God's unsearchable unfathomable transcendence, on developing the intellect, on ethical sophistication, on the role of the arts and social (and natural) sciences and on the need for cultural maturity. But we should interpret all over again the issue of the way in which philosophy shapes our attitude to biblical authority. The Scriptures are far more sophisticated than the neo-Kantianism, the existentialism, the positivism – or some-times the neo-pragmatism – that are lazily, falsely and precrit-ically deployed by some liberals in order to marginalize the Bible or in order to justify unbiblical lifestyles. Hermeneuti-cally speaking, how can one move 'beyond' the Scriptures if one has not yet fully or finally arrived *at* the Scriptures? *Bildung*, or self-cultivation, should not displace applied biblical-relational sanctification-wisdom, even if psychosocial tools such as transactional analysis and the drama triangle – coupled with a myriad of other insights from the arts and social (and natural) sciences – genuinely *do* flesh out that wisdom. And up-anchored or decontextualized biblical symbols can be as limiting to the divine voice as charismatic jingles, and need to be re-anchored in their biblical matrices, even though we still need biblical symbols in order to show us in a self-involving manner that God is great beyond all human understanding.[86]

(e) We should keep post-evangelicalism's emphases on multicultural variety, on inclusiveness, on the arts and on community. But we need to look again at the ways in which post-evangelicalism's unbiblical, postmodern neo-pragmatic foundations easily lead to authoritarianism. Such authoritarianism, moreover, shape-shifts at the whim of dominant personalities and leaders, and is far more insidious and covert than its modernistic predecessors, since it disguises itself beneath a politically expedient semblance, artifice or imposture of 'right relating'. Particular attention should be given to what Thiselton identifies as celebrity-seeking narcissism or local heroism amongst leaders and, therefore, to what Thiselton identifies as the unchallenged development of distorted home-grown local theologies that are designed to win applause from local audiences and patrons so as to project 'image' and gain local status and power. Such practices sacrifice the positive biblical shape of Christian religion and seriously distort the content and operative character of sermons – sermons that could otherwise help bring transcendental biblical revelation alive in a formative way. The gospel is a message about Jesus Christ, not about oneself or one's clique.

(f) We should keep a biblical paradigm of church authority, but should re-examine all over again the philosophical and theological ideologies that are implicit in our actual practice of church authority, since these ideologies will often turn out to be unbiblical. Biblically speaking, church authority is not primarily about policing conformity to systems, but is primarily about organizing systems that conform to promoting unique persons (including their unique gifts and ministries) and to promoting right relating. We must re-ground church authority in a relationally wise biblical theology that allows church authority to flex as it serves true, ever-developing, every-member ministries and true right relating, which lead to unique church profiles in every particular instance of church.

(g) We should perhaps keep certain notions of 'form' and of 'freedom' in our biblical theology of worship, but we should reinterpret all over again our theology and practice of worship so that our worship comes to reflect 'the human as it really is before the real God'. Squashing down all the various dimensions of personhood and of relationship – whether divine or human – into only 'form' (conformity to system) or only 'freedom' (hedonistic celebration of celebration itself) effectively blocks relational contact with God, both at the level of experience and at the level of expression. Worship is not the place for over-realized eschatology – for attention-seeking displays of pretend show-cased rapture or of pretend show-cased doctrinal or practical perfection. Again, worship should not suppress the operation of biblical language or, thereby, stress only the 'mystical' dimension of worship, for such practice hinders maturity, leads to the abuse of so-called 'prophetic pictures', and undermines the correct discernment of spirits. But nor should worship be reduced to the hymnic or spoken repetition of flat 'doctrinal' statements, since such practice loses the self-involving, relational, formative or *liturgical* function of biblical language.[87]

(h) We should completely revise our pastoral practice – *and thence our witness* – in the light of points (a) to (g) above. Broadly speaking, Christianity is about right relating to God and neighbour, for 'love sums up the law and the prophets' (even environmental issues relate to our love for God, to our love for each other, and to God's love for us). Pastoral practice, therefore, should model and train people into the art and science of right relating, and should become wise at interpreting and correcting the distortions that pervade our actual relating – distortions that the Bible calls 'sin'. True pastoral practice proceeds on the basis of its ability to interpret and correct distorted-relating, first to God, second to neighbour. Moreover, right relating, pastorally speaking, is inseparable from the practice of promoting individuals in their unique personhoods, identities, giftings, callings and ministries. Only a church that is characterized by such right pastoral practice and by such right relating will generate the biblical, relationally wise, discourse cultures – in preaching, teaching, pastoring, and conversation generally – that alone can function, through the Holy Spirit's ministry, as true prophetic discourse that can break the self-legitimizing and culturally habituated spells perpetuated by the discourse-worlds that hold non-believers captive. Conversely, pastoral practice and discourse are not to be marked by a pious inability to interpret relationally or wisely, by oppressive doctrine tests or application schema, by the mirage of false asserted hopes, by the pseudo-cultivated evasion of biblical wisdom for relational sanctification, by the expedient rhetoric of unfaithful, 'political' relating, by the infantilizing, lifelong suppression of maturity and of individuals' gifts and ministries, or by the blocking of worshipful formative relational contact with God through the Bible at every opportunity. Such aberrations throw up truly absurd, abusive and embarrassing church cultures and discourse cultures or 'phrase-regimes'[88] (in preaching, teaching, pastoring and conversation generally). Such distorted church cultures – and their accompanying distorted discourse cultures – can only function so as to mimic and even to extend worldly patterns of sin, and so as to undermine the witness of the church. It is not our task, however, to offer to the world an irrelevant *abstract (i.e. de-relationalized) salvation* that remains unrelated to, and that even potentially harms, people's personal and relational realities.

Part Three

Relating Faith: Mission

7.

Mission Distorted by Five Distorted Church Cultures

In Chapter 6, we have already begun to comment on how the problems of distorted theological persuasions, distorted church structures, distorted worship styles and distorted pastoral practices *de facto* produce distorted witness. If the ideologies implicit in our church cultures are not biblical – despite lip-service being paid to the Bible – then the shape of our religion isn't truly Christian. Today's Western culture, with its philosophical heritage, brings together the 'modern' and the 'postmodern'. Unfortunately, though, the shape of Western Christian religion is also often too modern and/or too postmodern, as we have just argued in Part Two above.

In particular, we also argued in Part Two above that neither modernity nor postmodernity had overcome the problem of oppressive hierarchical 'systems' – systems that, in effect, suppress both right relating and unique persons beneath conformity to those same systems. This means, however, that the church, insofar as it is wrongly shaped by modernity and/or by postmodernity, can also tend to suppress both right relating and unique persons and their unique gifts, callings and ministries beneath conformity to systems, as we have just argued in Part Two above.

The problem, though, is that since true biblical Christianity centres on Jesus' revelation of the Trinitarian God of 'unique-Persons-in-relation', and on God's desire to restore us as his imagers through restoring us to him through Jesus' death and resurrection, then to suppress 'unique persons' (including their unique gifts, callings and ministries) and 'right relating' beneath 'systems' is to resist the gospel.

And what, then, does our mission become? What, then, are we attempting to bring others into? The answer: gospel-suppressing systems derived from modern and postmodern ideologies that we have been too anti-intellectual to resist.

This charge, of course, is not the whole truth of the matter. There are many great Christians and churches out there. But this charge is still true enough of us for us to be very, very concerned indeed. In the end, God ensures that the church prevails; but it will go better for us if it turns out that we are not amongst those who have unwittingly resisted God in this matter.[1]

The current crisis in the church over the true shape of Christianity, then, is manifest in the current crisis in the church over the true shape of mission. Furthermore, those who 'do mission' tend to reproduce their own image in those reached, which means that the shape of future disciples and of future 'church' is also at stake.

That is, to the extent that the church is shaped by factors that reflect the cultural models – or the distorted church cultures – that we have dubbed Reformaca, Evangelica, Charismatica, Liberalica and Post-Evangelical Neo-Pragmatica, then to that same extent the church is succumbing to the surrendering of the true shape of Christianity, of mission, of discipleship and of the future church.

By contrast, as we have seen, *love* sums up the law and the prophets, and so the true shape of Christianity, and hence of true discipleship and of true church, has to do with love as biblical lawfulness. This means that the true shape of mission has to do with love as biblical lawfulness trying to reproduce its own shape in others who are outside the church. By definition, then, true mission understands others as a precondition for the possibility of helping those others to move from where they are at now and towards love as biblical lawfulness.

Naturally, since love as biblical lawfulness is love for God and neighbour, then true mission helps others to come to love God – which involves their right response to the gospel of Jesus Christ – and, in turn, to come to love others, which (as with their love for God) involves their rejection of distorted relational patterns, and their embracing of right-relational patterns.

Love as biblical lawfulness also inextricably links love for neighbours *to* love for God: apart from our communion with God, in which God loves us and we love God, we are thrown onto the created order alone, onto the flesh alone, and potentially into the hands of demonic forces, such that our love for others becomes radically distorted. Not that we are always conscious of this distortion, for we behaviourally mimic patterns of action and speech from the cultures around us, such that we adopt sinful strategies of relating and of self-deception without realizing it – often before we go on to sin more deliberately. We also said – in Chapter 3 on biblical lawfulness above – that we hide from the fact of our distorted loving by distorting God's law itself in order to create new 'rights and wrongs' according to which we self-deceptively claim to be righteous 'law-abiding citizens'.

And so, we are brought back to John Stott's point about 'double listening': listening to 'the Word', so that we know what Christianity is; and listening to today's culture, so that we know not only the ways in which non-believers are 'un-Christian', but also how we ourselves – *even as Christians* – have become un-Christian.[2] Therefore, listening to today's culture does not at all mean becoming compromised by cultural sins but, rather, means that we should do sufficient cultural studies so as to be able to repent of being *already* compromised – as a Christian church – *by* cultural sins.

Thus, as John Stott says, it will not do to remain only in the Scriptures, since then our cultural corruption will continue to shape how we read the Scriptures. Whilst the Scriptures can eventually overturn our cultural heritage, it speeds things up if – in addition – we read the cultural critics. Why take ten years to realize that a cultural distortion is present in one's life and discipleship when reading a good critical book about Western culture can expose that same distortion in ten minutes? Unfortunately, though, some *want* to suppress the knowledge of their cultural sins.

True mission to Western culture, then, understands *both* the positive shape of Christianity as 'love for God and neighbour as biblical lawfulness' (in discipleship, church and mission) or as 'right relating to God and others via a right response to the gospel of Jesus Christ' *and* where people in the West – *including ourselves* – are actually at.

In Chapter 3 above on biblical lawfulness we said much about (a) the positive shape of Christianity. In Chapter 9 below on modernity and postmodernity we shall say much about (b) where people in the West – *including ourselves* – are really at. And in Chapter 6 above on church-hopping, we argued that the church was thus very often much closer to (b) than to (a), which distorts its mission, as follows.

Reformaca

Thus the mission of Reformaca rightly seeks to win people over to an initial conversion event, yes, but otherwise seeks to win people over to conformity to assent to a system of doctrines that are repeatedly affirmed each week. The standard of doctrine may indeed be very high – except for the rather glaring problem that it is love that sums up the law and the prophets, not cognitive content abstracted from relational wisdom and turned into a tool by which to perpetuate moribund elitism or even by which to abuse power.

Clearly, to an extent, we are using caricature here – but there is sufficient truth in this caricature for us to be worried. We applaud the Reformed emphases on the Scriptures and on the gospel – but not Reformaca's *de-relationalizing* of the Scriptures and the gospel.

Evangelica

The mission of Evangelica also still rightly focuses on winning people over to a conversion event, but then sometimes goes on to seek to conform those people to a system of activisms that apply the results of discourses about strategies for evangelism *itself*. However, evangelism does not – in such a church culture – derive its shape from true Christianity; rather, in such a church culture, true Christianity is reduced in its content to discourses about evangelistic strategies – strategies that are then self-perpetuating. Evangelica's mission thus becomes almost a matter of converting people *to* mission, rather than *through* mission. But this means that the positive shape of biblical Christianity is reduced to 'actualizing mission strategies in order to win people to actualizing mission strategies'! The result is loads of meetings about mission strategies coupled with no biblical exposition concerning the actual relational shape of Christianity – the latter being supposedly presupposed but, in effect, being perpetually deferred.

Again, we are using caricature or characterization here – and evangelicalism, like the Reformed Church, has many good, noble and right qualities. But there is still sufficient truth in our characterization for us to be worried.

Charismatica

The mission of Charismatica, sometimes, seems like a plea that invites actors to a theatrical audition (though normally a real conversion event takes place). Often, there is a moment of awkwardness as one transitions from normal life in the world into the acting or dramatic mode of: pleas for succour; pretences to do with receiving eschatological levels of rapturous experience; theatrical shows of love marked by paraded gestures of hugging, but which are often not matched by any real off-stage strength of community or faithfulness; super-spiritual demonstrations of tongues that, as St Paul says, then serve to make some in the congregation feel like 'outsiders';[3] and so on. Meanwhile, the Scriptures are marginalized – except as a kind of stage-prop held in the hand – and biblically-formed right relating and the wise discourse associated with biblically-formed right relating are assigned to a profoundly off-stage realm (if they persist at all). Thus, a kind of system or game displaces, replaces and suppresses the true positive shape of biblical Christianity, and of mission.

Now of course, again, we are using some characterization or caricature. But our points are sufficiently true for us to be concerned. Certainly, one does not ordinarily *associate* Christian charismatic religion with 'missional awareness of Western postmodern culture'; rather, one ordinarily just sees Christian charismatic religion as being unaware of the fact that it very often *is* Western postmodern culture.[4] Nevertheless, some Christian charismatic mission is very practical and serving, and should be commended.

Liberalica

The mission of Liberalica, as we have already implied, does not (in its own eyes) involve anything as 'uncouth' as evangelism.

Liberalica is embarrassed by anti-intellectual Christianity and – to prove that it is the opposite – becomes an expert in the arts and human sciences. Thus, its mission often reflects this expertise, and easily aligns with well-known social action causes such as Amnesty International, and often rightly so.

The problem, though, is that – and as we shall see in Chapter 9 below on modernity and postmodernity – a predominant Western trend that we dub 'naturalistic humanistic utopianism' is part of the cause of the philosophical, political, humanitarian, environmental and economic crises to which such social action is addressed. But what is the point of being involved in commendable social action if one's church also *promotes* at least some of the premises that pertain to the ideologies that *produce* the crisis-situations that one's church's social action is trying to address? Liberalica, then, can end up perpetuating a self-defeating mission.

Now, of course, Liberalica is quite right to applaud aspects of the spirit of counter-cultural protest that we find in the Romantic Movement.[5] And yet, to us, Liberalica's mission still seems to promote something other than 'love as biblical lawfulness through a right response to the gospel of Jesus Christ'. Discourse on the biblical sanctification of relational patterns is often replaced by a mission that is all but assimilated to the curricula of university arts and human sciences departments – which are a mixed bag to say the least.

Post-Evangelical Neo-Pragmatica

The mission of Post-Evangelical Neo-Pragmatica, to us, seems like a matter of winning people into a club that aims to assimilate Christianity to contemporary political correctness – into a jet-set that perpetuates sanctioned, manicured, pseudo-critical pseudo-awareness of social, political, philosophical and theological issues. Consequently, and additionally, in Post-Evangelical Neo-Pragmatica there is both a desire to communicate intellectual savvy and yet also, simultaneously, a missional desire to become inclusive by becoming post-doctrinal, multi-doctrinal or multicultural, 'Green-Belt-style' – which leads to some very odd liturgy, as we have said.

What happens then, though, is that the post-evangelical neo-pragmatic intellect – in its attempt to become relevant (and avoid persecution) – assimilates itself to 'allowed' cultural rhetorics – for example, rhetorics to do with liberal democracy and its social outworkings, environmental sustainability and 'sanctioned-protest art-forms' that are, in reality, assimilated *to* allowed cultural rhetorics, and so on. (We will briefly outline these and other allowed rhetorics in Chapter 9 below on modernity and postmodernity). Such rhetorics make an art-form out of inclusive language but, as we shall see, are actually authoritarian in their purpose. Both the art of inclusion and the authoritarianism, though, then become part of Post-Evangelical Neo-Pragmatica. The result is an awkward juxtaposition of exclusion strategies (when people don't play the neo-pragmatic game) and a maintained semblance, artifice, or imposture of polite 'PC' inclusiveness.

Probably, as well, we would have to agree with Anthony C. Thiselton's complaints about how neo-pragmatism – through its post-doctrinal or multi-doctrinal emphasis – can descend towards perpetuating 'unchallengeable' power bases that won't admit challenge precisely because the very same biblical doctrine and criteria that should referee relating have been suppressed or marginalized so as 'not to offend'.[6] The result, though, can be a nepotistic culture that indulges in empty hyperbole, weeping celebrity-at-the-Oscars sentimentality, routinized flattery, glowingly positive false 'prophetic' divinations, and a superfluity of applauding adjectives – which all result in near-eschatological levels of gratitude over the realization that one has been clique-included – when commending any who are to be, or who are already, promoted within the often-unacknowledged clique hierarchy – regardless of levels of actual deservedness according to biblical-doctrinal criteria.[7] Admittedly, though, there are certainly those who really do seem to be far too genuine and loving to actually go all the way to where the mission of Post-Evangelical Neo-Pragmatica inevitably leads (on which, see Chapter 9).

To my mind, then, the five kinds of distorted mission that we have just highlighted: first, put Christians off from doing mission because they feel unhappy with what they are winning people *to*;

and second, put non-Christians off the church because there really *is* something odd about what they are being asked to join. In fact it is interesting to see just how many people *do* respond positively to the unmatched profundity of the gospel of Jesus Christ but who then, when faced with the 'next bit', fall away because the next bit is 'conformity to some sub-standard, non-Christian system' when it should be the biblical art and science of right relating – first to God, then to neighbour.

And so, if I were to offer five counter-intuitive ways to promote mission and evangelism, then I would say: repent of the five kinds of 'mission and evangelism' that aim to perpetuate and to win people to the five distorted versions of Christianity that we have just outlined and characterized – namely, Reformaca, Evangelica, Charismatica, Liberalica, and Post-Evangelical Neo-Pragmatica. It is *sin* to evangelize people into that which is inconsistent with biblical Christianity, and so we shouldn't do it!

8.

Mission and What Evangelism *Doesn't* Involve

These days, we live in a predominantly postmodern culture that claims to be more community-oriented than modernity, but that in fact still promotes modernity's individualism (see our analysis of this point in Chapter 9 on modernity and postmodernity). This problem of individualism then affects the church – which brings us to the first of our next seven counter-intuitive ways to promote mission and evangelism, as follows.

Against Standardizing Disciples and Discipleship

Thus, first, churches sometimes seem to promote *cloning*. Each active church-member is expected to conform to a system that turns each person within it into a standardized disciple. Part of the standardized disciple's profile is 'doing evangelism'. So, each person within the system is expected to 'do evangelism'. Ironically, though, it is *this* approach that is in a sense individualistic – even though it is also this approach that labels those who resist its imperializing tendencies as being the 'real individualists'. That is, pseudo-Christian collectivisms,[1] in seeking to make everybody the same, impose a singular *individualistic* model of discipleship on everybody.

Real biblical maturity, though, is about finding one's own unique identity under God, one's own unique gift profile, and one's own unique calling and ministry. A mature Christian will *want* to do what he or she is really *called* to do. We're not promoting hedonism here, for there was even a sense in which Jesus wanted the cross – not for heroic or masochistic reasons, but for what it would achieve – i.e. the salvation of the world.[2]

Pseudo-Christian collectivisms, however, suppress the diversity of every-member ministry beneath conformity to a cloning system. Thus, they rob people of their passion for Jesus, which is tied in closely to what they can do for Jesus using their unique gifts. Ironically, by trying to turn everybody into evangelists, churches kill evangelism.

So, step one for encouraging mission and evangelism is: stop trying to make everybody do evangelism. Since I stopped feeling obliged to become what I was not, I have become a much more effective witness for Jesus, because I am now happy with the true Jesus and with what he actually wants of me. I do far more evangelism by obeying Jesus and the apostles – which means for me, as it will for many people, *stopping* trying to be an evangelist.

Against Standardizing Churches and Mission

Our second point is similar to our first point. Our first point attacked the imposed standardization of disciples and discipleship; our second point attacks the imposed *standardization of churches and mission*. That is, churches often seek to impose a preconceived system of ministries upon their congregations. They look at the Bible, decide what 'church' should look like, draw up a chart of different roles and then ask people to fulfil those roles.

Oh dear! Such an approach standardizes church! Surely, though, each church has different individuals with different gifts in it; therefore, each church community is a unique combination of unique individuals and gifts, and is thus – wait for it – unique! But this means, surely, that church leaders have to:

(a) Look at who they have got;
(b) Ask what it is that those unique individuals are uniquely good at and actually want to do; and
(c) Submit to the unique historical factuality of what *their* church will *then* have to look like.

Imposing a standardized model on unique churches is oppressive, gift-suppressing, ministry-killing, relationally alienating and turns church communities into a total charade.

In fact, imposing standardized models of church on uniquely shaped groups is one of the main causes of 'churchianity'. Churchianity is characterized by that rather fake discourse-world – that pseudo-fellowship – that arises when people suspend their unique identities in order to participate in, and in order to speak the received language of, a pseudo-community that is built upon suppressed individuality and suppressed ministries. This kind of pseudo-community differs from a true biblical community. A true biblical community accepts, promotes and benefits from each person's cherished uniqueness and true ministry – and so will not conform to the *a priori* categories of a standardized model.

Such standardized models, though, are routinely imposed upon churches when it comes to mission. That is:

(a) Mission is defined in a standardized way: 'all "mission" is such and such'.
(b) A programme is devised on the basis of 'what all "mission" is'.
(c) People are cajoled into involvement in such 'mission', but normally hate it.
(d) People are then castigated for being 'half-hearted' or for being 'without passion for Jesus'.

The reality, though, is this: when people have standardized models imposed upon them, they become despondent. Real mission, again, is born out of people's actual unique gifts and ministries. Thus, yes, real mission always includes sharing the gospel at some point; but real mission will also be tailored uniquely in each instance of its occurrence according to the unique identities, unique giftings and unique ministries of those who, thereby, *want* to be involved. (Somehow, I fear that this point will never be understood.)

Step two for encouraging mission and evangelism, then, is to desist from all attempts to promote or impose standardized models of church, or of mission, or of evangelism. Never impose standardized models of anything onto churches. Rather, look at who you've got and ask, 'What does each unique person here rightly and uniquely *want* to do that he or she also uniquely *can* do?'[3] Then, build your church, your mission and your evangelism around that.

Against Embarrassing Breaches of Social Etiquette

Third, the church has turned evangelism into *embarrassing breaches of social etiquette* when evangelism should be a matter of biblically-wise relating – even though the offence of the gospel, which is something else entirely, remains.

Everybody loves being related to wisely, but everybody hates being evangelized. Why is that? It is because the loss of the true shape of Christianity has led to the loss of the true shape of evangelism. The true shape of Christianity is love for God and neighbour as biblically wise or biblically lawful relating – in discipleship, church and the world. This true shape should then shape our evangelism. But, if everybody hates being evangelized, then we must have turned both our Christianity and (thence) our evangelism into something that they are not supposed to be.

Admittedly, 'we are the smell of death' to 'those who are perishing', and are only 'the fragrance of life' 'among those who are being saved' (2 Cor. 2:15–16). But it is not bad etiquette that should cause our 'bad odour' amongst the perishing, but 'the aroma of Christ' (2 Cor. 2:15)! Christ was the very embodiment of love for God and neighbour, for he 'was without sin'.[4] So, it could not have been bad etiquette – or bad-relating – that caused Jesus to offend some folks. Rather, it was the content of his message and his challenge *to* bad-relating – particularly his challenge to the abuse of power – that caused offence. If Jesus did breach etiquette, then it was only that particular kind of etiquette that was relationally abusive that Jesus breached. Etiquette that embodied good-relating, then, was not what Jesus challenged.[5]

Therefore, there is something wrong with both our Christian religion and our evangelism if we start calling embarrassing etiquette breaches 'the offence of the gospel'. When Christians shy away from the embarrassing etiquette breaches of what often passes for 'evangelism', though, then they are often berated for 'unwillingness to be persecuted for the offence of the gospel', or for 'being embarrassed about Jesus'.

It's not Jesus who is embarrassing, though; it's *us*. Jesus understands how to relate well, and Jesus understands the times. During his earthly ministry, Jesus engaged with the culture of the time, understood it with a level of critical awareness that made Freud, Nietzsche and Marx look like critical beginners, and then somehow challenged that culture whilst not sinning relationally.

Step three for encouraging mission and evangelism, then, is to learn to relate wisely in/to today's culture in all its complexity so as to challenge it in a critically astute way (which will involve sharing the gospel at some point and in a wise manner) and to allow *this* to do the offending – for it is *this* that is the offence of the gospel, the aroma of Christ, and not embarrassing etiquette breaches. As for the embarrassing etiquette breaches themselves – well, they're too embarrassing to mention. (Christians each have their own stories to tell).

Against Obscurantist Sloganeering that Resists Biblical Wisdom and Apologetics

Our fourth point follows on from our previous point. If we are to learn to relate wisely in/to today's culture in all its complexity so as to challenge it in a critically astute way, then *we need to put biblical wisdom and apologetics back into our evangelism.*

In some churches, though, you'd think I'd uttered a *faux pas* in mentioning biblical wisdom and apologetics. Why is that? It is because we often have a false view of evangelism that says that 'we do not have to understand the Bible or our culture' so long as we 'share the gospel'. In such a counterfeit notion of evangelism, it is actually thought that the gospel of Jesus Christ can be reduced to a few slogans. Counterfeit Christianity thinks like this because it has actually *become* just a few slogans.[6]

Biblically, though, the gospel is roughly three hundred pages of text in length. It is called the New Testament. Even if one were to name just the Gospels of Matthew, Mark, Luke and John as 'the gospel' – which would be an error since Romans is also a gospel presentation – then one would still be left with 125 pages of text. Moreover, the biblical gospel engages critically with the surrounding culture of the time at every turn of the page. The one thing you *don't* see in Scripture is sloganeering.

Now, admittedly, when involved in evangelism, one cannot simply read out more than a hundred pages of New Testament text. But the great thing about evangelists like Billy Graham is that they can give short messages based upon a profound knowledge of the entire Bible. They speak simply, but they think profoundly.[7] A church that reduces its religion to anti-intellectual sloganeering, though, will also *think* simply – which will turn *its particular kind* of simple speech into obscurantist error. There is more than one kind of simple speech.

Furthermore, the most effective speakers I have heard also have a profound knowledge of apologetics that is born out of learning about Western culture. Thus, somebody such as Donald A. Carson is steeped both in knowledge about Western culture and in biblical understanding. That is why he is such an interesting and effective speaker and evangelist: he comes across as somebody who actually knows something – a bit like Jesus did, I imagine. He can be found online – and within thirty seconds of listening to Carson, you'll realize what you've been deprived of.[8]

You see, it is when evangelists actually *know* something that Christianity looks interesting and attractive. This is because God, the gospel of Jesus Christ, the Bible and true Christianity turn out to be not only very important but also to be very interesting indeed when one engages with them properly; and Western culture is a fascinating study in itself as well. People *want* the veil to be lifted on their postmodern disorientation; they *want* the curtain to be drawn back on what is actually happening in their lives and in this world. Those who don't want to know these things are those who want to remain in their 'darkness' because their 'deeds' are 'evil', Jesus says.[9] It is unfortunate that, these days, it is the *Christians* who often seem to fit this description best.

Step four for encouraging mission and evangelism, then, is to put biblical wisdom and an apologetics that understands Western culture back into evangelism. Such biblical and cultural insights are fascinating, both for those imparting them, and for those hearing them. But a brute pseudo-evangelistic sloganeering activism devoid of all interesting content is an abusive oppression. Only sin-deniers want such claustrophobic darkness.[10] No wonder many Christians and most non-Christians can't stand such activism.

Against Pseudo-Evangelistic Infantilization that Resists Content and Vocabulary

The fifth point, following on from the last point, concerns the *church's embarrassing confusion of evangelism with infantilization*. It is assumed that ministers and elders are mature and can take profound biblical content, that seasoned churchgoers are almost as mature and can take moderate biblical content, but that most Christians can only take 'the basics', and that non-Christians – well – *Thomas the Tank Engine* is too advanced for them. What a load of old patronizing and offensive drivel.

It is shameful that I and many others even have to point out that many non-believers have degrees, read text-books, do professional jobs that involve technical language, are familiar with current affairs, and are – quite frankly – very, very often much further on in their thinking than the Christian sloganeers are. But the sad fact is that, these days, many of us *do* have to point this out to the church. Worse – when I and many others do point it out, what we say is even often rejected as being irrelevant thinking 'by intellectuals' who 'only have academic knowledge'.

Earlier, we linked infantilization to the standard strategies of those in power who wish to keep people immature so that their power bases and systems of privilege are not challenged. Such abusers need to mislabel people who think as 'mere academics' so that they can falsely cast aside the genuine criticisms that thinkers bring to the table. Moreover, such patronization even assumes that academics or thinkers actually have 'less real-life experience' from which to contribute, which is also both false and an abuse of power.

Furthermore, it is a genuine breach of etiquette, register and of politeness generally when evangelistic mission deploys speakers who sound like nursery-school teachers. Frankly, it is insulting to those unfortunate enough to be listening. Every day, people hear what some sloganeering believers think of as 'the dreaded long words' on television. And yet, I have even been rebuked in some church contexts for using vocabulary that would be commonplace on *Blue Peter*. Only anti-intellectuals and power-hungry infantilizers resist vocabulary, however, for an extension of vocabulary often brings an extension of wisdom and an exposure of sin. Indeed, it's funny how anti-intellectuals and power-hungry infantilizers are happy to learn a compound word like 'video-recorder', which has *six* syllables; but if one dares to articulate a *three*-syllable word such as 'redemption', then suddenly it's 'a long academic word'. Oh, grow up!

Step five for encouraging mission and evangelism, then, is to take the infantilization out of evangelism and put some cognitive content and some vocabulary back into it. I'm not saying that we should read out a paper on post-structuralism – I'm just advocating that we say something interesting that doesn't insult people's intelligence. It is often *the church* that has become infantile, not the world.

Against the False Evangelistic Promises of Counterfeit Worship Cultures

Sixth, *the church is turning to making false promises in its evangelism*, and needs to repent of this practice. Sometimes God miraculously heals people; normally he doesn't. If this were not true, the National Health Service and the body's immune system would be irrelevant. As it is, the former is stretched beyond capacity, and the preservation of the latter proves to be necessary enough for us to need enough sleep ongoingly. In any case, and as we argued earlier, since when did God ever heal people who ongoingly reject his true prophets and who set up false prophets in their place?

Frankly, it is embarrassing and saddening to watch certain so-called evangelists routinely and fraudulently use false proclamations concerning false revivals, false movements of the Spirit and false miracles to undermine the reputation of Jesus Christ and his gospel (see also Chapter 6 on church-hopping above). Such 'revivalist' meetings displace actual gospel proclamation and actual Christian religion by propagating a harlequinade of counterfeit glory-seeking theatrics.

Some churches, though, are immersed in such shallow and false pseudo-evangelistic cultures. Biblical wisdom, wise-relating, cultural understanding, developed gifts and ministries centred on different kinds of social action, and mature discipleship generally are habitually suppressed. Meanwhile, hypnotic strategies, psychosocial impressionism, emotivism, hedonistic 'worship of worship itself', pseudo-self-objectifying narcissistic introspection and spurious anecdote are repeated *ad nauseam*.

This is not Christianity. Actually, it is closer to occult in its use of trance states and soothsaying. At best, it is a short-term strategy for pulling in a big crowd, for manipulating them out of their cash and for capitalizing on Western therapeutic culture.[11] At worst, in the long term, it is a demonic strategy for alienating people from the church. People are always attracted to fairgrounds, lights, carousels, happy noises and a party atmosphere that says, 'This is where the action is'. The problem, though, is that this kind of carry-on is not real Christianity. At best it is *only* a party – though, admittedly, the God of forbearance may sometimes act into such circuses despite this fact.

Step six for encouraging mission and evangelism, then, is to remove from both the fraud, the false promises, and the use of cheap 'this is where the party is' tricks to get people in through the door. That is, evangelism needs to be lifted out of counterfeit worship cultures (on which, see also Chapters 3 and 6), even if much of the church is busy immersing itself into the same. If we offer something with *true* content and gravity, *then* we'll be taken seriously.

Against Fleshly Legalistic 'Evangelism at Spiritual Gunpoint'

Finally, a lot of inappropriate pressure is placed on people to become evangelists, as we have already said. What we haven't yet said, however, is that one of the mechanisms for doing this is that people are often told that others' eternal salvation depends upon them 'doing evangelism'.

Of course, though, this is just fleshly legalistic oppression all over again. For just as the doctrine of justification by faith so takes the colossal pressure off good works that they become a joy to do instead of something done at spiritual gun-point, then so the doctrines of election and predestination so take the colossal pressure off mission and evangelism that they too become a joy to do and not a spiritual kidnapper's ransom demand.

There are some things that are, frankly, beyond us. Just as we saw how securing our own justification was so utterly beyond us that fleshly legalism was ridiculous, so also securing other people's justification is so utterly beyond us that to think that it depends on us is a demonically orchestrated, pompous elitist's category mistake, grounded in boasting filtered through a rescuer's complex, and then sifted through a wall-to-wall, Evangelica-style, unbiblical, relationship-suppressing, fleshly, legalistic activism that is designed to impress peers and patrons so as to advance one's ecclesial career and that has, additionally, been fashioned from a modernist's anthropocentric Nietzschean delusion of power and from a postmodernist's model of accelerated culture.

Why not try to be biblical instead? Relax! God has it under control. Think of Jesus asleep in the boat. Remember that it is *God* who created and who redeems the universe. Stop confusing your modernist system with righteousness. Learn to relate to people. Have a cup of tea, and take some time to reflect. (And, if necessary, see an exorcist). Christianity is faith expressing itself in love, or trust in God that learns to relate to people properly. Christianity is not about becoming Robo-vicars; God has already got the whole 'justification' and 'election'/'predestination' thing covered.

Now, of course, Robo-vicars will say that I'm now falling into the old ultra-Reformed trap of using the doctrine of election as an excuse not to do evangelism. Actually, though, I'm using the doctrine of election as an excuse not to do *their kind* of Robo-evangelism, which is not evangelism anyway, but a heart attack trying to win people to something unrelational, un-Christian, unbiblical and unlike Jesus.

Step seven for encouraging mission and evangelism, then, is to realize that others' justification does not depend on you any more than your own justification depends on you. I've done so much more witnessing for Jesus since I realized this. '[O]ur struggle is not against flesh and blood' (Eph. 6:12). If we could see the forces we were really up against, we'd drop dead on the spot. Only the Holy Spirit can hold back those forces so as to enable us to do any evangelism at all. So then, the way forward is to discern the *particular place* that *God* has for you in *his* mission of redemption, and then to be obedient as a witness for Christ *in that*.

9.

Mission and Understanding Modernity and Postmodernity

Modernity and postmodernity are difficult to define but may be seen as historical trends that are especially associated with both Western culture and Western thought – though modernity and postmodernity are not just confined to the West. Certainly, a broader understanding of these almost-global historical trends is integral to most if not all effective Christian mission and evangelism today. In the present chapter, therefore, we will aim to move towards such a broader understanding; but, we will do so by expounding eight angles of view on the *Western* expression of the shift from modernity to postmodernity, as follows.

Rise of the Knowledge of God versus Death-of-God Utopianisms

Thus, first, modernity and postmodernity are associated with how Western culture and Western thought relate to humanism, to naturalism and to 'technological progressivism',[1] as follows.

Thus, to begin with, we should note that contemporary *humanism*, in emphasizing the human and not the divine, tends to manifest as *secular* humanism,[2] and thus endorses visions of humanly constructed utopian futures, even though dystopias are also envisaged.[3] Thus, today's humanism often slips into unrealism – arguing, in effect, that humankind can create its own heaven. Arthur C. Clarke's visions of the future even involve ET helping humankind to build its utopias – and yet such visions have been treated seriously by many: Clarke is described in one newspaper's response to his book, *2010: Odyssey Two* (1982), as 'truly prophetic'.[4]

Christianity, though, rationally and realistically argues that only God could create a heaven, and that it is futile to try to construct a humanly 'designed' future (or 'designer reality'[5]) on God's building site – for 'Unless the LORD builds the house, its builders labour in vain'. Today's humanism, however, abstracts human creativity from co-operation with divine creativity and re-contextualizes the former within a delusional setting in which humanity, in effect, unwittingly builds against God. The future, however, is biblical, for 'the Scriptures must be fulfilled' and 'cannot be broken'.[6]

Humanism is not all bad, of course, and rightly stresses human creativity, human value, and the need to understand that which is human – all of which are biblical emphases. Much of the contemporary emphasis on human rights is also good and biblical; setting certain minimum standards for how people are treated respects our created role as God's 'imagers', and civlizes us.

Humanism, though, also distorts certain biblical emphases, borrowing realistic, eschatological pilgrimage from Christianity, and then distorting it into escapist, utopian odyssey – even into escapist, utopian, *space* odyssey in recent times.[7]

Moving on, then *naturalism* emphasizes that which is impersonal about the universe, and either marginalizes God (cf. deism) or rejects God altogether (cf. atheism). Naturalism, though, like Christianity, rightly emphasizes: some kind of creative event horizon (wrongly secularized in naturalism as 'the big bang'); a primordial chaos; physical laws of order; and entropy or 'decay unto chaos'.

Christianity, however, is more realistic than naturalism in that Christianity stresses that physical laws of order could only come into existence through divine creative miracle: since order and chaos are antithetical and not co-extensive, then it is more rational (or more logically and internally coherent) – and mathematically far more probable – to say that 'the rational *imposed* rational order onto primordial chaos' than it is to say that 'time and chance caused rational order to *evolve from* primordial chaos'. Admittedly, though, Christianity does allow that God's imposition of rational order could constitute a process that could be mistakenly identified *as* 'evolution' by Darwinists and others.

Naturalism, then, in its secularization of *beginnings* or of creation processes, ends up making 'primordial chaos' and physical 'laws of order' too basic, or too foundational, when such realities are really built on a more fundamental foundation, namely an ongoing divine creative miracle that extends well beyond an initial 'big bang' and on into the future (as recent findings in relation to 'dark energy' now seem to allow). That is, the future does not yet exist, and yet the future constitutes the precondition for the possibility of the existence of all future 'natural' mechanisms. Therefore, since mere mechanism cannot be its own precondition of possibility, then we must rationally invoke ongoing 'divine creative miracle', in line with the Scriptures.

Naturalism, furthermore, in its secularization of *endings* or of eschatology, is also too pessimistic in that it makes 'decay unto chaos' as (or even more) fundamental or basic than physical 'laws of order'. In naturalism, then, there is a 'chaos attractor at the end of time'.[8] By contrast, Christianity rationally argues that since God created physical laws of order from primordial chaos, then God can also redeem physical laws of order from a less-than-primordial 'decay unto chaos'. In Christianity, 'decay unto chaos' (as opposed to the primordial chaos) is not at all foundational, but is even less basic or fundamental than physical laws of order, since it is parasitic upon the latter and pertains to the fall. In Christianity, then, the end of history is not chaotic, but is ordered – and is actualized in God's coming kingdom, in a new heaven and a new earth.

Again, though, as in the case of humanism, naturalism is not all bad. Its emphases on an initial creative event, primordial chaos, physical laws of order and decay unto chaos are partially compatible with biblical teaching on the creation and the fall, and have proven to be sufficiently realistic to allow great advances in the 'natural' sciences.

Naturalism, however, also distorts certain biblical emphases: naturalism borrows aspects of the doctrines of creation and of the fall, and then distorts these into a pessimistic, foundationalist determinism of 'chaos–evolution–order–entropy–chaos' that – from a modernist's perspective – engenders a view of 'nature' according to which 'nature' can only be challenged and mastered (on naturalism's own terms) by an irrationally optimistic, humanistic, escapist utopianism – for naturalism itself admits no hope, and so humanism has to borrow Christian eschatological hope and secularize it.

That is, and moving on, *modernity* – or (post-) Enlightenment culture and thinking – in combining humanism with naturalism, is (in its own view) compelled to create its utopias in the face of the 'natural order' and the latter's decay unto chaos. Assuming absolute ownership of the so-called 'natural order', modernity seeks to completely master the 'natural order', through the ever-advancing development of technology, so as to overrule 'decay unto chaos' and impose its utopian 'designer realities' upon the 'natural order' in a Godlike manner. Thus, 'natural' resources are consumed in order to create utopian designer realities that, biblically speaking, futilely ignore a divine building programme that is already in progress.

Modernity thus locks itself into a *'technological-progressivism'*[9] that seeks to empower humankind with Godlike capacities for mastering – and even for overruling – the 'natural order'. Whilst Christianity acknowledges that humankind is to subdue and govern the earth and develop technologies to that end, modernity can never rest in that it seeks to develop technology so as to *become* Godlike, rather than so as to *serve* God. Thus, modernity becomes locked into a frenetic competitive bid for total Godlike control of the 'natural order', and for this purpose purloins the earth's resources for futile, greedy and grandiose projects that such resources were never meant to resource. Both material resources and people are exploited to these ends, which generates both ecological problems and a slave trade. Greed leads to consumerism, whilst competitive power struggles lead to wars and, as technology develops, to world wars and nuclear threat. The result is genocides, humanitarian disasters and economic crises – not to mention the 'rape of the planet', global warming and other impending environmental problems.

Moving on, then the *'postmodern'* or the 'late modern' relates to modernity's failure to create its envisaged utopias in the concrete world: note how Arthur C. Clarke's *Odysseys – 2001, 2010, 2061* and *3001* – are dated exponentially further and further into the future.[10]

Negatively, when faced with its failure, modernity creates an escape-hatch into a virtual world. Modernity's desired concrete utopias – to an extent – become desired virtual digitopias. Several often-negative characteristics or shifts associated with this 'digi-topianism' then constitute often-negative aspects of the 'post-modern'.[11] Thus, for example, we may think of shifts:

(a) From exploitation of earth's *resources* to exploitation of *information*;
(b) From '*manufacturing* and *heavy industry*' to 'networked *digital communications*';[12]
(c) From *caring engagement* with real issues in the community to *apathetic 'disengagement'* from real issues in the community;[13]
(d) From *realisms* to various *escapisms* (whether consumerist, digital, tribal, hedonistic, sexual or substance-abuse-related);
(e) From *patient responsible relationality* (i.e. relating well to others) to *impatient accelerated impulsive reflexivity or reactivity* – a kind of *road-rage reaction* to everybody and everything;
(f) From *stable* linguistic systems to *rapidly changing and disintegrating* linguistic systems;
(g) From *stable* belief systems to *unstable* belief systems;
(h) From *optimistic co-operation towards common* goals to *suspicious tribalism* in pursuit of *privatized* goals that are more susceptible to becoming *fundamentalist or extremist*;
(i) From *responsibility in relation to social or ethical contracts* to *irresponsible 'play' or hedonism*.[14]

The list goes on.

Negatively, then, postmodernity strives to keep naturalistic humanistic utopianism and its self-empowering technological progressivism alive. This, in effect if not in intent, is a narcissistic attempt to block the rise of the knowledge of God, and says, 'We've learned the lessons from the past, we can see the way ahead now, all will be well – and, in any case, our knowledge of the past is so uncertain.' This rhetoric, however, then becomes mere propaganda about aims such as democratic globalization, digital revolution, environmental sustainability, economic development and humanitarian awareness. Speech or rhetoric about such often-laudable aims becomes mere propaganda because the very same naturalistic humanistic utopianism that undermines the realization *of* such aims is left unaddressed.

Conversely, positively, modernity's failure to create its designer utopias in the concrete world has sometimes led to a more realistic postmodernity – both politically and socially. Thus, for example, today we see genuine renewed concern for the environment and genuine advances in the social sciences. There are real advances in relation to the question of clean energy; better treatments and policies are now available for caring for those with various disadvantages or disabilities; there is a greater awareness concerning the kinds of inner-city housing projects that are needed if the alienating and deperson-alizing effects of 1960s housing projects are to be avoided; the list goes on.

'Good postmodernity', then, potentially promotes the rise of the knowledge of God because it is more realistic about human-kind in that it sees that naturalistic, humanistic utopianism has not produced a utopia, but rather has produced greedy consum-erism, exploitation of people and resources, wars, genocides, the nuclear threat, and humanitarian, ecological, and economic disasters.

Thus, on the one hand, modernity's 'death of God' utopia-nism[15] – its 'post-Christian' dream of a humanly-constructed heaven in which 'humankind conquers space travel and the stars' – is in crisis. God gave us enough resources to steward the earth, not enough resources to try to become heavenly gods ourselves. Therefore, the fact that modernity's utopianism – which it frequently hides behind its more-realistic naturalism – is being exposed by certain postmodern trends is good! In time, the death of idolatrous human narcissism could lead to the rise of the knowledge of God.

On the other hand, the tenacious persistency of modern 'death-of-God' utopianisms – in their shape-shifting transposition into a postmodern, digitopian guise and in their self-contradictory, self-cloaking, 'wolf in sheep's clothing' rhetoric about demo-cratic globalization, digital revolution, environmental sustain-ability, economic development and humanitarian awareness – is concerning, particularly given how destructive naturalistic humanistic utopianism has proven to be. This trend causes the potential rise of the knowledge of God to falter.

Turn to Relationality versus 'Play' and Conflict

Second, a new postmodern emphasis on dialogue, or on a 'philo-sophical turn to relationality' (i.e. relationships or the relational), contrasts with modern individualism.[16]

Thus, the philosopher H.-G. Gadamer examines the notion and practice of conversation with 'the other', highlighting contrasts between the openness of genuine conversation and the modern imposition of prior, overly formal and illegitimately unchallenge-able concepts onto the other that characterizes what Gadamer identifies as being (post-) Enlightenment 'Method' (see also Chapter 6 above).[17] We all know doctors who have prematurely imposed diagnoses upon us, only to be proven wrong by other doctors whom we see subsequently. Due to power imbalances, however, we found that it was initially difficult for us to challenge the original doctors. Well, from early on, modernity was like this on a grand scale. With respect to 'eighteenth-century' modern-istic society, M. Foucault identifies 'disciplines' as 'techniques for assuring the ordering of human multiplicities'[18] that:

> define . . . a tactics of power that fulfils three criteria: firstly, to obtain the exercise of power at the lowest possible cost (economically, by the low expenditure it involves; politically, by its discretion, its low exteriorization, its relative invisibility, the little resistance it arous-es); secondly, to bring the effects of this social power to their maxi-mum intensity and to extend them as far as possible, without either failure or interval; thirdly, to link this 'economic' growth of power with the output of the apparatuses (educational, military, industrial or medical) within which it is exercised; in short, to increase both the docility and the utility of all the elements of the system.[19]

The 'political' emphases on 'discretion . . . low exteriorization . . . relative invisibility [and] little resistance' (cf. 'docility'), here, are telling. If there were any abuses of power in what Foucault is describing (which there certainly were – e.g. people are deperson-alized and called 'elements of the system'), then 'zero exposure' of these abuses was certainly an aim of those in power. Thus, J. Habermas writes of 'the emergence of institutions from structures of distorted communication'. A right postmodern emphasis on genuine conversation, though, exposes modern systems of oppression and their 'distorted communication'. Indeed, power abuse is therein *exposed as being* – to some extent at least – 'distorted communication'.[20]

Notably, Gadamer also emphasizes conversation with *the past*. Yes, the past is different from the present, but not so different that it cannot be understood. Genuine communication and understanding can occur between the past and the present.[21] Thus, for example, Pharaoh's pride in Moses' day is not so alien that we cannot still learn from the Exodus narrative today. A great deal of time has passed, yes, but we all still know what pride is! Thus, whereas the modern individualistic 'isolated knower' is over-suspicious of tradition, being in conversation with past tradition through texts actually helps us since such conversation textually transmits received wisdom to us[22] – wisdom that can *referee* how we relate today. That is, how we relate to one another today can be regulated through our reading today about how Pharaoh related to others in the distant past. The horrors resulting from Pharaoh's pride *back then* can help us to choose humility in *the here and now*.

That is, a postmodern emphasis on genuine conversation, as opposed to the distorted communication of power abuse, and on genuine conversation with the past, as opposed to modern suspicion of tradition, helps us to referee our relating by promoting our openness to the textual communication of wisdom grounded in corporate memories of lessons learned in the past, and hence to a new respect for the Scriptures. Thus, a person's self-understanding is these days seen to develop through their relationships, including their relationships with past traditions of wisdom transmitted in texts, rather than through solitary individualistic introspection.[23]

Negatively, though, another side to postmodernity causes the turn to relationality to falter – and does so by emphasizing 'play' which, in this context of discussion, is relating to the other that is *not* refereed by wisdom from the past. Since, in this darker side of postmodernity, textually transmitted historical truth and textually transmitted historical wisdom are deemed to be inaccessible, then there are deemed to be no true grounds upon which somebody else, or even texts from the past, can expose abuses of power in our relating. We can supposedly simply relativize any challenge

by saying, 'That's just your opinion', and we can thereby supposedly always justify ourselves.[24]

Of course, though, non-refereed relating leads to bad relating.
And if we relate badly to others, but reject all confrontation,
then we will offend and enrage others. Similarly unchecked by
truth and/or by textually transmitted wisdom, others may then
seek Lamech-style revenge.[25] Since we have chosen self-justification, however, we will see their revenge as even more without
just cause than revenge already is, and will take great offence
ourselves. Being un-refereed by truth or wisdom, we may then
adopt a similar, brutal, Lamech-style, tabloidesque or chav-style
approach to vengeance ourselves.

Thus, 'play' inevitably leads to factions, to conflict, and to the
death of true relationality, dialogue and conversation. Modern,
centralized forms of distorted communication and power
abuse then merely fragment into competing localized forms of
distorted communication and power abuse within and between
factions, feudal tribes, guilds, political parties, protest groups,
interest groups and other cliques. Meanwhile each faction, in
justifying itself, constructs a rhetoric by which it perpetually
boasts and asserts how 'righteous' it is, even as it descends into
denied sin.[26]

Thus, the postmodern 'turn to relationality' is good and coheres
with Scripture; but in the dark side of the postmodern, 'play' turns
love into war.

Arguably, though, if modern 'death-of-God' utopianisms failed
completely, and the knowledge of God did rise again, then there
would indeed be a turn to relationality. In Chapter 3 above on
biblical lawfulness, we noted that 'love for God and neighbour
sums up the law and the prophets'. Love, though, is right relating,
or right relationality. Thus, largely, Christianity is right relationality – though, since we live in a fallen world, such relationality
must retain a critical aspect that is guided by and formed through
received biblical wisdom, and that referees our relating. Certainly,
then, if the world turned to God, then there would indeed be a
turn to right relating that was formed and refereed by the Holy
Spirit's deployment of received biblical wisdom.

But, as Billy Graham said on the day I became a Christian,
'We live in a spiritual battlefield.'[27] What, though, would such

a battlefield look like today? Well, if a turn to God involves a turn to right relating that is formed and refereed by the Spirit's deployment of received biblical wisdom, then demonic resistance to this 'turn' would oppose and corrupt right relating or right relationality, and would do so by opposing received biblical wisdom.

But that is precisely what we have just highlighted: a battle between a turn to relationality (dialogue, conversation, and received wisdom from the past by which our relating is formed and refereed) and 'play' (non-refereed bad relating resulting from the suppression of received wisdom from the past, and leading to factions, conflict and war).

Let us not remain naïve: it is not at all super-spiritual to argue that changes on the scale of the Western shift from modernity to postmodernity relate to dynamics involving spiritual 'powers and authorities'; 'For our struggle is not against flesh and blood, but against the rulers, against the authorities, against the powers of this dark world and against the spiritual forces of evil in the heavenly realms'.[28]

Domesticated middle-class Christianity, though, is embarrassed by belief in the demonic, and often transposes the entire conflict we are highlighting into the merely human plane – sociology is much cooler than demonology, no doubt. But what if we then fail to 'take [our] stand against the devil's schemes', or become 'unaware of his schemes'?[29] In my view, this has now happened – globally: we are 'unaware of his schemes'.

That is, whilst human agencies are certainly involved, the postmodern emphasis on 'play', as we have defined it here, is in our view nothing less than a demonic counter-attack against the potential rise of the knowledge of God that is co-extensive with the equally postmodern (but also biblical) turn to relationality.

There is spiritually good and biblical postmodernity consistent with dialogue and love. But there is also spiritually evil postmodernity consistent with 'play' and war.

Admittedly, some define 'postmodernity' more in line with what we have called the 'spiritually evil' side of these two opposing trends, whereas others define postmodernity as a questioning of modernity – a questioning that leads in both good and bad directions. To a large extent, of course, the 'good' and the 'bad' are mixed together in practice. We are oversimplifying matters somewhat here in order to highlight contrasts between 'good' and 'bad' aspects of a more complex historical 'whole'.

It is interesting to note, though, that Anthony C. Thiselton – in the later 1990s and more recently – tends to use the term 'post-modern' and its cognates for developments that are more nega-tive than positive. By contrast, in his earlier work, *New Horizons in Hermeneutics* (1992), Thiselton also strongly hints that the term 'postmodern' and its cognates can be used to signal more positive developments as well. Here, in this book, we more closely align with Thiselton's earlier strong hints in terms of working defini-tions, but more closely follow Thiselton's later emphases when we attack what we call here 'bad postmodernity'.[30]

Our point, though, is that 'bad' postmodern emphases on 'play' (in our use of this term here) and on the supposed inaccessibility of received, textually transmitted, biblical (and other) wisdom and historical report from the past, cause relationality itself to be undermined, leading to factions, conflicts and wars. 'Play' and war cause the biblically positive turn to relationality to falter.

Rise of Historical Consciousness versus Historical Negationism

Third, a still-continuing trend that began in modern times is called 'the rise of historical consciousness'.[31] One problem with the legacy of ancient Greek thinking and of modern trends in the West was (and is) an overemphasis on so-called 'upper storey' concepts – e.g. oneness, unity, substance, a Greek timeless 'God', ethical absolutes, reason, properties, ideal forms, timeless truth, formal language, static systems, the abstract, the logic 'behind' everything, generalization, totality and so on. Conversely, in the same legacy, so-called 'lower storey' concepts – e.g. diversity, movement, change, event, process, the particular case, difference, the concrete, life, language-uses and developing traditions – were (and are) problematically under-emphasized.

With the rise of historical consciousness, however, all this changed. The whole thing was turned upside-down, and then fell on its side. The previously 'lower storey' concepts were emphasized, whilst the previously 'upper storey' concepts were de-emphasized. Moreover, this change of emphasis meant that time came to prominence, rather than space. Thus, the overall focus was no longer so much on an 'upper storey' and a 'lower storey', but more on 'back then', 'now' and 'not yet'.[32] These changes marked the rise of historical consciousness.

The problem then arose, however, of what to do with all the previously emphasized 'upper storey' concepts. Moreover, another problem arose: how should the newly emphasized 'lower storey' concepts be interrelated with one another?

Now, of course, the de-emphasizing of the notion of 'a Greek timeless "God"' meant that our understanding of God changed. Negatively, some reduced God to a humanly projected construct, which led to the so-called 'death of God' and to so-called 'post-Christian' Western culture. Positively, others conceived of God more biblically, distinguishing the biblical 'time-*full*' God from the now-defunct 'Greek "time*less* God"'.

Less obviously, human persons had also been seen in terms of 'upper-storey' or 'idealist transcendental' (as opposed to 'historical transcendental') categories – for example, 'reason'. Negatively, then, the collapse of the 'upper storey' led in some circles to the deconstruction of the self or to the so-called 'death of the self' (or 'death of the subject', or 'death of the author'). This development was complex because it was actually the collapse of formal 'upper storey' concepts, and hence of formal stable language, and hence (supposedly) of stable linguistically constructed 'human selfhood' or 'consciousness' that led to the 'death of the self'.[33]

Positively, though, others reconfigured – i.e. reconceptualised – human selves more biblically as 'unique historical one-offs who are realized in relationships with others over time'. The stability of human identity was then anchored in more historical notions, such as narrative,[34] and in a comparatively stable historical view of language (and thence of consciousness) that, moreover, was emphatically not a return to ahistorical formalist or 'upper storey' idealist views of language (or of consciousness).

Similarly, our understanding of logic was also reconfigured. Negatively, some dismissed logic as being only an arbitrary human construct. However, positively, others saw logic as having to do with after-the-fact internal coherence, and as still being of great use in historical reconstructions, mathematics and systematic theologies – which is a development that is also true to biblical Christianity.[35] This latter development, though, still prioritized 'life' over 'logic' and 'system', which allowed human personhood and human relationships – once freed from the problems to do with the deconstruction of selves noted above – to be re-prioritized in line with biblical emphases on unique human persons and their unique gifts, callings and ministries, and on love or right relating.

We could go on. Our point, though, is that just like the turn to relationality, the rise of historical consciousness brought positive developments. Our reality really *is* historical and is:

(a) moving and changing;
(b) diverse and full of particularity and difference;
(c) that which combines movement, change and difference within a unified whole in which there are degrees of continuity and stability;
(d) a conditioning force that shapes us as Bible-readers;
(e) characterized by an open future that is to an extent uncertain.

Having said all this, however, and turning again to the darker side of the postmodern, then the destabilization of older frameworks of thought also allowed certain *malformed historicisms* to develop that:

(a) over-stress movement and change – or 'flux' – at the expense of stability;
(b) over-stress diversity, particularity and difference at the expense of unity, continuity and similarity;
(c) combine movement, change and difference in such a way as to produce absolute historical 'dislocation' or 'dissociation' between moments in time;
(d) view conditioning one-sidedly as prohibiting objectivity (e.g. about the historical past), when in fact conditioning also aids objectivity (including objectivity about the historical past);
(e) over-stress future-related indeterminacy, when in fact divine promises and other factors shape the future in ways that combine indeterminacy with degrees of predictability and/or of probability.

Now, of course, biblically speaking, it is true that some truths change: I used to live in Manchester, but now I don't; Genghis Khan used to be a leader, but now he isn't. And so on. It is this postmodern and biblical emphasis on change – and hence on movement – that differs from older modernistic emphases on non-historical or constant truth (e.g. laws of 'nature', or fixed static – or at least cyclic – deterministic systems that describe even sociological patterns as being scientifically predictable, and so on). Biblically speaking, God brings about change and movement, animating and breathing life into creation by his Spirit.

And biblically speaking, historical truth – including historical contingencies – is diverse, and full of particularity and difference. A hedgehog is not a peanut. The wind is not a solid. Blue is different from red. A person is different from a snail. And so on. Such thinking is biblical, for God has made the world rich in variety and exceedingly complex.

Moreover, biblically speaking, emphasizing diversity, movement and change does not rule out the created unity of history or the fact that some things only change very slowly over time and thus form comparatively stable continuities. Thus, for example, geological rock formations, wisdom concerning right relating, the facts about JFK's assassination and so on are stable historical realities (even if the details of JFK's assassination are not fully known yet). And, as we said above, pride now looks very much the same as pride in Pharaoh's day! History is unified throughout, even if it is far from being uniform.

Negatively, though, some forms of postmodernity emphasize historical difference, change and movement so much that they preclude historical unity, stability and continuity by positing radical dissociations between historical moments or between (what we would call) 'horizons'. But this approach not only contradicts the notion of the unity of history, but also the notions of the unity of creation and of the space–time continuum.

Furthermore, if Bible-readers – according to what we are calling 'bad postmodernity' – are conditioned by present horizons that are supposedly radically dissociated from the horizons of the biblical texts, or if present horizons are supposedly radically dissociated from past horizons, then (in bad postmodernity) historical conditioning becomes that which prohibits historical objectivity – even about such horrors as the Holocaust.

And yet, if creation, history and the space–time continuum are in fact a unity, then such dissociation is impossible.[36] That is, and as we indicated above, historical conditioning can actually involve the shaping of Bible-readers by textually transmitted biblical wisdom as well as by textually transmitted reports about historical facts such as the Holocaust, which means that historical conditioning can aid objectivity ethically and factually as well as hinder objectivity ethically and factually.

And finally, whilst the future is unknown at one level, it is not totally indeterminate, but only partially indeterminate. Yes, human rationality cannot deduce what the future will be, since human rationality is confined to considerations drawn from the past and the present. And yet, divinely created history is not simply going in any and every direction but, rather, involves a future that is shaped by personal agencies, notably by *God* who fulfils his promises.[37] Negatively, though, some postmodern trends emphasize total indeterminacy, and are thus consistent only with atheism.

Therefore, broadly speaking: the modern and postmodern rise of historical consciousness is good and coheres with Scripture; but some 'bad postmodern' emphases – especially on 'flux' and on 'dissociation' – turn historical consciousness into historical-negationism, even into Holocaust-negationism.

Thus, the philosopher Paul Ricoeur writes, 'The paradox of the situation created by the Holocaust is to oblige the champions of a rhetoricist interpretation of history to answer the suspicion that they are unable to refute negationism, because of their failure to discover any firm line between fiction and reality in respect of the historical past.'[38] That is, if postmodern flux and dissociation turn historical consciousness into historical-negationism, then that is immoral. Here, we may cite Ricoeur again: if the postmodern 'masters of suspicion, with their password of "referential illusion"' (Ricoeur calls their approach 'rhetoricism') and 'the negationists, and their password of the "official lie"' are 'suddenly brought up against each other', then the result is a new, postmodern, 'rhetoricist' historical 'negationism' that finds itself unable – on the basis of its own theory at least – to find any way of speaking truly about the Holocaust through texts![39]

But how, then, will future generations learn of the horrors of the Holocaust so as to avoid repeating them?[40] That is, historical-negationism causes the biblically right rise of historical consciousness to falter.

Rise of Liberating *Concientización* versus Historical Relativism

Fourth, the previous point leads on to our next point: the rise of historical consciousness properly leads to the rise of historical knowledge. Becoming aware of the past lets us learn from the past so that we can referee our present actions so as to bring about a better future – not the utopianisms of modernity, but the kingdom of God. Otherwise, 'Those who cannot remember the past are condemned to repeat it.'[41] The rise of historical consciousness is biblical and right, for it is essential that we come to a proper confessional awareness of how modernism *itself* (and not just some more ancient legacy that extended into modernity) largely caused *its own* catastrophic errors – not least, the Holocaust, the world wars and other disasters.

Certain postmodern trends, however, have not turned over-abstract, formal, ancient Greek or positivist-style notions of truth into sobering awareness of historical truth, but have dismantled the former without re-establishing the latter. Admittedly, abstract, formal, ancient Greek or positivist-style notions of truth, being idealist, do not relate in any simple sense to accessible realities or truths. However, historical truths transmitted in texts are in principle accessible to us. One hundred years from now, texts will not convey the full horrors of the Holocaust; but texts will certainly transmit much of the terrible truth about the Holocaust. And it would be immoral for them not to do so.[42]

Certain postmodern trends, however, espouse historical relativism which, ultimately, produces authoritarianisms which, when fully grown, will produce further terrible oppressions.

That is, in Western postmodernity, there is sometimes thought to be no such thing as truth, but only different interpretations of what truth might be. This popular view is what Thiselton calls a 'neo-pragmatic' 'mood'. It is sometimes not a 'serious' philosophical viewpoint, but this popular mood remains part of Western postmodernity nonetheless.[43]

In this neo-pragmatic postmodernism it is said that since an interpreter is always located in a historically unique cultural and traditional setting then that interpreter will always view truth in line with received views from that same cultural and traditional setting. Thus, Martin Luther related 'his Bible' to his inherited historical concerns, and so the way in which he understood 'his Bible' was different from the ways in which, say, different communities within the contemporary church understand 'their Bibles'.

And, to an extent, of course, this is right. The problem, however, comes when it is said that exposure to texts, or to other cultures through texts, cannot then *alter* the perspectives of one's own culture. This is like saying that water cannot be added to cordial to make squash. But just as it is true that adding water to a cordial changes both liquids, it is also true that neither liquid entirely becomes the other liquid. Rather, a new liquid is formed. In the same way, since thought and language are closely intertwined, then reading, in introducing new combinations of concepts – and hence new hybrid concepts – into the reader's mind, potentially alters the reader's thinking. Thus, Bible-reading does not make our thinking instantly totally biblical, but it can make our thinking more biblical. One *begins* from one's own cultural perspectives; but one need not *remain* there.

This process of having one's cultural perspectives altered by the biblical texts is sometimes closely related – in liberation theology – to a kind of awakening known as *concientización*.[44] We all experience a kind of *concientización* when we have some sense of unease in some relationship or situation, but then go on to identify the cause of the unease, and thereby become empowered to tackle the cause as an objectifiable problem. The process and experience of *concientización*, then, is like the breaking of a spell. And it is the reading of texts – especially the Bible – that often initiates this process and experience of *concientización*.

On the basis of 'dissociation' (see above), however, certain neo-pragmatic postmodern strands (a) preach a historical relativism that says that we cannot access historical truth through texts, but then (b) practice an absolutism that says that, therefore, their community's beliefs cannot be challenged by historical truth that is supposedly 'accessed' through texts. They then say (c) that anybody who tries to challenge them with such truth is therefore actually being imperializing, or is trying to gain power over their community. Thus, (d), they equate 'truth' or 'knowledge' claims with colonializing power bids. After all, modernity claimed to know truth, and was indeed abusive with power.

The problem here, though, is that those who testify to the accessibility of historical truth and knowledge on non-modern, or on non-formal, provisional, historical grounds, are not necessarily objectivists or imperializing fundamentalists. Modernity claimed to have absolute knowledge that was formal; but a right kind of postmodernity – which only admits the possibility of having provisional historical knowledge that is incomplete and non-formal – does not claim to have absolute formal knowledge.

Thus, a right kind of postmodernity – just like true biblical Christianity – accepts that the challenger can also be challenged by historical truth that is accessed through texts. Thus, it is the neo-pragmatists, who refuse to be challenged by historical truth that is accessed through texts, who in principle are being authoritarian: their power base, on their view, could only ever be overturned by a pragmatic decision on their part – or by an act of war, threat or of pragmatic overruling on the part of another community.

Thus, ordinarily, and until it pragmatically suits him, the neo-pragmatist blocks *concientización* by an argument centred on the inaccessibility of historical truth, and does so in order to immunize his power base from threat – which is why some neo-pragmatic pastors try to keep their congregations infantilized, as we argued in Part Two. This kind of situation, though, is a breeding ground for unchallengeable fundamentalisms, extremisms and even terrorisms.

Thus, the postmodern rise of historical knowledge is good and coheres with Scripture; but postmodern, neo-pragmatic historical relativism immunizes absolutist authoritarian – and potentially extremist – communities from challenge by historical knowledge, and thereby greatly hinders the victims of (and/or within) such communities from attaining liberation through *concientización*.

One problem with neo-pragmatism is that it radicalizes the Cartesian 'subject–object' model of knowledge. Neo-pragmatism rightly stresses that the 'knowing subject' of Descartes was too individualistic, and that it is also communities of people who do the perceiving. However, neo-pragmatism then radically dissociates the corporate subject from the object in cases where the object in question is textual content and function. Neo-pragmatism then says that a present community's inherited interpretative norms entirely determine what a reader within that community perceives to be 'in the text'.

Thus, neo-pragmatism removes the epistemic distance from between the reader and his or her community, but radicalizes the epistemic distance between the community and the text. But this is like saying that the reader is 'entirely "one" with the present horizon', but 'entirely "dissociated" from the past textual horizon'. But this is like saying that the mere passage of time makes something different and unknowable in principle. (It is also like saying that a reader cannot do other than utterly submit to their community).

The problem though, again, is that this viewpoint – its authoritarianism to one side – transgresses the criteria of the unity of creation (biblically speaking), the unity of history (philosophically speaking), and the space–time continuum (scientifically speaking). When it comes to understanding the past through texts, neo-pragmatists thus ignore biblical doctrine, Continental philosophical tradition since Heidegger (and earlier), and recent science.

When asked to justify their stance, neo-pragmatists simply assert that one cannot access philosophical (and, presumably, other kinds of) texts in order to contradict their stance. Thus, they presuppose their argument's conclusion at the start of their argument, which means that their 'argument' is only a circular assertion that, being immunized from challenge, is also – and as we have already indicated – authoritarian.

Thus, neo-pragmatists base a circular, authoritarian assertion on an impossible, dichotomous split in creation, history and space–time. Their disowned and projected authoritarianism thus immunizes cultural oppression from intellectual challenge. This is called fundamentalism, which easily decays into extremism.[45]

That is, we said earlier that if a rise in the knowledge of God involves a turn to right relating that is refereed by received wisdom, then spiritual opposition to this would promote bad relating that was not refereed because, in addition, received wisdom was blocked by such opposition.

Now, though, we have said that received wisdom allows people to come to awareness (*concientización*) of oppression so that they can be liberated. So then, what would spiritual opposition to *this* look like? It would look like authoritarianism trying to keep people unaware of its presence and of its abuses by using fine-sounding rhetoric to dismiss the possibility of receiving wisdom through texts, and to deny charges of authoritarianism by projecting those charges back onto those who make them.

Neo-pragmatism is thus – in effect (if not in intent) – a post-modern cloaking device that perpetuates oppression by blocking historical knowledge and *concientización*.

Demonic powers resist the rise of the knowledge of God by attacking the received wisdom and knowledge that could liberate us from the 'self-justifying autonomy' spell of modernity. Therein, historical relativism causes the biblically right rise of liberating *concientización* to falter.

Linguistic Turn to Enfleshed Word versus Docetic-Rhetoricist Flux

Fifth, another potentially positive aspect of the modern–post-modern shift is the linguistic turn. In part, this shift occurred when the later Wittgenstein and other philosophers, such as J.L. Austin, recovered a view of language that resonated with a biblical view of language. Biblically speaking, Christ is the 'enfleshed Word'; and one implication of this teaching is that Jesus shows us what his words mean by his embodied actions.[46]

That is, actions give concrete currency to the meanings of language-uses. What does Jesus' use of the word 'love' mean? Well, look at how Jesus acts. What does Paul mean when he uses the word 'redemption'? Well, look at God's redeeming actions in the Old Testament, and Paul means something similar, since his background training involved the study of Old Testament texts. What do certain, modern-day, charismatic Christians mean when they use the phrase, 'experience of the Spirit'? Well, look at how they use the phrase, and in what contexts of action or behaviour. If they do not mean what Paul would have meant when using the same phrase, then that might be depressing. But at least their actions will have shown – or disambiguated – what *they* mean by *their* use of the phrase.[47]

In modernity, however, words and concepts tended to be given supposedly absolutely formal meanings that were supposedly independent of people's actions in/when using those words and concepts. Modernists, especially logical positivists, and against the background of ancient Greek thinking, imagined what was in effect an 'upper storey' realm of absolute concepts or logic to which our language uses and meanings at least 'should' (supposedly) correspond. There was supposedly a 'blue-print in the sky' so to speak – a kind of 'exalted dictionary' – that said what our words and concepts should supposedly 'really' mean.

Clearly, this was nonsense. Language derives its meaning from conventions of how words and phrases are used, as we have just said above. Even when God speaks to us, he uses human language according to human conventions of language-use; otherwise we could not understand him. Undoubtedly, within the Trinity, there is an exalted language involved in perfect intra-divine communication. But we do not know that language. When God spoke *to us* in the past, he used Hebrew, Aramaic and Greek. And when he speaks to us today, he uses that same Hebrew, Aramaic and Greek – or else he uses translations of what he says in these languages.

So, when modernity's view of language proved to be nonsense, the hunt was on for an adequate philosophy of language. And, as just noted, it was the later Wittgenstein who hit on the view of language that Jesus (and the rest of us) actually presupposed in practice.

Others, though, namely the post-structuralists, and particularly Jacques Derrida and the later Roland Barthes, came up with a different view of language – and it was this different view of language that created the problems to do with flux and dissociation that we noted above. Thus, broadly speaking, post-structuralism turns 'enfleshed word' into 'en-worded flesh'. In the case of enfleshed word, historical action by persons 'contains' language and so constrains linguistic meanings (sign relations) to historically concrete meanings (horizonal relations). But in the case of en-worded flesh, language 'contains' historical action by persons, such that historical action by persons no longer constrains linguistic meanings. Thiselton calls this latter view of language 'docetic' after the heresy called Docetism, which denied the enfleshed reality of Christ's body and death.[48]

An illustration will help us here. Imagine being in a room in which different images and words are being continuously projected at a fast pace on all the walls, the ceiling and the floor. It is not hard to see that this would be very confusing! But now imagine that there was no exit from the room, such that your only reality was the room. This would mean that there would be no constancy, no stability but only constant flux – since the different words and pictures would be changing all the time.

And to an extent, the post-structuralists are right. This is how our postmodern age actually looks! Until recently, our frameworks for thinking and speaking were comparatively fixed and stable; but now, everything constantly changes – especially since the advent of television and of the digital age. These days, language seems no longer to connect us to firm ground, but rather seems to obscure firm ground. Accordingly, language seems to be trivialized and used ever-more irresponsibly, as in the mass media, advertising and some party politics.[49]

The problem, though, is that post-structuralism is describing a culture that it helped to create. It is a self-fulfilling prophecy. Culture *can* use language in a post-structuralist kind of way. But need it *necessarily* do so? Somewhere, a cultural choice has been mistaken for a philosophical necessity. Yes, language and history are irrevocably interrelated; language is not an imitation of an abstract 'reality' in the sky. But language and history are not interrelated as post-structuralism says they are: ultimately, it is history that contains language, and not the other way around, for all language is historical action (any unknowable intra-divine languages aside), but not all historical action is language.

That is, even if language in our culture *is* up-anchored from tradition, trivialized and digitally accelerated into a 'play' of changing meanings, then this is because we have *chosen* that course of action. (NB: this use of the word 'play' is different from our earlier use of the word 'play' [50]). That is, post-structuralists are complicit in:

(a) *suppressing* tradition by calling all texts that purport to communicate from the past mere 'rhetoric' (this is called 'rhetoricism', and even threatens to suppress true historical report about the Holocaust);[51]

(b) *trivializing* our language-use through this up-anchoring of our language from continuities with past traditions of stable language-use and of the stable ethical criteria of wisdom;

(c) the postmodern *use of digital technology* to create a *virtual* realm in which these trivializing changes of language use and foolish wisdom-suppressions can be *accelerated*;

(d) the postmodern, apathetic decision to choose to be *passively conditioned* by this digital onslaught of trivial, present-moment, foolish non-wisdom so as,

(e) to become *so confused about 'the real'* that our consciences can no longer internalize any stable ethical criteria by which we can be convicted of sin.

Naturally, of course, post-structuralists argue that it is those who try to fix language and meanings who unwittingly come under power structures, who impose power structures on others, and who perpetuate those power structures through the use of rhetoric about 'speaking truly' – a rhetoric that (supposedly) serves merely to reinforce prior oppressive ideologies. After all, is that not what modernity did with its 'Method',[52] its formal concepts and formal definitions – its propaganda of oppressive 'phrase-regimes' that you weren't allowed to argue with?[53]

Again, though, the problem with the post-structuralist approach is that there ends up being no way of exposing the truth about oppressive regimes if all purportedly concientizing language is only a rhetorical power bid itself. Post-structuralists would no doubt reply that oppression is manifest precisely *by* fixed phrase regimes – and indeed there is truth to this. The problem, though, is that freedom is actually secured by discourse that is salted with wisdom concerning how things actually work. Oppression can be caused by unpredictable, ever-changing, arbitrary false language just as easily as it can be caused by fixed false language. It is false language that oppresses – regardless of whether the falsehood is arbitrary expanding meanings or arbitrary fixed meanings – for all false language isolates and alienates.

'The truth', however, 'will set you free.'[54] True language manifests both stability and creative change – for its historical point of origin (and object, when it has one) also manifests both stability and creative change. Thus, those who expose oppressive regimes by using language tend to expose similar kinds of abuses to those exposed by other prophetic voices exposing other oppressive regimes. And yet the details in each case differ and alter with time. *Both* real history *and* this true language that liberates are *both* stable *and* changing.

Post-structuralism, however, threatens to banish such liberating language and merely replace an oppression of false fixed terms with an oppression of false fluxing terms. One of the false assumptions behind this post-structuralist approach, however, is the hyper-suspicious view that power interests constitute the only motive for the decision to stabilize language-uses. Human beings, though, often stabilize language-uses for good reasons as well – for example, to warn future generations about what oppression looks like, or to pass on corporate memories concerning ethical lessons learned from bitter national experiences, or to pass on to future generations the celebration of what is good in life, and so on and so forth.

Thus, the postmodern linguistic turn can be good and can cohere with Scripture; but postmodern, post-structuralist, docetic rhetoricism up-anchors language-uses from traditions of transmitted wisdom and truth so as to produce a counterfeit or falsely marketed 'freedom from false, fixed oppressive phrase regimes' that is in reality a different kind of isolating and alienating oppression that is caused by false, arbitrarily expanding language uses and meanings, and that banishes truly liberating discourse that is salted with wisdom concerning how things actually work.

Demonic powers, in order to suppress the received wisdom that liberates us from modernity's deadly utopian spell, attack the very linguistic structures that transmit that wisdom. Thus, docetic rhetoricist flux causes the biblically right linguistic turn to falter.

Rise of Democracies versus Fragmentation and Authoritarianism

Sixth, further observations about the modern–postmodern shift can be made with respect to Western culture. Earlier, we argued that some postmodern cultural developments were good, where we cited renewed environmental concerns, advances in the social sciences, better systems of care and improvements in housing. Here, we could extend this list by citing renewed concerns for the Third World, for oppressed groups at home and abroad, for human rights (which we also noted earlier, in a slightly different context of discussion), and so on.

That is, if modernity developed the hard sciences so as to bring technological advances, postmodernity develops the social sciences (as well as the hard sciences) so as to bring humanitarian and other advances as well. It is right that people in Britain generally now tend to have the basic necessities: food, water, clothes, shelter, provisions, electricity, gas, sanitation, the vote, education, access to justice, social equality – and so on (though just recently, as always, this positive trend is in some cases under threat). And even if modernity helped to create Third World poverty,[55] at least postmodern awareness of modernity's failings is a good thing, isn't it? Cultural 'goods' *have* arisen with the modern–postmodern shift.

Nevertheless, and before we lapse into too much Olympics-2012-style self-congratulation, we should note that much of the postmodern constitutes an almost worldwide turning to sin that is so dangerous that it threatens to swallow such cultural 'goods' whole and even to derail the global rise of humanitarian democracies.[56]

Thus, the bad, neo-pragmatic side or outcome of the modern–postmodern shift brings very serious *political* problems. If there is supposedly no handle on truth, or supposedly no stable, true way of speaking, then rational argument that appeals to publicly accepted criteria (i.e. tested truths) is undermined. Rhetoric and party-political pragmatic powerplays – or propaganda – then tend to displace sound rational argument, and political speeches often then become devices that merely capitalize on popular sentiments.[57] Such neo-pragmatism presents us with a rhetoric about 'freedom' and 'democracy' that is really what D.A. Carson calls 'philosophical pluralism'.[58]

At first, philosophical pluralism seems liberating – like a policy of 'live and let live' that accommodates 'where different people are really at'; like a policy of tolerating the empirical fact that people simply believe different things; and even sometimes like a policy of setting people free to find the real God, the accessible truth and genuine wisdom for themselves.

But, as Carson rightly notes, such purported 'democratic tolerance' and purported 'empirical pluralism' really amount to a 'philosophical pluralism' that encourages 'intolerance' of anybody who makes a truth claim, or who doesn't toe the relativist line. The claims concerning 'freedom' are not true. 'Philosophical pluralism' hides the real God, the accessible truth and genuine wisdom in a sea of supposedly 'uncheckable', arbitrary 'possibilities' that are all, supposedly, 'equally valid but equally not true'. 'Philosophical pluralism', through this assertion of cognitive 'arbitrariness', thus actually tends to greatly hinder our access to that which can lead us to the Saviour – namely Jesus Christ – who heals and frees us.[59] According to Thiselton this neo-pragmatic situation has 'four possible' outcomes: 'paralyzing skepticism . . . the view that "might is right" . . . sheer intuitionism, or a self-situating contextualism. None of these four alternatives provides a critical theory for social action, as Rorty and Fish concede'.[60]

That is, in the case of full-blown neo-pragmatic culture, we end up with either hyper-critical disengagement, or domination of the other, or slavish submission to domination by others, or tribal warfare between groups that are each characterized by authoritarian power structures. In plain English: in full-blown neo-pragmatic cultures one either dominates others, goes to war in order to dominate others, submits to domination, or runs away. Everything is 'dominate, submit, fight or flight', or reduced to the animal. When they are full-blown, negative neo-pragmatic postmodern developments, once globalized, lead to a choice between authoritarianism and violence. This is not 'freedom'.

The bad, neo-pragmatic side or outcome of the modern–postmodern shift also causes *consumption* (cf. consumerism) to replace contribution. If there is supposedly no objective overarching story that says what life is about, but rather if there are only multiple, arbitrary visions of designer realities – i.e. reactions to and instrumentalizations of the shattered and fragmented remains of what used to be modernity's more-unified utopian vision(s) – then there is less of an authentic sense of building something together in a way that involves each person's vocational contribution. People will die for a vision, but if there is no vision, then they will live for themselves. Vision breeds sacrificial contribution; 'no vision' breeds self-centred consumption.[61]

Moreover, as modernity's 'Arthur C. Clarkean' visions of, or odysseys towards, humanly created (and sometimes supposedly ET-directed) technological utopias become ever-more unrealistic and fragmented in the concrete world, consumers become ever-more seduced by the computerized 'phantasmagoria' of the virtual world – i.e. by a 'trapdoor' into a fantasy 'digitopia' of perfectly 'connected' 'community' in which, actually, individuals are trained out of patient relating to others and into impatient, impulsive, road-rage reactivity to everything and everybody – and into a 'brutally insincere', disengaged and objectifying mode of perception that can view 'Gulf-War' 'bombing' 'as yet another "special effect"'.[62] A digital culture only accelerates neo-pragmatic processes of cultural fragmentation into conflicts between competing tribal interest groups and between their respective, radicalized group visions and self-legitimizing rhetorics.[63]

The bad, neo-pragmatic side or outcome of the modern–postmodern shift also brings disastrous *economic* consequences. An economy of providing for necessities deteriorates into an 'economy of signs' geared towards competitive status attainment, and then deteriorates still further into an 'economy of sign systems' based on 'information' 'and entertainment', not on 'manufacturing' and production.[64]

Above, we noted the turn to consumerism. Consumerism is that culture whereby people – according to largely arbitrary hierarchies of sign systems related to taste, discretion or preference – select, procure, consume or otherwise deploy various products, pleasures and performances so as both to symbolize and generate both their particular social class or sub-group and their position *within* their particular social class or sub-group so as, in turn, to solicit differential, discriminatory, exclusivist distinctions and social dynamics that confer upon them certain privileges, rewards or empowerments.[65] In other words, people put on increasingly elaborate displays of affluent living in order to secure their social advancement – and will stop at nothing in order to do so.

This consumerism then becomes that which the expanding economy has to finance – namely, a very expensive life-paradigm that is about a lot more than 'putting bread on the table'. A status-seeking, consumerist, life-paradigm is about multiple four-wheel drives, exotic holidays, huge television sets, large mansions with gaudy black and gold iron gates, and so on. Middle-class status-generating symbol deployment costs the earth – literally; and so a culture of borrowing develops.

Furthermore, this form of concrete consumerism, this non-sustainable, non-distributable, affluent cocoon of escapist abstraction that is absurdly divorced and disengaged from the real state of the world internationally, is accompanied by, and is vulnerable to collapse into, an even more escapist disinhibited virtual consumerism.

The latter is that culture whereby people – according to largely hedonistic hierarchies of sign systems related to indulgence, indiscretion and preference – impulsively select, procure, consume or otherwise deploy various online products, pleasures or performances so as both to symbolize and generate: their online social class, sub-group or tribal allegiance; their position *within* their online social class, sub-group or tribe; and their personas that disguise their disintegrating true self-hoods (see below). The purpose of these behaviours is to solicit or derive differential, discriminatory, exclusivist 'tribal' recognition or affirmation and/or persona-related, private personal gratification. In other words, people indulge in increasingly elaborate and abstracted private or tribal virtual online worlds in which they gratify increasingly bizarre – and potentially dangerous – construals of persona-selves.[66]

This kind of disinhibited virtual consumerism then becomes what the expanding economy *also* has to finance. The problem, though, is that whilst people are in the virtual world, they aren't producing much in the concrete world. Only certain products can be constructed from data, notably products related to 'information' 'and entertainment'. But who then produces, or for that matter pays for, concrete consumerism – for the ongoing, middle-class, status-generating symbol deployment, which requires 'heavy' 'manufacturing' and real wealth? It is easy to see how a culture of borrowing then accelerates and collapses.[67]

Sustainable stewardship of the earth is right; irresponsible exploitation of earth's resources – or of digital information – in pursuit of humanistic utopias or digitopias is not. The development of technology in order to steward the earth responsibly is right; the development of technology in order to create an entirely virtual environment that trains people out of right relating and into impatient impulsive reflexivity is not.[68] Lifting the poor out of poverty through an expanding economy of provision for necessities is right; the distortion of material emancipation into a greedy exclusivist materialism of competitive consumerism involving an unsustainable expanding 'economy of signs' that 'cannot be universalized' (to use Moltmann's language) is not. Healthy competition for opportunities for enterprise and endeavour within a broader co-operative setting that allows for social mobility is right; tribalism, hyper-suspicion and the fragmentation of society into competing interest groups 'at war' with each other in a hyper-accelerated culture is not.[69]

Only the Bible keeps its feet on the ground when it comes to warning us against this catalogue of modern and postmodern distortions. If the 'good', more biblical side of the postmodern encourages the rise of humanitarian democracies then, by contrast, the fragmentation and the authoritarianism of the 'bad', more demonic, neo-pragmatic side of the postmodern cause the rise of humanitarian democracies to falter.

Rise of True Self-Awareness versus Avoidant 'Deconstructed Selves'

Seventh, the modern–postmodern shift also brings the rise of biblically truer self-awareness through a better understanding of human selves.

The modern self was often perceived as a conquering hero. Through science, technology and the relentless advance of knowledge, we would eventually supposedly be able to control our own destinies and create our utopian futures. Technological advances would allow us to master 'nature', sociological advances would allow us to achieve self-mastery, and we'd come of age, in modern Kantian or Nietzschean autonomy from God. As 'free' 'adult' selves, we would make up our own minds on ethical matters, and would impose our 'brave new world' upon the universe.[70]

Certain postmodern trends, however, consider such self-perceptions and self-aspirations to be naïve. If knowledge itself is under threat, then how can it relentlessly advance? If people are the victims of manipulative power-plays, whether politically, at the workplace, or even in churches, interest groups and families, then how can they control their own destinies? Psychoanalysis has shown that we deceive ourselves: we don't even know ourselves. Before we even mention demonic forces, often-unseen sociological and psychological forces threaten to construct or at least condition our very identities.[71] Are people not routinely herded into arbitrary behavioural patterns through manipulative advertising, films and the media?

Thus, certain postmodern interpretations of the self are right to attack modernity's delusional notions of human selfhood. Psychological, sociological and other forces do indeed undermine individualistic (and even corporate) notions of 'self-mastery' or of 'ethical autonomy' or of 'control of one's own destiny'.

Again, though, other postmodern trends have negative effects on the philosophy of human selves. Post-structuralism acknowledges the reality of a concrete biological animal entity that is traditionally called 'the human self', but then reduces this self to a primate bombarded by shifting or fluxing cultural and/or linguistic signs that repeatedly 'write', 'overwrite' and thus constantly change the self that modernists once saw as a stable entity – as though our 'programming' was constantly being altered. Thus, supposedly, according to post-structuralism, even our very selves, including our minds, since they are largely linguistic, are the fleeting and changing products of accelerated linguistic bombardment by cultural signs, of momentary convergences of varying cultural and other forces.[72]

This view, though, conveniently absolves us of responsibility. If there is no 'me', but only an ever-changing cultural construct, then can't I say, 'Culture made me do it', when anything goes wrong?

Of course, again, post-structuralism tries to take the moral high ground by arguing that it 'frees' human selves from 'fixed' linguistic categories and descriptions – from 'fixedness' itself.[73] And indeed, modernity often *did* oppress people by imposing upon them fixed diagnoses, definitions, phrase regimes, concepts, and so on – as already noted.

Nevertheless, we also indicated earlier on that people are liberated by true speech about them and in relation to them. This is what 'being known in relationship' *is*. But, if language is supposedly so divorced from reality that it can no longer 'speak truly' at all, then persons are effectively silenced when it comes to speaking truly about themselves, or when it comes to speaking truly about others. The result is an irreconcilable breakdown of relationships, whether between individuals or between groups or even between nations.

Furthermore, as we said earlier, people are not liberated by 'arbitrary flux'. Both false fixed language and false arbitrarily fluxing language can oppress because they both fail to correlate with historical actualities, which manifest *both* stabilities *and* changes.

Human selves, then, find social liberation when they are socialized through participation – over time – in common discourse-worlds that, in addition, map onto their personal realities empathically and in line with traditions of received wisdom.

To make a related point, then the reason why constant post-structural irony and unpredictability is so dull is that it constantly draws attention to itself. Some contemporary music is extraordinarily clever in its constant unpredictable discontinuities. And yet, it is often the artist's cleverness, rather than the feeling-states of the listener, that is on show. Of all the human feeling-states that could be expressed empathically by the music, the only feeling-state actually expressed by such 'post-structuralist' music is non-empathic you-can't-catch-me ironic vanity, which soon becomes boring.[74] There is something embittered, hyper-critical and vengeful about such 'I told you so' cleverness. There is, correlatively, a schism between attempts to get attention in our celebrity-seeking culture, and attempts to sidestep relationship or 'being known': one sees flirtation, but little or no faithfulness.

By contrast, music that resonates with its listeners flexes to fit multiple feeling-states and multiple narrative-configurations of feeling-states, and is forever fresh and delightful, since it gives empathically to the other and is thus relational and not narcissistic.

Biblically speaking, then, both the monolithic, modern, conquering heroic self and the postmodern, embittered-victim, shape-shifting vain self are sub-relational individualists who are preoccupied with the will-to-power.

'The Holy Spirit', though, can free us from 'manipulation' such that the 'will-to-power' can become the 'will-to-love' in a way that remains critical enough to expose the relational distortions of power abuse. 'The Holy Spirit' can thus move us away from individualistic autonomy and into relationship, such that the self finds itself in a kind of living narrative of faithfully laying itself down for the other, in 'giving' and 'receiving' love in relationship with 'the Other'.[75]

Post-structuralism, though, evasively insists on ignoring more biblical, relational 'narrative' conceptions of selfhood. As C.E. Gunton puts it, 'Alongside the main stream there is an alternative tradition of philosophizing about the person, and it is to be found in the works of those whose names are entirely absent from the bibliography and index of Derek Parfit's mammoth exercise in deconstruction [i.e. *Reasons and Persons*].'[76]

Thus, the postmodern recovery of a more realistic notion of selves as being at the mercy of psychological, sociological (and other) forces that are often beyond their control is good; but the post-structuralist decision to perpetually sidestep being known is a counterfeit, individualistic conception of freedom that serves vanity and the will-to-power, and that traps and isolates people away from the empathic right relating made possible by truthful communication within common, ethically formed discourse-worlds over time.

Being thus disaffected, postmodern selves become embittered and despair of ever having close or fulfilling relationships. As A.J. Torrance notes, even the self-help culture that then develops tends to objectify relationships as a problem to solve, and therein still presupposes a 'unipolar' conception of selfhood according to which the self is supposedly able to actualize itself through 'managing' relationships aright.[77]

With Torrance, though, it is right relating itself, first with God then with neighbour, rather than the objectification of relationships, that brings healing. A self can only be fully actualized through the non-manipulated loving actions of others, actions that – by definition – the self cannot control. Torrance thus cites W.H. Auden's brilliant line, 'Love's possibilities of realization require an otherness that can say *I*.'[78]

Naturally, of course, immersion in fallen relationships demands that critical, objectifying, biblical wisdom should accompany that immersion. One cannot simply intuit right relating from behavioural training alone since one could be immersed in an insular

local cultural world that had initially-invisible damaging and/
or oppressive effects on those within it, and/or on those not
included within it. Relating in a fallen world always requires a
biblical 'referee' to be on hand. Otherwise one could seemingly
'relate brilliantly' but still end up either suffering – or causing –
subtle (or not so subtle) oppression.

Thus, in Chapter 6 above, we provided a list that paraphrased
(alongside some of our own points) R. Howard's analysis of the
strategies of power abuse that were operative in the cult known
as 'the Nine O'Clock Service' (NOS) in the 1980s to 1990s in Sheffield, UK. From our list (pp. 135-6), it might seem that such strategies would be obvious to those oppressed by them. But that is
not how oppression always works. Oppression is often invisible
to those under it. Only when oppressed people see the 'world'
that is oppressing them from the perspective of a different world
(i.e. a world that is very often new to them) do they – sometimes suddenly – experience the spell of such oppression being
broken. And even then, oppressed people's liberation is often not
a pleasant sense of release. Since oppression has its own language-
worlds that (to an extent) can form and constitute the very identities of those persons who are oppressed, then a sudden liberation
can cause a catastrophic collapse of those persons' identities. Thus
Howard, citing A. Teale, reports regarding the 'collapse' of the
'cult' of 'the Nine O'Clock Service': 'two worlds or realities' 'met'
'head-on, and as NOS reality met normality it simply collapsed';
'NOS members' trauma was such that some people were hitting
themselves against walls and mutilating themselves.'[79]

Some postmodern strands, then, bring a biblically positive rise
of truer self-awareness. But the other, darker, side of postmodernity deconstructs the biblically and/or ethically refereed common
discourse-worlds that are preconditional for the possibility of the
formation and actualization of selves in right relating over time.
Faced with only different local or tribal contexts for relationship
– contexts that, being biblically and/or ethically *un*-refereed, are
often distorted by cliquey or cult-like relational dynamics – postmodern selves are often only given the choice between isolation
and a crippling succession of very traumatic rude awakenings
from which there is no ultimate escape (other than by divine inter-
vention). Such deconstructed selves then understandably flee from

such traumas, remain isolated and so unwittingly contribute to causing the biblically truer rise of self-awareness – which depends on *good* relationships – to falter.

Rise of True Interpretation versus Deceit over 'Impossible Objectivity'

Eighth, the modern–postmodern shift brings a potentially very positive new emphasis on interpretation – an emphasis that, additionally, brings together some of the points from our previous seven sub-sections.

Thus, in modernity, there was often no room for differences of interpretation. Complete authority was often attributed to the evaluations of those who had institutional status – for example, governments, courts, doctors, scientists, councillors, teachers, philosophers, military officers, clergy, and so on. Even today, institutional position is often mistaken for proof of objectivity.[80]

Admittedly, official viewpoints were often challenged even back in the days of high modernity. Nevertheless, broadly speaking, modernity's objectivism still said that, whatever was being studied, the right method of empirical observation and rational deduction would produce 'objective truth'.[81] And, of course, advances in the 'natural' sciences seemed to support this perspective: knowledge and language seemed to have an unchallengeable formal connection to 'the real' – methodological mistakes aside. Modernity's technological utopias thus seemed to be an imminent evolutionary certainty.

Over time, however, modern objectivism itself was challenged. It was seen that, at best, scientific paradigms only progressed *towards* objectivity. Of course, many realized that there must be *some* possible objectivity. Without objective aerodynamics knowledge, for example, we couldn't regularly jet people safely across the Atlantic! But the reality of paradigm-shifts – for example, the often-cited Newtonian-Einsteinian paradigm-shift – showed that, at best, we only achieve increasingly accurate *interpretations* of the real that, to an extent at least, we *project onto* the real.

In addition, the scientific model of knowledge and understanding – or Cartesian subject–object thinking – proved to be inadequate for the human sciences. There was a problem when it came to understanding human selves. Understanding 'me' as 'object' is impossible for me, because the place from which I 'understand myself' is also me! So, I try in vain to be both object and subject, since the 'objectified me' is only my mind's projected interpretation of me, and is never actually 'me'. Even Hume and Kant failed to solve this problem adequately.[82]

The psychoanalytical tradition, as noted earlier, also discovered that the unconscious delivers a self-deceptive and sanitized perception of 'the self' to the conscious mind.[83] So, now, even conscious reflection is no longer seen as a sure means by which we arrive at truth, but as a potentially problematic activity that can block true self-understanding. And even the unconscious is hardly a key to objective truth since it is shaped by the unconsciously received perspectives of traditions. Even though traditions certainly can transmit received truth and wisdom, they can also transmit distortions of received truth and wisdom.[84]

Earlier, moreover, we noted how the rise of historical consciousness confirmed that some truths are constantly changing. Even if one momentarily attains objectivity, then historical movement can quickly make such objectivity out of date. Under the spell of the ancient Greek legacy, modernity often saw truth as static, formal, cyclic, mechanistic, deterministic or predictable. But once truth was seen to be historical, and also partly human, then interpretation had to account for difference, movement and unpredictable change.

We also noted earlier that language can obscure truth as well as communicate truth. Language emerges in traditions, and traditions can transmit error. Thus, traditions can transmit deceptive ideologies that are motivated by power interests. That is, language can convey faulty perceptions, certainly; but the very categories and concepts at the heart of language can simply be ideologically motivated metaphors that 'pretend' to be formally true. And when we read ancient texts, then there are two possibly distorted ideologies – our own and the author's – and the historical distance between them to account for.[85]

We also noted earlier that digital culture accelerates the deployment of, and bombards us with, linguistic fragments. Superficially speaking, the age of monolithic world-views at first appears to be over. To an extent, there are now many world-views, competing sub-cultures, interest groups and 'tribes' of various other kinds in our culture. In our digital age, moreover, slow-paced change is over, and accelerated change has arrived. Keeping up with the changes is making politicians younger and younger, because only the comparatively youthful can do it! And, finally, since many no longer believe in accessible truth then language is often used carelessly, manipulatively and/or irresponsibly.

Summarizing, then when we attempt to interpret truly we have to account for: paradigm-shifts, in-part-projected interpretative models, the problem of self-understanding, the self-deceiving unconscious, distorted traditions, difference, movement, unpredictable change, truth-obscuring language, power-serving ideologies, historical distance, the fragmentation of monolithic world-views into multiple ideologies, acceleration of change, and careless, irresponsible and/ or manipulative language. No wonder that hermeneutics – i.e. the philosophy of interpretation or of understanding – is on the ascendancy.

Interestingly, the Bible allows for all these and for other problems that pertain to true interpretation. If modernity sets us up as the knowers, then the Bible says that we are the known. If postmodernity has us as the interpreters, then the Bible says that we are the interpreted. Even Christianity, then, is doing hermeneutics! In fact, it was originally Christians who were trying to interpret the Bible who were instrumental in starting the whole 'interpretation' emphasis off. So, we can't even retreat behind the walls of the church in order to hide from hermeneutics!

In my view, moreover, it is God himself who is calling us to interpret ourselves – or rather to be interpreted – again. (Here comes the paradigm-shift). You see, the above 'barriers to objectivity' are not barriers at all. To call them 'barriers' is partly panic, and partly deceit, since these so-called barriers to objectivity are actually, in my view, factors that have emerged from God's accelerated disclosure to us of what we need to know in order to interpret ourselves truly, or rather to be interpreted truly. Once we recover from the panic and the deceit, we will cease to be overwhelmed and deceived, and will realize that we have just been shown, by God, how to see.

That is, we were under modernity's spell, thinking that modernity led to utopias, when really it led to disasters. We thought our 'Method' of looking at ourselves led to objectivity, but it was blindness. Modernity was blinding narcissism that claimed to be able to see. Modernity was so blind, that it took two world wars, several genocides, the Holocaust and the nuclear threat to wake us up to the fact that modernity was deadly – and still is.

Indeed, in the twentieth century this situation became an emergency. Modernity nearly destroyed us, and still might. We were on the very brink but then, in my view, the Lord intervened. In his mercy, he has now given us all the philosophical tools that we need in order to build a new pair of spectacles through which to look at the Scriptures – and thus at ourselves – again. It is time to look at the Scriptures again, this time without the old, positivist, historical-critical glasses or any other such philosophically over-simplified spectacles or lenses. We need to become the interpreted before it is too late. There is just about still time for us to snap out of the spell of modern hubris, interpret ourselves aright with the Scriptures and with the true prophets of today, and prevent our own self-destruction.

The interpretative 'barriers' listed above are not barriers at all. They are *clues*. God, in my view, is saying, 'Wake up and examine yourselves, before it is too late. Here's what you've missed in the *way* you're looking at things.'

Traditionalist church, though, by shunning philosophy and hermeneutics, has blinded itself to its own ancient Greek, modern and (these days) bad-postmodern distorted perspectives or frame-works. It has then read the Scriptures through these distorted perspectives or frameworks as though through the wrong prescription spectacles. Thus, it has faithfully interpreted the Scriptures in some ways, but has also made terrible and terrifying errors as we have argued in our earlier chapters above.

Our use of the phrase 'bad-postmodern', here, alerts us to what we have been presenting all along as the dark side of post-modernity. For every move of God, there is a counter-attack by the enemy. Good postmodernism wants us to wake up from our modernist slumber and reinterpret ourselves objectively before it is too late. This is surely from God himself. Bad postmodernism, however, will bend over backwards to say that this can't be done, to show that this can't be done, and to actually prevent it from being done. Bad postmodernism throws everything possible in the way of humanity's coming to saving self-awareness, and is therefore evil.

Like the evil one, though, bad postmodernism markets itself with a propaganda that says, 'Hey, we're the good guys – we liberate people from oppressive, objectivist, fixed interpretations and phrase regimes!' But it is from the pit. So let's expose it still more clearly. To this task we now turn.

Today's Postmodern Spiritual Battlefield

And so, let's paint a still-clearer picture of today's postmodern spiritual battlefield. Let us summarize our findings above as a series of contrasts between good, more biblical postmodernity and bad postmodernity – (even though we realize that these trends are in fact mixed together historically) – as follows.

Thus, first, good postmodernity potentially promotes the rise of the knowledge of God by interrogating naturalistic, humanistic utopianism which, despite its technology and its positive achievements, is therein shown to have also produced wars, genocides, and humanitarian, ecological and economic disasters.

Bad postmodernity, though, promotes 'death of God' ideologies that: block the rise of the knowledge of God; revive naturalistic, humanistic utopianism; and use self-deceiving rhetoric about democratic globalization, digital revolution, environmental sustainability, economic development and humanitarian advances to disguise – unwittingly – their unconscious adherence to the demonic agenda of 'becoming like God, without God'. That is, creation without God is 'nature' (cf. naturalism); the Western vision of humanity without God encourages secular humanism; and 'becoming like God, without God' replaces eschatological pilgrimage with utopian space odyssey. Naturalistic, humanistic utopianism, or modernity, is thus – largely (if not entirely) – obedience to the original demonic temptation.[86]

Second, good postmodernity promotes love, healthy relating, dialogue and/or conversation, and keeps these healthy and non-abusive through the 'refereeing' application of accessible, textually transmitted received traditions of (especially biblical) wisdom and historical report from the past.

Bad postmodernity, though, stresses the inaccessibility of textually transmitted, received traditions of wisdom and historical report from the past, and so facilitates non-refereed relating or 'play', which becomes abusive and thus descends into factions, conflicts and war.

Third, good postmodernity promotes the rise of historical consciousness, stressing: change and stability; diversity and unity; conditioning that both hinders and aids objectivity; and both future uncertainty and the certainty of God's fulfilment of promises. Thus, good postmodernity facilitates people's growth into an awareness of history – for example, the Holocaust.

Bad postmodernity, though, hinders the rise of historical consciousness, stressing: only change (radicalized as flux); only diversity (radicalized as dissociation); only conditioning that hinders objectivity (radicalized as absolute historical relativism); and only future uncertainty (radicalized as indeterminacy). Thus, bad postmodernity actively hinders people's growth into an awareness of history – as, for example, in rhetoricist Holocaust-negationism.

Fourth, good postmodernity allows historical knowledge to increase our awareness *of* the terrible destructive characteristics and consequences of modernity's evils, and of evil oppressions generally, so that we may use this *concientización*, this coming-to-awareness, to liberate ourselves *from* terribly destructive modern and other evil oppressions. Thus, good postmodernity seeks to learn lessons from the horrors of modernity's history, notably the Holocaust, whilst remaining aware that only those experiencing such horrors could understand them most fully.

Bad postmodernity, however, denies the possibility of growing in historical knowledge through reading texts, and thus promotes a historical relativism that prohibits *concientización* – i.e. that prohibits a growing critical awareness of modernist and other strategies and regimes of oppression. Bad postmodernity inverts reality, arguing that historical truth claims *cause* authoritarian oppression, and citing modernity's objectivism and oppressions as proof. However, historical truth claims that remain open to challenge by truth are neither 'modern' nor objectivist. It is resistance to challenge that *by definition* characterizes authoritarianism. Thus, bad postmodernity facilitates oppressive and extremist regimes by immunizing them from challenge by historical truth and by projecting their sin of authoritarianism onto their challengers. The 'persecutors' thus pretend to be 'victims' and 'rescuers'.

Fifth, good postmodernity attacks modernist approaches to language and meaning that oppress people beneath often-false fixed and formal language-use that immunizes itself – by its formality and fixedness – from challenge by truth.

Good postmodernity in effect promotes a biblical view of language and meaning according to which language and meaning are: enfleshed or grounded in stable-yet-flexible patterns of historical action by persons – patterns that, in having such a character, can embody and transmit – via texts – stable-yet-flexible historical frameworks of criteria of true ethical-relational wisdom and historical report that can, in turn, function today so as to enable us to interpret and evaluate similar-yet-variable historical oppressive regimes, and that can, thereby and/or additionally, enable ethical formation, *concientización* and liberation.

Bad postmodernity also attacks oppressive modernist often-false fixed and formal language and meaning that are immunized from challenge by such formality and fixedness, but then replaces such language and meaning with equally oppressive often-false arbitrary language and meaning that are fluxing and immunized from challenge by that very fluxing. Bad postmodernity thus replaces one kind of linguistic oppression with another: fluxing-arbitrary linguistic worlds are just as false and oppressive as modernity's fixed linguistic formalism.

That is, bad postmodernity's post-structuralism and neo-pragmatic rhetoricism sinfully promote an approach to language and meaning in which a docetic, digitally accelerated, arbitrarily expanding, dissociating unstable flux – falsely marketed as 'freedom' – actually: seeks to contain, constantly alter and overwrite 'stable-yet-flexible patterns of historical action by persons', so as to preclude the possibility of the formation of, and thus the possibility of access to, the 'transmitted stable-yet-flexible frameworks of criteria of true ethical-relational wisdom and historical report' that would otherwise structure and inform conscience, and thereby prevents liberation-through-*concientización*, so as to leave people under the power of oppressive regimes that are therein immunized from challenge through the suppression of awareness of sin itself.

Sixth, good postmodernity contributes towards realizing the realistic vision of a civilized society that rightly and progressively seeks to release the oppressed from poverty, inequality, injustices, sickness, human-rights abuses, poor housing, poor education, and so on; and rightly and sustainably stewards God's created environment to these ends. Good postmodernity, to these human-itarian and environmental ends, actively seeks:

(a) technological and humanitarian advances through the pursuit of developments in the 'natural' and social sciences;

(b) a democratic government that – within a framework of law shaped by textually transmitted ethical criteria grounded in corporate memories and historical report of lessons learned in the past – accommodates a tolerant empirical pluralism that sets people free to find the real God, the accessible truth, genuine wisdom and thus healing for themselves; and

(c) an expanding market economy of manufacturing that provides for necessities for all.

Bad postmodernity, though, still promotes a sinful, self-centred, consumption-based, redirection of technological advances and of an unrealistically overstretched, borrowing-dependent, bank-ruptcy-threatening, expanding market economy of manufac-turing: on the one hand, in the service of a continued, modernist, escapist utopianism marketed as the middle-class dream in which competitive, self-centred, status-generating symbol deployment manifests in consumerist greed; and, on the other hand, in the service of an even worse, manufacturing-neglecting, escapist, hedonistic, disinhibited, virtual, digitopian consumerism that fosters increasingly bizarre, elaborate, impatient, impulsively reflexive and relationally disengaged, self-justifying, brutal, individualistic or tribe-centred, potentially extremist, false-persona-based, arbitrary, chaotic, culture-fragmenting designer realities and/or designer selves.

Bad postmodernity, in order to hold such a society together, promotes a covert, chaos-necessitated and '-justified', creeping authoritarianism that deploys an intolerant, philosophical pluralism that masquerades as 'tolerant empirical pluralism' and that oppresses people by hiding the real God, the accessible truth, genuine wisdom and the way to healing deep within an 'infinite' multi-narrative of uncheckable possibilities.

Seventh, good postmodernity recovers a less anthropocentric and more realistic view of the human self according to which human selves are de-centred and relationally actualized over time, and according to which human selves are not bound to inevitable scientific progress, not ethically autonomous, not individualistic conquering heroes, not the forthcoming masters of the universe, and not in control of their own destinies, but who are vulnerable to psychological, sociological and spiritual forces greater than themselves, and who are in need of the real God, the accessible truth, genuine wisdom and (therein) healing.

Bad postmodernity, though, promotes a tradition-shunning, deconstructed self – a mere fluxing, linguistic product of changing social forces and changing cultural signs 'who' is supposedly no longer responsible for those changing social forces and changing cultural signs, and 'who' is supposedly 'liberated' from former modern linguistic oppression by passive submission *to* those changing social forces and changing cultural signs.

Bad postmodernity, however, is largely *responsible* for these changing social forces and changing cultural signs, and its deconstructed self is not free but is oppressed by the same changing social forces and changing cultural signs through the disintegration of the common discourse-worlds through which individuals are brought out of isolation, ethically formed, socialized, and thus relationally liberated. The result is: creeping isolation and relational breakdown; shape-shifting catch-me-if-you-can irony that sidesteps being known; deeply unhappy, alienated, disaffected embitteredness; lack of empathic, relational joy coupled with cynicism over the possibility of ever having any such joy; and an unaddressed will-to-power of narcissistic addiction to clever-clever, attention-seeking, celebrity-seeking vanity that makes popular art initially entertaining but ultimately dull. Bad postmodernism, then, merely transposes modern sub-relational individualism and the will-to-power into a different key.

Eighth, good postmodernity calls us to reinterpret ourselves and our culture before God so as to explode the previously unchallengeable, dangerous illusions of modernity's naturalistic, humanistic, utopian, objectivist self-deception – illusions that hid modernity's immense destructiveness from us. Good postmodernity does this so that we can wake up before it is too late.

Good postmodernity, in order to break modernity's deadly blinding spell, exposes factors that modernity's false way of interpreting the world didn't take into account – namely: paradigm-shifts; projected interpretative models; the problem of self-understanding; the self-deceiving unconscious; the problem of distorted traditions; the problem of difference, movement and unpredictable change; the potential of language to obscure truth; the problem of power-interested ideologies; the problem of historical distance; the issue of the fragmentation of monolithic world-views into multiple ideologies; the acceleration of change; careless, irresponsible and/or manipulative language; and the need to become the interpreted rather than the interpreters.

Good postmodernity says that our proper understanding of these factors is a crucial part of our arriving at a true perception of ourselves before God. God shows us the way to salvation by exposing to us that which impedes our understanding of ourselves.

Bad postmodernity, though, markets these same factors, these ways forwards towards a true understanding of ourselves before God, as 'absolute barriers to a true understanding of ourselves before God'.

Bad postmodernity bends over backwards through the strategies outlined above in order to prevent us from coming to saving self-awareness, as a human race, before God, until it is too late. Its proponents do not consciously seek this, but the demonic forces behind it do.

Good postmodernity says, 'You're blind, things are not OK, here's the way to see truly'; bad postmodernity says, 'We can see, things will be OK, and we can see that there is no way to see truly.'

Modernity and Bad Postmodernity: Disasters and False 'Solutions'

Modernity, then, combined naturalistic, humanistic utopianism with an older, Platonic legacy that fostered oppressive, hierarchical systems. Thus, modernity attempted to 'become like God, without

God', following the satanic temptation recorded in Genesis 3:1–5. Eschatological pilgrimage became utopian space-odyssey, stewardship of the earth became conquering the heavens, and the sustainable technological utilization of created resources became the unsustainable technological mastery of 'nature'. The earth and most of the people on it did not benefit from these distorted aims, however, but were subjugated by them. Naturalism and humanism are not bad in *every* respect; but J. Moltmann bemoans modernity's 'fortresses of wealth planted in a sea of mass misery'.[87]

That is, twentieth-century advances in the 'natural' sciences and in technology accelerated so fast that Nietzsche's exalted overlord – his 'godlike' Übermench – seemed to be on the ascendancy. After Satan we said, 'I will ascend to heaven; I will raise my throne above the stars of God; I will sit enthroned on the mount of assembly, on the utmost heights of the sacred mountain. I will ascend above the tops of the clouds; I will make myself like the Most High.'[88] Indeed, the powerful, isolated centred-self of Nietzschean mythology is described by Karl Barth in similar terms, for Barth sees Nietzsche as 'the prophet of . . . humanity without the fellow-man',[89] of the

> man of 'azure isolation', six thousand feet above time and man; the man to whom a fellow-creature drinking at the same well is quite dreadful and insufferable; the man who is utterly inaccessible to others, having no friends and despising women; the man who is at home only with eagles and strong winds . . . the man beyond good and evil, who can only exist as a consuming fire.[90]

That is, the twentieth-century advances in the 'natural' sciences and in technology also *armed* Nietzsche's Übermench and *resourced* humanism's attempt to build its utopian citadel in the sky. The result was world wars, genocides and weapons of mass destruction combined with an insanely accelerated exploitation of people and resources, depletion, pollution, hoarding, Third-World poverty, misery, famines, starvation and diseases. Even *within* the 'fortresses of wealth', systems of 'industrialized' manufacturing streamlined to maximum efficiency oppressed, instrumentalized, 'dehumanized' and 'alienated' millions.[91] Even this rate of productivity, however, could not produce wealth fast enough for utopian consumerism, which led to borrowing, debt and economic crises.

Like Satan, we did not 'ascend to heaven', but were 'brought down to the grave, to the depths of the pit . . . "Is this the man who shook the earth and made kingdoms tremble, the man who made the world a desert, who overthrew its cities and would not let his captives go home?" '[92] Isaiah could be speaking about modernity here – for it is *our* bombs that 'shook the earth and made kingdoms tremble', it is *we* 'who made the world a desert', and it is *we* who 'overthrew' and enslaved millions so that the 'captives' could not 'go home'.

Bad postmodernity, though, despite this catalogue of modern catastrophes, still exonerates naturalistic, humanistic utopianism, and so blames only the Platonic legacy of 'ideologically driven oppressive hierarchical systems of power' for all modernity's disasters. In reality, however, *both* these strands produced our environmental, humanitarian and economic disasters – as well as the political disaster of oppressive authoritarian systems themselves, and the philosophical-ideological disaster of ideologies claiming to have formal fixed truth. Bad postmodernity, though, blames the whole mess of modernity on fixed ideologies in order to keep its deadly and delusional, naturalistic, humanistic, utopian dream alive – its deadly and delusional mass psychosis of 'playing God'.

Bad postmodernism says, 'Fixed ideologies *alone* led to authoritarian power systems that exploited people and resources, that oppressed and killed millions, and that did so at a rate that even such power systems could not afford: ideological disaster spawned political disaster, leading to humanitarian, environmental and economic disasters.' Bad postmodernity is thus a pseudo-critique that ignores much of the real cause of modernity's mess – namely, the disastrous affects of naturalistic humanistic utopianism.

Nevertheless, bad postmodernity threatens to hold sway, and now suggests – and claims that it implements – the following five-fold 'solution' to the modern crisis:

(a) to avoid environmental disaster, practise eco-friendly sustainability;
(b) to avoid philosophical disaster, banish fixed ideologies with their fixed truth and fixed language, instigate 'shifting truth and fluxing language', and yet preserve naturalistic, humanistic, utopian optimism;

(c) to avoid political disaster, banish authoritarian power, and bring in worldwide freedom through spreading constantly changing democratic governments globally;

(d) to avoid humanitarian disaster, spread fairness by spreading capitalist expanding economies and development globally;

(e) to avoid economic disaster, harness the digital revolution in order to create the needed expanding economies.

Bad postmodernity then labels any who challenge these 'five pillars' as being ideologically authoritarian imperialists, formalists, foundationalists, fundamentalists or extremists.

Bad Postmodernity Deployed: Twenty-Five Resulting Problems

The fact that bad postmodernity threatens to hold sway, however, means that bad postmodernity has already begun to afflict Western societies with the following twenty-five superimposed problems.

Fivefold cognitive, relational and ethical disintegration

Thus, first, aspects of the second of bad postmodernity's five pillars – aspects to do with 'shifting truth and fluxing language' – lead to a fivefold cognitive, relational and ethical disintegration, as follows.

(a) *Human minds*, since they are linguistically structured, disintegrate if 'built' from 'fluxing language' rather than from stable language.

(b) *Human relationships*, since they presuppose stable common discourse-worlds, disintegrate if 'built' using 'fluxing language' rather than stable language.

(c) *Ethical criteria* for 'refereeing' human relating depend on textually transmitted corporate memories that embody historical report, ethical wisdom from lessons learned in the past and theological grounds for ethics. 'Fluxing language', though, disintegrates textual transmission, and so disintegrates that upon which ethical criteria depend. 'Fluxing language', therefore, disintegrates ethical criteria themselves.

(d) *Ethical conscience* (individual and corporate) depends upon textually transmitted ethical criteria. Thus, 'fluxing language', in subverting and disintegrating textually transmitted ethical criteria, subverts and disintegrates ethical conscience and any possibility of *concientización*. This situation leads to a culture of corrupted consciences and to being trapped within that culture of corrupted consciences.

(e) The Holy Spirit deploys the biblical texts as speech-acts in order to build the Christian and the church as 'right relaters'. Thus, 'fluxing language', in subverting and disintegrating textually transmitted ethical criteria, subverts not only ethical formation, but threatens to subvert *biblical* ethical formation, such that *Christianity itself comes under attack*.

Fivefold cultural 'fragmentation–authoritarianism' dipole

Second, this fivefold cognitive, relational and ethical disintegration then leads to an oppressive fivefold cultural fragmentation-authoritarianism dipole, as follows.

(a) *Fragmented or deconstructed selves* degeneratively develop an '*incurvatus in se* self-relation'[93] (a key concept in this context of discussion) that results from their experience of cognitive dissonance and ethical malformation. Psychological disintegration and/or cognitive dissonance cause confusion, anxiety, and can lead to obsessive-compulsive disorders. Ethical malformation can cause selves to develop anything from a hyper-sensitive conscience to a disposition of shameless, self-righteous self-justification. Responding to these problems, selves may then withdraw socially and end up experiencing and suffering isolation, de-relationalization, disaffection, alienation and despair. Patterns of escapist self-anaesthesia – potentially substance abuse and self-harm – can then often develop. Additionally, and through desperate 'authoritarian', assertive or maladaptive attempts to reimpose order, counterfeit 'constellations' of self-imposed and/ or of culturally construed self-integration then arise that involve the manufacture of 'pseudo-objectified' persona-selves. These persona-selves can then indulge in anything from celebrity-seeking, to individualistic hedonism, to flirt-not-commit syndrome, to manipulative strategies, to inter-net-'disinhibited' 'pseudo-self'-gratification, to life-evading virtualism, to the dull vain irony of post-structural atten-tion-seeking that perpetually sidesteps being-known, and so on.[94]

(b) Disintegrated common discourse-worlds – and the resulting disintegration of ethical-relational criteria – cause *relation-ship-fragmenting anti-socialization* that results in feuding, domestic abuse, broken marriages, antisocial behaviour, and so-called chav culture.[95] Problem-cliques – such as 'problem families', gangs and partners-in-crime – which manifest the counterfeit intimacy of a shared suspicion of outsiders, then impose authoritarian order upon this relational chaos – an authoritarian order configured as ego-extensions of dominant leader-type personas.[96]

(c) Reacting to such *social fragmentation*, cults, corporations, and fundamentalist or extremist groups impose – via hostile take-overs, cultic conversions, extremist recruitment, pres-sure-group tactics, expansionism, self-advertising rhetoric, threat or self-interested exploitation of others – self-impe-rializing authoritarian corporate tribalisms, which exhibit 'in-house' controlled speech or discourse (cf. 'corporate speak'), corporate narcissism, indoctrination, vision radical-ization, 'distinctive tribal smells' and spell-binding, herme-neutically sealed sub-cultural worlds (corporations can be as destructive as terrorist groups).[97]

(d) The resulting *conflicting cultural groups* – born also out of of cultural separatism, ethnic non-integration, an alienated underclass, and competing value-systems – bring us riots, interracial hatred, honour killings, forced marriages, reli-gious hatred and extremist nationalist groups. Order is then imposed by Olympics-2012-style, boastful, self-congratula-tory, nationally propagated, authoritarian, neo-pragmatic 'philosophical pluralism', which – through intolerance disguised by an 'allowed rhetoric' of multicultural tolerance – relativizes all views as 'equally valid, but equally untrue'.

This situation then leads: to 'homogeneities' of sanctioned or politically correct media-controlled, consumer-normalized, pseudo-market-driven, cultural difference-suppressing tastes, pastimes, arts or pursuits; and to eroded civil liberties (notably the erosion of freedom of speech), not least through increased surveillance.[98]

(e) On a still-larger scale, *national separatism* manifests itself in authoritarian dictatorships, self-interested nationalism that is suspicious of other nations, devolving unions, 'independence at any price' attitudes, wars and cold wars. Order is then imposed by pseudo-democratic, authoritarian, globalizing, international bodies that overrule national sovereignty, regime-change at will, blacklist 'axis of evil' nations, and market wars and invasions over resources as 'the spread of democratic freedoms'.

Due to the aforementioned disintegration of ethical criteria, ethical formation and ethical conscience, this fivefold, cultural fragmentation-authoritarianism dipole then remains inadequately challenged.

Five problematic 'allowed rhetorics' that control speech

Third, bad postmodernism, in hiding from this situation, deploys a fivefold rhetorical control over freedom of speech – a control which is then exerted through the media and through the arts. Thus, fixed speech habits are encouraged in relation to:

(a) environmental sustainability;
(b) 'shifting truth, and fluxing language' and naturalistic, humanistic utopianism;
(c) global and national, multicultural, liberal, democratic freedom and its humanitarian outworking in health care, education, civil and human rights, the justice system and so on;
(d) global, capitalist, economic expansionism and humanitarian fairness through worldwide development;
(e) utopian progress and economic expansion through technological – especially digital, space programme-related and hard science-related – advances.

Certain cultural 'prophets' on television (e.g. Richard Dawkins) can even speak in an authoritarian mode and yet remain comparatively unchallenged – so long as they stay within the bounds of these five 'allowed rhetorics'. The West is so programmed or shaped by these allowed rhetorics and by their prophets, that there is no need to police the propagation of either: other views are shouted down precritically by the general population, and are stigmatized as 'authoritarian ideology'. Thus, bad postmodernity disowns its own sin, and projects it onto its challengers.

Moreover, many of the older counter-cultural protest voices of the popular arts have now become culture-affirming icons. Even punk-rock stars are now part of the establishment. More subtly, certain *sanctioned* 'protest voices' are still marketed as *genuine* protest voices in the arts – as if to prove that our society allows freedom of speech and expression. Sanctioned 'protest voices' in the popular arts are both lauded as brilliant, when often they are not, and are promoted unceasingly through the media – often at the expense of more talented acts. Even musical intellectuals are sometimes spell-bound into applauding the emperor's new clothes in this respect. Musical intellectuals have always – authentically – liked some pretty weird avant-garde classical and jazz music. But now, some musical intellectuals are so conditioned by socially engineered tastes that they hail rock bands who can't write music as 'brilliant'.

Now, of course, we applaud the four 'goods' of environmental sustainability, democratic freedom, economic fairness and technological progress. But those who also peddle 'shifting truth, fluxing language' and 'naturalistic humanistic utopianism' cannot properly deliver these four 'goods', and so their heralding of these four 'goods' becomes empty propaganda.

Five problems resulting from modernity remain unaddressed

That is, and fourth, peddling 'shifting truth, fluxing language' and 'naturalistic humanistic utopianism' leaves the fivefold philosophical, political, environmental, humanitarian and economic disasters of modernity unaddressed, as follows.

(a) Escapist, naturalistic, humanistic utopianism – marketed as the middle-class dream – continues to produce rampant consumerism. But now, the 'shifting truth, fluxing language' obfuscation facilitates denial of the past and present consequences of this consumerism.

(b) Bad postmodern authoritarianisms threaten to persist in causing oppressions. But now, 'shifting truth, fluxing language', neo-pragmatic philosophical pluralism (see above), and the allowed rhetorics of propaganda perpetuate the denial of this sin by projecting it onto challengers and calling it 'the challengers' sin'.

(c) Ongoing rampant consumerism perpetuates and deepens environmental problems. But now, propaganda about environmental sustainability and local-sourcing functions as asserted self-absolution in the face of increased indulgence in luxury.

(d) Ongoing rampant consumerism continues to exploit resources and people and continues to cause conflicts over resources. But now, propaganda about globalizing democracy and about helping the developing world makes us look caring (to ourselves at least, if not to outsiders).

(e) Ongoing rampant consumerism continues to create a culture of borrowing and debt that exceeds sensible, enterprise-necessitated borrowing (and debt) tied into productivity. And yet, even in the present economic climate, naturalistic humanistic utopian optimism – the very cause of the problems – still creates false hope in a better future, and is all that underwrites the borrowing and the debt.

Five problems associated with digital culture

Fifth, this entire disastrous degeneration is only *accelerated* by naturalistic, humanistic utopianism's shift into a digitopian key, which brings a further fivefold problem, as follows.

(a) *Digitalization* itself moves us away from 'industry', 'manufacturing', and earth-stewardship to mouse-clicking, virtual products and exploitation of 'information'.[99] Productivity and long-term wealth creation are lowered, whilst consumerism continues apace, leading to debt, and to a skills deficit. Meanwhile, Orwellian-style online surveillance by governments is born around about, or probably before, 2012.

(b) Digital *distraction* undermines holistic rounded education and world awareness born of experience in the concrete world, and increases narrowed, virtualized education regarding the cyber-world.[100] However, the digital multi-narrative artificially seems to confirm the post-structuralist, neo-pragmatic viewpoint of 'shifting truth, fluxing language': the sheer sea of signs hides the real God, real truth, real ethical wisdom and the way to healing amidst 'infinite' options. But as broader, stabilizing discourse worlds based on corporate memories from the past are disintegrated, so are persons, relationships, ethical criteria, ethical conscience, ethical (and biblical) formation and dissenting viewpoints. Meanwhile, politically correct, present-horizon fixed allowed rhetorics and authoritarian corporate-speak (see above) are everywhere presupposed and disseminated.

(c) Digital *distancing* trains people out of real, community-immersed, patient, empathic right relating and perspectives and into virtual-community, cliquey antipathy and a 'brutal insincerity' of objectifying perspectives that 'can treat the bombing of the Gulf War . . . as yet another "special effect"'.[101]

(d) Digital *'disengagement'* brings 'apathetic' resignation when people are faced with real 'political', 'social' and cultural problems.[102] This relates to the skills deficit or deskilling that we noted above.

(e) *Disorder* results, as the fostering of intensely self-serving self-centredness and expectations of instantaneousness trains people into impulsive, impatient, reflexive 'road-rage' reactivity towards everybody and everything; and as 'disinhibited' persona-'constellations', problem cliques and extremists commit online and offline crimes.[103] Such disorder then allows authoritarian measures, such as surveillance, to be voted in democratically.

That is, bad postmodern authoritarianism seeks to ensure and to justify its own perpetuation and advance through a threefold 'disorientation, dependency and divide-and-conquer' strategy: dissent-disintegration and allowed-rhetoric-dissemination serve to disorientate; debt and diskilling serve to add dependency to disorientation; and disorder creates the societal division that – in effect – allows the divide-and-conquer principle to be voted in democratically, in that authoritarian order is made to look better than the supposed 'only alternative' of (demonically engineered if not so much humanly engineered) disorder. Modern authoritarianism thus re-emerges in a different, more insidious, form.

Moreover, digitopianism is naturalistic, humanistic utopianism's last stand. The real-world utopia has failed; when the virtual digitopia fails, we'll be ejected back out into the 'even-more-broken real'.

Again, though, we are not describing the whole of our situation here by any means, but are just describing what is bad about the kind of postmodernity that, in our view, threatens to hold sway. Furthermore, we are not at all anti-government, as we made clear in Chapter 3 above. Rather, it is precisely the government, amongst others, that needs to become aware of these dangers – dangers to which the church, unfortunately, has often already succumbed.

Biblical-Relational Evangelism and Promoting Good Postmodernity

But what constitutes mission in / to such a culture? Well, certainly, the church will not attain to right mission whilst it remains conformed to its current non-biblical modern or 'bad postmodern' shape. To do mission aright, we need to recover the positive shape of biblical Christianity.

Do not be deceived: the Western church today often does not have a biblical shape. Since love sums up the law and the prophets, then biblical Christianity's positive shape is inextricably linked to biblically-defined love for God and neighbour, or to biblical lawfulness. The latter, in turn, closely reflects what true mission, and true evangelism, should look like.

What true mission to Western postmodern society does not look like

Thus, true mission, or love as biblical lawfulness that reaches out beyond the church, is incompatible with fleshly lawlessness – and is thus especially incompatible with manipulative strategies and imposed role performances that instrumentalize others in order to gratify oneself or one's clique, tribe, institution, government or global authority.

True mission, or love as biblical lawfulness that reaches out beyond the church, is also incompatible with fleshly legalism – and is thus especially incompatible with elitist, authoritarian judgmentalism that confronts without self-criticism and that devalues people unless they conform to some kind of oppressive, de-relationalized system of beliefs, actions, experiences, politics or patterns of self-cultivation.

True mission, or love as biblical lawfulness that reaches out beyond the church, is also incompatible with the suppression of maturity and of wisdom – and is thus especially incompatible with:

(a) the suppression of the transmitted biblical texts, corporate memories and ethical criteria by which persons, relationships, ethical conscience, liberating consciousness and right relating are formed and refereed through the action of the Holy Spirit;

(b) the promoting and show-casing of conformity to systems of infantilizing indoctrination that proceed according to projected propagandas of self-righteous, utopian positivity shaped by distorted ideologies – whether naturalistic-humanistic or pseudo-Christian;

(c) the neo-pragmatic use of the 'shifting truth, fluxing language' argument, since the latter contributes to the perpetuation of the disintegrations, authoritarianisms, allowed rhetorics and modern disasters – and to the acceleration of these factors through digitopian culture – that we have noted above;

(d) the marginalizing and alienating of intellectuals that accompanies the desire to remain unchallenged in relation to any of these sins.

If only the church was not almost as guilty as 'bad postmodernity' in relation to such matters. No wonder the church is often capable of only a crude, distorted kind of love that, in its often-championed, anti-intellectual ignorance, can have the same effect as hate.

The general characteristics of true mission to Western postmodern society

By contrast, true mission, or love as biblical lawfulness that reaches out beyond the church, is in part characterized by ongoing, Spirit-wrought, biblically formed maturing unto biblically wise relating – within appropriate agreed boundaries – that involves:

(a) caring Trinitarian inclusiveness and positive regard for others that confers freedom from non-agreed 'obligations', and that promotes others in their unique otherness (identities, giftings, callings, vocations, ministries and so on);[104]
(b) where appropriate, situation-specific, redemptive, merciful, practical action towards others – sometimes but not always in accordance with one's gifts – that includes (but that cannot be reduced to) helping to train others: out of crippling isolating introversions, abstractions, self-anaesthesia, and self-harm; out of sinful patterns of relating; and into the freedom of right relating to God and neighbour;
(c) where (a) and (b) will often involve sharing the gospel of Jesus Christ at some point.

Moreover, true mission, or love as biblical lawfulness that reaches out beyond the church, is in part characterized by a prophetic discourse that is:

(a) truthful, relationally wise, biblically salted, healing, gracious, merciful and forgiving;
(b) a critically astute, reflective 'language of the real' that is characterized by awareness of distorted relational patterns, of right-relational patterns and of how to build others up into right relating and into the uniqueness of their personhoods, gifts, callings and ministries;
(c) gospel-centred, and yet moving beyond maturity-shunning, neutered repetition of 'the basics';
(d) able to confront, having the self-critical transparency that makes such confrontation non-judgemental;
(e) able to care, having the framework sophistication that is necessary in order to do so.

With respect to the state, then true mission, or love as biblical lawfulness that reaches out beyond the church:

(a) does not 'impose' itself in an authoritarian manner but – by default – submits to authorities, testifying about what is right and working together with others and with the state in order to refine society from within;[105]
(b) remains self-critical about matters of conscience, defaulting (in the first instance) to respect for human courts;[106]
(c) is law-abiding by default – for conscience's sake and for the sake of our witness – allowing the principle of 'not causing offence' to overrule fleshly legalism (but not justice itself), and wisely discerning between submission to right principles and submission to good outcomes according to particular circumstances.[107]

The specific characteristics of true mission to Western postmodern society

In our particular cultural situation, then, true mission, or love as biblical lawfulness that reaches out beyond the church, is specifically aware of and able to address pastoral needs that emerge from the situations expounded in our earlier analysis of the five contemporary sets of fivefold cultural oppressions that afflict us in the West today (see above).

This will mean that culturally sensitive love, as missional biblical lawfulness, will promote 'good postmodernity' (since it is biblical) and confront 'bad postmodernity', desiring:

(a) *a turn to humbled humanitarianism*, against humanistic hubris – allowing the rise of the knowledge of God;
(b) *a turn to right relationality*, against un-refereed 'play' and conflict – promoting refereed love and dialogue;
(c) *a rise in historical consciousness*, against historical negationism – allowing awareness of the historical truth of our past failings;
(d) *a rise in 'concientizing' ethical wisdom*, against a historical relativism that immunizes authoritarian power from challenge – allowing liberation from oppression;

(e) *a turn to enfleshed stable-yet-flexible language*, against oppression
     by arbitrarily fixed or arbitrarily fluxing language – allowing
     the textual transmission of formative 'concientizing' histor-
     ical truth and ethical wisdom;
(f) *the rise of realistic humanitarian societies*, against grandiose,
     consumerist, humanistic middle class utopianism or digitopi-
     anism – allowing both material and cognitive emancipation,
     and environmental and economic sustainability;
(g) *the rise of true self-understanding*, against both anthropocen-
     tric and deconstructed individualisms – allowing sobriety
     regarding our de-centred-but-valued relational 'narrative'
     selves;
(h) *the rise of true interpretation of the human plight*, against the
     deadly spells and obfuscations of modernity and of bad post-
     modernity – allowing the healing of minds, relationships and
     cultures through knowing the real God, the accessible truth
     and genuine wisdom – before it is too late.

After all, Jesus would hardly want our missional loving to be blind
to its cultural object. Indeed, for the most part, Jesus' message in
the New Testament *is* cultural criticism, and certainly does not
reduce the gospel to a few slogans.

   And finally, and with respect to the spiritual battle, then true
mission, or love as biblical lawfulness that reaches out beyond the
church:

(a) exposes bad postmodernity's promotion of naturalistic,
     humanistic utopianism as being direct obedience to the
     demonic temptation to 'become like God, without God';[108]
(b) exposes bad postmodernity's promotion of the 'shifting
     truths, fluxing language' philosophy as being direct obedi-
     ence to a demonic strategy designed to keep us blind:
     (i) to the great sin of modernity that is destroying others, the
          earth and ourselves; and
     (ii) to the real God, the genuine wisdom and the accessible
          truth who/that could save us – through the Person and
          work of Jesus Christ our Lord.

Endnotes

1. Being Formed by God's Biblical Speech-Acts

1. I follow Anthony C. Thiselton's approach to speech-act theory. See his *New Horizons in Hermeneutics: The Theory and Practice of Transforming Biblical Reading* (London: HarperCollins, 1992), pp. 283–312.
2. On 'self-involvement' see, Thiselton, *New Horizons*, pp. 272–312.
3. Anthony C. Thiselton, *The Two Horizons: New Testament Hermeneutics and Philosophical Description with Special Reference to Heidegger, Bultmann, Gadamer, and Wittgenstein* (Exeter: Paternoster Press, 1980), pp. 115–39, 357–438.
4. Anthony C. Thiselton, 'Predictable, Domesticated and Tamed', *CEN* (8 Feb. 1974), p. 7.
5. Compare: Matt. 7:12; 22:34–40; Rom. 13:8–10; Gal. 5:14. On 'training' see, Thiselton, *Two Horizons*, pp. 376–9.
6. See Rom. 12:7.

2. Communion with Christ in the Central-Room

1. On models see, Anthony C. Thiselton, *The Two Horizons: New Testament Hermeneutics and Philosophical Description with Special Reference to Heidegger, Bultmann, Gadamer, and Wittgenstein* (Exeter: Paternoster Press, 1980), p. 432ff.
2. On Heidegger's notion of 'worldhood' or 'world' see, Thiselton, *Two Horizons*, pp. 30–1, 297, 312, 338, 344.
3. Matt. 6:6.
4. 2 Tim. 3:12.
5. Thiselton, *Two Horizons*, pp. 133–9.

6 Thiselton, *Two Horizons*, pp. 370–9.

7 Dan. 4:34; Mark 14:49.

8 Thiselton, *Two Horizons*, p. 307.

9 So, Thiselton, *Two Horisons*, p. 292; cf. 83–4; cf. Robert Knowles, *Anthony C. Thiselton and The Grammar of Hermeneutics: The Search for a Unified Theory* (Milton Keanes: Paternoster, 2012), pp. 515–21.

10 John 7:17.

11 Anthony C. Thiselton, *New Horizons in Hermeneutics: The Theory and Practice of Transforming Biblical Reading* (London: HarperCollins, 1992), pp. 111–2; 344–50; cf. Anthony C. Thiselton, 'Sigmund Freud and the Language of the Heart', *CEN* (13 Feb. 1976), pp. 12, 14; cf. Anthony C. Thiselton, 'Truth', in *The New International Dictionary of New Testament Theology*, Vol. 3 (ed. C. Brown; Exeter: Paternoster, 1978), pp. 879, 883–6, 892.

12 Sara Tulloch, ed., *The Reader's Digest Oxford Wordfinder* (Oxford: Clarendon Press, 1993), p. 1047.

13 Thiselton, *Two Horizons*, pp. 370–9; cf. 335–47.

14 We follow Thiselton here. See endnotes 1–3 of Chapter 1 above.

15 Anthony C. Thiselton, 'The New Hermeneutic', in *New Testament Interpretation: Essays in Principles and Methods* (ed. I.H. Marshall; Exeter: Paternoster, 1977), pp. 321–2.

16 Matt. 23:10.

17 Compare: Matt. 7:12; 22:34–40; Rom. 13:8–10; and Gal. 5:14.

18 Anthony C. Thiselton, '1 Corinthians', in *New Dictionary of Biblical Theology* (ed. T.D. Alexander and B.S. Rosner; Leicester: IVP, 2000), pp. 298–9.

19 cf. Matt. 5:23–4.

20 Gen. 4:24; Matt. 7:6.

3. Love for God and Others: Biblical Lawfulness

1 Matt. 5:18–20; cf. Rom. 3:31; 13:1; 1 Cor. 9:20–1.

2 Heb. 7:11–9; cf. 7:11 – 10:18; cf. 1 Cor. 9:20–1; Gal. 2:16; Col. 2:14–5; Rom. 8:2.

3 Jas. 4:11–7; Matt. 22:37–8.

4 Matt. 15:1–9; cf. Mark 7:1–13; Jas. 4:11–7; John. 16:5–11.

5 Jas. 4:11–2; cf. Job 32:1–3; Matt. 22:37–40; cf. 7:1–6.

6 Matt. 15:1–9; cf. Mark 7:1–13; Luke 18:9–14.

[7] e.g. Matt. 23:23–4; cf. 5:27–8; 21–2.

[8] cf. Matt. 23:23–4; cf. 5:27–8; 21–2.

[9] Matt. 12:24–9; cf. John 8:42–7; Col. 2:8–15; Gal. 4:1–11; 5:1–6; John 9:35–41.

[10] For this point and the previous point see Anthony C. Thiselton, *Interpreting God and the Postmodern Self: On Meaning, Manipulation and Promise* (Edinburgh: T&T Clark, 1995), pp. 25–6, 78–97, 121–35; cf. Anthony C. Thiselton, 'Communicative Action and Promise in Inter-Disciplinary, Biblical, and Theological Hermeneutics', in *The Promise of Hermeneutics* (R. Lundin et al.; Carlisle: Paternoster, 1999), pp. 133–7, 214–22, 234–6; Colin E. Gunton, *The One, The Three, and The Many: God, Creation and the Culture of Modernity* (Cambridge: CUP, 1993), p. 35.

[11] Matt. 22:40; cf. 34–40; Rom. 13:10; Gal. 5:14; 1 John 4:8,16; 3:1,16.

[12] Mark 10:19; cf. Matt. 19:19; 23:23.

[13] Matt. 5:27–8; Exod. 20:17; Matt. 15:11–20.

[14] Matt. 5:21–2; cf. Mark 10:19; Jas. 4:2–3.

[15] Mark 7:9–13; cf. Matt. 15:4–6.

[16] Robert Knowles, *Anthony C. Thiselton and The Grammar of Hermeneutics: The Search for a Unified Theory* (Milton Keanes: Paternoster, 2012), pp. 444–564; cf. Anthony C. Thiselton, 'Signs of the Times: Towards a Theology for the Year 2000 as a Grammar of Grace, Truth and Eschatology in Contexts of So-Called Postmodernity', in *The Future as God's Gift: Explorations in Christian Eschatology* (ed. D. Fergusson and M. Sarot; Edinburgh: T&T Clark, 2000), pp. 17–8; 27–8; Matt. 12:24–9.

[17] Jeff Lewis, *Cultural Studies: The Basics* (London: Sage Publications, 2002), pp. 83–4, 267–9, 412–8; cf. Eccl. 7:29; Ps. 127:1; Jas. 4:15.

[18] See endnote 10 above; cf. Gunton, *One*, pp. 117–9; E. Behler, *Confrontations: Derrida, Heidegger, Nietzsche* (California: Stanford University Press, 1991), p. 159.

[19] Ps. 23:1–4.

[20] Lewis, *Cultural Studies*, p. 413; cf. Jürgen Moltmann, 'Progress and Abyss: Remembering the Future of the Modern World', in *2000 Years and Beyond: Faith, Identity and the 'Common Era'* (ed. P. Gifford et al.; London: Routledge, 2003), pp. 16–34; Thiselton, *Interpreting God*, pp. 83–4, 121–35.

[21] John 16:8.

[22] Rom. 3:20.

[23] Rom. 7:7–13.

[24] Rom. 7:21–4; cf. 7:13; Gen. 4:7.

[25] For points (a) to (n) see Eph. 2:3; cf. 4:17–9; Rom. 1:18–32; Col. 2:8–19; Gal. 4:1–11; 5:1–26; John 8:34; 1 John. 2:16.

[26] Roger Lundin, 'Interpreting Orphans: Hermeneutics in the Cartesian Tradition', in *The Promise of Hermeneutics* (R. Lundin et al.; Carlisle: Paternoster, 1999), pp. 1–64; cf. Thiselton, 'Communicative Action', pp. 133–43; Heb. 1:3.

[27] Rom. 7:24–5.

[28] Rom. 7:10–21.

[29] Gal. 3:24–5.

[30] Acts 15:10.

[31] Anthony C. Thiselton, Contribution to 'Flesh', in *The New International Dictionary of New Testament Theology*, Vol. 1 (ed. C. Brown; Exeter: Paternoster, 1975), p. 681.

[32] Anthony C. Thiselton, *The Two Horizons: New Testament Hermeneutics and Philosophical Description with Special Reference to Heidegger, Bultmann, Gadamer, and Wittgenstein* (Exeter: Paternoster Press, 1980), p. 278.

[33] 1 Cor. 3:21; cf. Eph. 2:8–9; 1 John. 2:15–7; Col. 2:20–3.

[34] Col. 2:13–5.

[35] Gal. 5:1–5; cf. 4:3–9; Col. 2:8. The translation, 'elemental spirits' (cf. Gal. 4:9), is from James Moffatt's translation of the New Testament. See James Moffatt, *A New Translation of the New Testament* (London: Hodder and Stoughton, 1949), pp. 279, 296; cf. Beverly R. Gaventa, 'Galatians', in *Eerdmans Commentary on the Bible* (ed. J.W. Rogerson and J.D.G. Dunn; Grand Rapids: Eerdmans, 2003), p. 1380. Paul has 'demons' in mind, not just 'rules'.

[36] Gal. 4:15; cf. 5:2–4.

[37] Rom. 9:30–2; cf. 11:22–4; cf. 11–24; Gal. 5:10.

[38] Eph. 2:8–9; cf. Gal. 4:3–7.

[39] Gaventa, 'Galatians', p. 1380; cf. Luke 22:31–2; 1 Cor. 5:5; 2 Cor. 2:5–11; 1 Tim. 1:20; Job 1 – 2; 32:1.

[40] Luke 22:31; cf. Jas. 4:7; Gal. 4:4–9; 5:3; Col. 2:8–15; 20–3.

[41] 1 Thess. 3:5; cf. Rev. 12:10; Gal. 4:9; Matt. 12:25–9; John 8:42–7; 2 Cor. 2:11; 1 Pet. 5:8–9.

[42] Gal. 5:5; cf. Matt. 5:6.

[43] On points '(e)' and '(f)' see Matt. 22:37–8; cf. 12:26–9; Rom. 2:28–9.

[44] On points '(g)' – '(l)' see Rom. 7:7–25; Luke 8:29; Matt. 22:39.

[45] John 8:31–59; cf. Matt. 23:15.

[46] Gal. 4:5; cf. Rom. 7:7 – 8:4; 5:12–20; 6:23; Isa. 59:2; Matt. 19:17–9.

[47] Gal. 4:4–5.

[48] Rev. 19:14.

[49] Luke 14:32; cf. 2 Cor. 13:4; Matt. 24:30; 2 Tim. 4:1; Prov. 15:3; Heb. 4:13.

[50] Donald A. Carson, *The Gagging of God: Christianity Confronts Pluralism* (Leicester: Apollos, 1996), pp. 515–36; cf. Anthony C. Thiselton, *Life After Death: A New Approach to the Last Things* (Grand Rapids, MI: Eerdmans, 2012), pp. 145–84; cf. Rev. 19:15.

[51] Dan. 4:35.

[52] Matt. 13:49–50.

[53] 1 Thess. 1:10.

[54] John 14:13–7; cf. 1:1–2, 18; 20:28; Heb. 1:8; 5:9; 4:15; 11:26; Titus 2:13; 2 Pet. 1:1,16–7; 1 Pet. 1:19; 2:22; Phil. 2:6–11; Matt. 5:48; Rev. 5:12; Bruce Milne, *Know The Truth: A Handbook of Christian Belief* (Leicester: IVP, 1982), pp. 59–64; 128–41.

[55] Matt. 1:1–25; 4:1–11; 9:36; 11:19; 21:18; 26:37; 27:42–50; Luke 2:7, 40–52; 3:23–38; 7:9; 10:21; 11:15–20; 19:41; 22:63; 23:33; Gal. 4:4; Heb. 5:8; Mark 1:24; 3:5; 6:1–6; 8:33; 14:33–6; John 2:17; 4:6; 11:5; 12:27; cf. Milne, *Know The Truth*, pp. 125–8.

[56] Gal. 4:4; cf. John 4:22; Rom. 9:1–5, 25–9; Heb. 7:1 – 10:18; Exod. 5:1.

[57] Matt. 5:17–20; cf. 15:1–9; 2 Tim. 3:16; Heb. 4:15.

[58] e.g. Lev. 6:25–6; 7:2–5; cf. R.T. Beckwith, 'Sacrifice and Offering', in *New Bible Dictionary* (ed. J.D. Douglas et al.; Leicester: IVP, 2nd edn, 1982), pp. 1045–54.

[59] Isa. 52:13 – 53:12; cf. Ps. 40:6; 110:4; Heb. 4:14 – 10:18; Rom. 1:32; Gal. 3:10–4.

[60] Ps. 45:6; cf. Heb. 1:1 – 2:9; 10:1–12.

[61] Heb. 2:5–18; cf. 4:15; 9:1–28; 1 Pet. 2:21–2; Isa. 53:9.

[62] 1 Pet. 1:19; cf. Exod. 12:1–5; Lev. 1:3; Mal. 1:6–14.

[63] Exod. 40:2; cf. 25:8–22; 29:42–3; 26:33; Heb. 9:1–28.

[64] As well as endnotes 55–63, see also Isa. 52:13 – 53:12; cf. 1 Pet. 2:22–4; Matt. 8:17; Mark 15:28; Luke 22:37; John 12:38; Acts 8:30–5; Rom. 3:21–6; Gal. 3:13; 2 Cor. 5:21.

[65] Matt. 19:17; cf. 6:12; 7:13; 8:22; Mark 10:18; 9:49; 7:20–3; Luke 18:19; 13:1–5; Gen. 3:14–9; 1:26–8; Rom. 3:9–24; 8:18–27; Rev. 11:18; John 1:29; 3:16; caveats to do with small children and certain others aside.

[66] Matt. 5:20; 6:13 cf. Exod. 33:20; 1 Tim. 6:16; Hab. 1:13; Isa. 59:2; Heb. 6:20 – 8:13; Gal. 3:1–25; John 8:34; 1 John 3:8; 5:19.

[67] John 3:1–21; cf. 2 Cor. 5:1–17; Gal. 6:15; Rev. 21:1–5; 22:2; Rom. 8:11; 1 Cor. 15:12–58.

68 John 3:16–21; cf. 5:24; 6:43–59; 11:25–6; 14:6; Rom. 10:9–13.

69 Rom. 3:21–6; cf. 4:25; 5:8; Heb. 2:9–17; 1 John 2:2; 4:10; Col. 1:20.

70 Heb. 7:1 – 10:18; cf. 2:17; Rom. 3:25, 26; 1 John 2:2; 4:10; Jer. 33:8–9.

71 Heb. 12:2; cf. William L. Lane, *Hebrews 9 – 13: Word Biblical Commentary* 47B (Dallas, Texas: Word Books, 1991), p. 428; Anthony C. Thiselton, '1 Corinthians', in *New Dictionary of Biblical Theology* (ed. T.D. Alexander and B.S. Rosner; Leicester: IVP, 2000), p. 298.

72 Rom. 3:25–6; cf. Matt. 5:17–8; Heb. 7:1 – 10:18.

73 Rom. 3:21–6; cf. 5:1–21; 9:10–8; 30–3; 10:1–13; Gal. 3:10–1; 5:1–15; Eph. 2:8–10; 1 Cor. 6:11; Heb. 7:1 – 10:18.

74 1 John 3:8; cf. 1 Cor. 15:24–6; Gal. 4:1–11; 5:1–15; Col. 2:6–23; Eph. 6:12.

75 1 Cor. 15:12–20; cf. Eph. 1:20; John 14:28; 16:10; Heb. 2:11; 4:15; 5:9; 7:11 – 8:13; 9:11–24; 10:1–18; 1 John 3:2; 1 Pet. 2:21–2; Isa. 53:1–12; 1 Tim. 6:16.

76 Heb. 7:1 – 8:13; 9:15; 12:24; cf. Rom. 2:28–9; 3:25; 8:1–4; 10:1–13; 2 Cor. 3:1–6; 4:16; Col. 1:13; Eph. 1:7; John 11:25–7; 14:1–2; Matt. 26:28; Gal. 4:21–31.

77 Heb. 2:17; cf. 6:13–20; 10:1–18; Rom. 4:23–25; 5:1–21; Eph. 1:1–14; 2 Cor. 1:22; 5:16–21.

78 Acts 20:32; cf. 26:18; 1 Cor. 1:2; 6:11; Heb. 10:10–39; Lev. 20:7–8; Exod. 29:43.

79 1 Cor. 6:2–20; cf. Rom. 6:22; 8:17; 2 Thess. 3:3; John 15:9–17; 17:15; 1 Pet. 5:7; 1 John 3:1–3; Eph. 1:5; Gal. 4:7; Matt. 19:28.

80 1 Cor. 6:11–9; cf. John 16:7; 14:16–7; 2 Pet. 1:9; Titus 3:4–7; 2 Cor. 5:17; Gal. 6:15; Eph. 5:25–6.

81 2 Thess. 2:13; cf. Eph. 1:13; Gal. 5:16 – 6:8; John 16:12–15; Rom. 8:1–17.

82 1 Cor. 3:16; cf. 12:1–31; 2 Cor. 6:16; 1 Pet. 2:4–10; Col. 1:18; Eph. 4:1–16; Titus 2:13–4.

83 John 5:24; cf. Jude 1:21; 1 John 5:13; Heb. 5:9; 9:12; 2 Cor. 3:18; Rom. 6:23; 2 Tim. 2:10.

84 Col. 1:13; cf. 2:15; Rom. 11:26; Gal. 4:1 – 5:15; 1 Cor. 5:1–13; 2 Cor. 2:5–11.

85 Eph. 1:15–23; cf. 2:19–22; 4:14–6; 5:9–33; Heb. 2:11; 3:1–6; 5:11–4; 10:14; 12:2; Rom. 3:31; 8:4; 15:14–6; 1 Thess. 5:23–4; 2 Thess. 2:13; 1 Pet. 1:2; 2:5; 5:10; 2 Cor. 3:18; 11:2; 1 John 3:2–3; Col. 1:22; 2:19; 2 Tim. 2:21; 1 Cor. 3:9; 15:21–58; Titus 2:13–4; Gal. 5:5; Luke 17:5–6.

86 Heb. 2:14–8; cf. 4:15; 5:7; 8:1–6; 1 John 2:1–2; 4:11–2; Rom. 8:26–7; 1 Pet. 2:18–25; John 15:12.

87 John 14:15–31; cf. 16:5–16; 1 Cor. 13:6; Phil. 1:9–10; 4:6–7; Col. 4:12; Heb. 10:22; Rom. 5:1; 12:2; 2 Tim. 3:15–7; on speech-acts see e.g. Anthony C.

Thiselton, 'The Supposed Power of Words in the Biblical Writings', *JTS* NS25.2 (Oct. 1974), pp. 283–99.

88 Heb. 10:13; cf. 12:2; Rom. 8:28–39; 9:10–8; 1 John 3:8; 1 Cor. 15:24–6; John 10:1–33; Eph. 6:10–8; 2 Thess. 2:1–12; Rev. 12:1 – 13:18; 20:1–10; 1 Pet. 5:8–9; Matt. 13:24–30; 1 Tim. 5:14–5; 1 Thess. 5:23–4; Gal. 5:5.

89 Eph. 2:10.

90 2 Pet. 1:5; cf. 3:14; Heb. 4:11; 6:10; Gal. 3:3; 5:22–3; Rom. 8:12–17; 14:19; John 5:44; 2 Tim. 3:16–7; Eph. 2:10; 4:16; 1 Cor. 4:12; Phil. 2:12–3; 2 Thess. 3:10; 1 Tim. 5:18; Jas. 2:14–26; 4:13–7; 1 Cor. 13:1–13; 15:58; Col. 3:22–4; 1 Thess. 4:3–8.

91 Col. 1:12–20; cf. 3:24; Rev. 21:1 – 22:6; 1 Cor. 3:8–15; 15:20–8; 1 Pet. 1:4; Heb. 9:15; 11:1–40; Eph. 1:14; 6:8; Luke 6:23; 2 Cor. 5:1–21; Prov. 8:27–31; Matt. 17:11; Mark 9:12–3.

92 See endnote 91 above and also: Rev. 4:7–11; cf. 5:1–14; John 5:21–3; Rom. 4:25 – 5:21; Job 38:4.

93 Jas. 4:1–12.

94 Gen. 4:23–4; cf. Jas. 4:1–11; cf. on S. Hall's comments see Christopher Norris, *The Truth About Postmodernism* (Oxford: Blackwell, 1993), p. 7.

95 Rom. 2:6.

96 Rom. 13:4; cf. 1 Cor. 5:5, 13; 2 Cor. 2:5–11; Deut. 25:2–3; Heb. 12:6–10; Ezek. 18:32; 33:11; Isa. 63.11.

97 Jas. 4:12; 2:13; cf. Luke 9:54–5; Matt. 6:15.

98 Jas. 1:20; cf. Gal. 5:19–21; cf. Norris, *Postmodernism*, p. 7; cf. Matt. 5:17; Rom. 3:21–6.

99 Gal. 3:11; cf. Rom. 3:20.

100 Rom. 3:22–6; 5:20–1; cf. Gal. 3:24; 4:4–5; Eph. 2:8.

101 Rom. 8:2; 6:14; cf. 3:31; 1 Cor. 9:21; Gal. 4:5.

102 Heb. 8:6–7; cf. 7:11–2; 5:7–10.

103 1 Cor. 9:20–1; cf. Rom. 8:2.

104 1 John 4:8–16; cf. Rom. 13:10; John 15:12.

105 cf. Jas. 1:25; John 15:12.

106 Matt. 5:48.

107 Rom. 8:1; cf. Luke 7:44–50; 1 John 4:18.

108 Luke 18:9–14; cf. Rom. 3:27; Eph. 2:8–9; 1 Cor. 3:21.

109 Gal. 4:3–9; cf. 5:1–6; Col. 2:8–23; Rom. 13:10; Gal. 5:14; Matt. 22:34–40; Luke 14:15–24.

110 Gal. 5:6; cf. Rom. 5:1; 3:21; 4:6; 2 Cor. 11:14.

111 Gal. 5:6.

[112] Matt. 13:12.

[113] Mark 12:30–1; cf. Matt. 22:37–40; 1 John 4:20–1; 5:3 cf. John 4:23–4.

[114] On points in and immediately before this list see John 4:23–4; 14:15–31; 15:1–17; 16:12–5; cf. Col. 2:9–12,19; Ps. 105:3–5; 1 Thess. 5:18; Rom. 4:20, 6:1–14; Heb. 8:6,10–1; Matt. 6:6; 1 Cor. 12:13.

[115] 1 John 2:23; 5:11–2; cf. Rom. 6:5; 10:9–13.

[116] John 15:1–17; Col. 2:16–19; 3:15–17; Eph. 5:18–9; Heb. 12:28.

[117] Ps. 145:3; cf. 1 John 2:3; Heb. 8:11; 1 Cor. 13:12; Eph. 5:22–33; Col. 2:19.

[118] Ps. 105:3.

[119] 1 John 4:1–6.

[120] Thiselton, *Two Horizons*, pp. 417–22; cf. Matt. 16:23. Thiselton made this point verbally at a conference celebrating his career, held in 2012, at Nottingham University, UK.

[121] Heb. 5:11 – 6:3; cf. 1 Tim. 3:9.

[122] See endnotes 114–20 and also: Ps. 104 – 105; John 17:17; Heb. 4:12–3; 8:1–13; Rev. 21–2; Eph. 6:17–8; 2 Tim. 3:16–7; Prov. 1:32–3.

[123] 1 Cor. 12:1–31; 1 Thess. 5:18; Gal. 5:16–26; Eph. 4:11–6; Acts 1:1–8.

[124] 1 John 4:19–21; 5:3; cf. Rom. 12:1–21.

[125] Rom. 12:3–8.

[126] Luke 10:25–37; cf. Mark 12:30–1; Matt. 22:37–40.

[127] Phil. 1:9–10.

[128] 1 John 3:18.

[129] Moltmann, 'Progress', pp. 23–6.

[130] Anthony C. Thiselton, *The Hermeneutics of Doctrine* (Grand Rapids: Eerdmans, 2007), p. xvi; cf. xvi–xxii.

[131] Rom. 12:2; cf. 1 Cor. 13:6; 14:20.

[132] Matt. 22:37–40; cf. John 17:17; 16:12–5.

[133] Mark 14:49; cf. John 10:35.

[134] John 16:5–15; cf. 14:16–27; Jas. 4:13–7; 1 Cor. 2:6–16.

[135] 2 Tim. 3:16–7; cf. Heb. 4:12; 5:11 – 6:3; 1 Pet. 2:2.

[136] John 7:37–9 cf. 4:15–8; Heb. 5:11 – 6:3.

[137] Phil. 4:6–7; cf. Prov. 3:5–6; 4:7; 1 Cor. 14:20; Matt. 22:37–40; Heb. 4:12; 5:11 – 6:3; 2 Tim. 3:16–7.

[138] cf. 1 Cor. 8:1–3; Jas. 1:5; 3:13; Eph. 5:15; Prov. 4:1–9; Gal. 5:16–26.

[139] cf. e.g. Eph. 5:26–9.

[140] Rom. 12:2; cf. Gal. 5:16–26.

[141] Gal. 5:16–26.

[142] I. Stewart, *Transactional Analysis Counselling in Action* (London; Sage Publications, 2007). We say more on this theme later on.

143 S.B. Karpman, 'Fairy Tales and Script Drama Analysis', *TAB* 7.26 (Apr. 1968), pp. 39–43. We say more on this theme later on.

144 2 Cor. 11:14.

145 Gal. 5:24.

146 John 10:17–8.

147 1 Cor. 13:5–6; cf. John 8:34.

148 Eph. 5:21.

149 1 Cor. 7:21–3.

150 cf. Eph. 4:17–9.

151 Paul Ricoeur, 'The Task of Hermeneutics', in *Hermeneutics and the Human Sciences: Essays on Language, Action and Interpretation* (ed. and trans. J.B. Thompson; Cambridge: CUP, 1981), p. 51; cf. Rom. 12:3–8.

152 Jas. 1:25.

153 Prov. 27:17.

154 1 Pet. 4:10; cf. 1 Cor. 12:1–31.

155 Rom. 13:1,2; cf. 2 Cor. 6:5; 11:23–33.

156 Rom. 13:3–4; cf. 1 Pet. 2:14; 4:12–9; 2 Cor. 11:23–33.

157 Exod. 2:11–7; cf. John 7:1–13; Lev. 10:1–2.

158 Eph. 2:10; cf. Rev. 13:10.

159 Jer. 27:1–15; cf. 28:1–17; 38:17–8; 42:7–22; 2 Chron. 12:8.

160 1 Cor. 5:12–3.

161 Anthony C. Thiselton, *The First Epistle to the Corinthians* (Carlisle: Paternoster, 2000), p. 417 (Thiselton's bold type removed).

162 Thiselton, *Epistle*, p. 417.

163 Matt. 5:39; cf. Thiselton, *Interpreting God*, pp. 154–5; Anthony C. Thiselton, *New Horizons in Hermeneutics: The Theory and Practice of Transforming Biblical Reading* (London: HarperCollins, 1992), p. 615.

164 1 Cor. 4:3–5.

165 Thiselton, *Epistle*, pp. 340–1; cf. 338–44.

166 Thiselton, *Epistle*, p. 340 (Thiselton's italics).

167 Heb. 8:10; cf. Rom. 13:5 (our italics).

168 e.g. Amos 2:7; 5:12,15; Prov. 29:7; 18:5; 21:15; 29:26; Isa. 5:7.

169 On points (a) – (c) see 1 Cor. 6:1–8; cf. Thiselton, *Epistle*, pp. 418–9ff.

170 Rom. 13:1; cf. 10.

171 Rom. 13:8–9; cf. 1 Cor. 9:21; Matt. 19:18–9; 5:17–48.

172 2 Cor. 8:21.

173 Anthony C. Thiselton, 'Biblical Classics: VI. Schweitzer's Interpretation of Paul', *ExpTim* 90 (Feb. 1979), pp. 133–5; cf. 1 Cor. 9:19–20.

174 John 16:5–11.

[175] Matt. 17:27.

[176] John 8:10–1.

[177] Exod. 2:11–5; cf. 3:1–22.

[178] Luke 7:47.

[179] Rom. 13:8–10.

[180] William L. Reese, *Dictionary of Philosophy and Religion: Eastern and Western Thought* (New Jersey: Humanities Press, 1980), pp. 156–7.

[181] The term 'socio-pragmatic' is Thiselton's. See Thiselton, *New Horizons*, especially pp. 393–409, 410–70, 535–55.

4. Church Distorted by Modernity

[1] Matt. 25:14–30; cf. Luke 19:11–27.

[2] Mark 6:5.

[3] Leonardo Boff, *Trinity and Society* (trans. P. Burns; Tunbridge Wells: Burns & Oats, 1988), pp. 4–7, 11–3, 16–24, 77–85, 200–7; cf. Colin E. Gunton, *The One, the Three, and the Many: God, Creation, and the Culture of Modernity* (Cambridge: CUP, 1993), pp. 6–8, 11–27, 37, 80, 106–25, 144–5, 221–30.

[4] cf. John 14:10–28; 17:5; 1 Cor. 2:11–2; 12:1–31; 1 John 4:7–21; Gen. 1:26–7; Gal. 5:14; Rom. 13:1–10; Matt. 22:37–40.

[5] Compare: Anthony C. Thiselton, 'Man Longs for the Status and Dignity of a 'Thou'', *CEN* (9 Jan. 1976), p. 9; Anthony C. Thiselton, 'An Age of Anxiety', in *The History of Christianity: A Lion Handbook* (ed. T. Dowley et al.; Tring, Hertfordshire: Lion Publishing, 1977), p. 600; Anthony C. Thiselton, 'Review of A. Hodes' *Encounter with Martin Buber*', *Chm* 90.2 (1976), pp. 138–9.

[6] Anthony C. Thiselton, *New Horizons in Hermeneutics: The Theory and Practice of Transforming Biblical Reading* (London: HarperCollins, 1992), pp. 388–9.

[7] Thiselton, 'Man Longs', p. 9; cf. Thiselton, 'Anxiety', p. 600; Thiselton, 'Rev *EMB*', pp. 138–9.

[8] Anthony C. Thiselton, *The Two Horizons: New Testament Hermeneutics and Philosophical Description with Special Reference to Heidegger, Bultmann, Gadamer, and Wittgenstein* (Exeter: Paternoster, 1980), p. 331.

[9] Gunton, *One*, p. 64; cf. 44–51; Jeff Lewis, *Cultural Studies: The Basics* (London: Sage Publications, 2002), pp. 107, 267–9, 412–4.

[10] Gen. 3:17–9; cf. Eccl. 1:1–11; 2:17–26; 3:9–22; 4:1–16.

11 Gunton, *One*, p. 64; cf. 44–6; 51.

12 cf. Gal. 5:14; Rom. 13:10; Matt. 22:34–40.

13 The Scriptures command the opposite of this. See 1 John 1:8–10; 1 Cor. 8:1–13; 12:1–31; Jas 2:1–13; Matt. 6:1–18; etc.

14 1 Cor. 12:1–31.

15 I. Stewart, *Transactional Analysis Counselling in Action* (London; Sage Publications, 2007); cf. endnote 12.

16 S.B. Karpman, 'Fairy Tales and Script Drama Analysis', *TAB* 7.26 (Apr. 1968), pp. 39–43.

17 Anthony C. Thiselton, '1 Corinthians', in *New Dictionary of Biblical Theology* (ed. T.D. Alexander and B.S. Rosner; Leicester: IVP, 2000), p. 298.

18 1 Cor. 12:1–31; cf. Eph. 4:14–6; Col. 2:19; 1 Pet. 2:4–5; 4:10; etc.

19 3 John 9.

20 Matt. 23:6–7; Mark 12:40.

21 Mark 4:19.

22 Thiselton, *Two Horizons*, pp. 372–9.

23 Anthony C. Thiselton, 'Keeping up with Recent Studies: II. Structuralism and Biblical Studies: Method or Ideology?' *ExpTim* 89 (Aug. 1978), pp. 329–35; cf. e.g. Thiselton, *New Horizons*, p. 395.

24 See e.g. Matt. 8:8–10.

25 Matt. 23:12.

26 Phil. 2:8–11.

5. Church Distorted by Postmodernity

1 Anthony C. Thiselton, '1 Corinthians', in *New Dictionary of Biblical Theology* (ed. T.D. Alexander and B.S. Rosner; Leicester: IVP, 2000), pp. 297–306; cf. 297, 305; cf. Anthony C. Thiselton, 'Can a Premodern Bible Address a Postmodern World?' (public lecture, University of St Andrews), in *2000 Years and Beyond: Faith, Identity and the 'Common Era'* (ed. P. Gifford et al.; London: Routledge, 2003), pp. 127–46.

2 Thiselton, '1 Corinthians', pp. 297–302, 304–5.

3 Gen. 3:5; cf. Rom. 1:18–3:20; cf. Phil. 2:5–11.

4 Gen. 1:26 – 2:25; cf. 2 Cor. 3:17–8.

5 Jas. 4:11–7; cf. Rom. 2:1–11; 9:30–3; 2 Thess. 2:4; Gen. 3:16; Eccl. 7:29; 2 Tim. 3:1–5; 4:3–4; Dan. 4:28–37; 1 John 1:8–10; 2:15–7.

6 Jeff Lewis, *Cultural Studies: The Basics* (London: Sage Publications, 2002), pp. 83–4, 267–9, 412–4; cf. Jas. 4:11–7; cf. Eccl. 7:29.

7 Jürgen Moltmann, 'Theology in the Project of the Modern World', in *A Passion for God's Reign* (J. Moltmann et al.; ed. M. Volf; Grand Rapids: Eerdmans, 1998), p. 14.

8 Lewis, *Cultural Studies*, pp. 267–9; cf. 412–4; 1 John 2:16.

9 Lewis, *Cultural Studies*, pp. 267–9; cf. Thiselton, '1 Corinthians', pp. 297–302, 304–5.

10 J. Suler, 'The Online Disinhibition Effect', *CP&B* 7.3 (2004), p. 321; cf. Thiselton, '1 Corinthians', p. 299.

11 The analysis above emerged from my study of Thiselton, '1 Corinthians', pp. 297–306. I have omitted most speech-marks for cosmetic reasons, but I should note that, mostly, this analysis expounds Thiselton's thinking, not my own – though I agree with Thiselton.

12 Thiselton, '1 Corinthians', pp. 304–5; cf. 298; cf. 297–306.

13 As for endnote 11.

14 Thiselton, '1 Corinthians', p. 305; cf. 297; cf. 297–306.

15 Thiselton, '1 Corinthians', p. 305; cf. 297; cf. 296–306 (our italics).

16 Pete Ward, 'The Tribes of Evangelicalism', in *The Post-Evangelical Debate* (G. Cray et al.; London: SPCK/Triangle, 1997), pp. 26–7; cf. Anthony C. Thiselton, 'Experience-Centred Religion: Harvey Cox on the Seduction of the Spirit', *CEN* (9 Aug. 1974), p. 8; Anthony C. Thiselton, 'Realized Eschatology at Corinth', *NTS* 24 (Jul. 1978), pp. 512–5; cf. 520–6 (our italics).

17 Thiselton, '1 Corinthians', p. 305; cf. 297; cf. Ward, 'Tribes', pp. 26–7; Thiselton, 'Experience-Centred', p. 8; Thiselton, 'Realized Eschatology', pp. 512–5; cf. 520–6.

18 Colin E. Gunton, *The One, The Three, and The Many: God, Creation and the Culture of Modernity* (Cambridge: CUP, 1993); cf. Leonardo Boff, *Trinity and Society* (trans. P. Burns; Tunbridge Wells: Burns & Oats, 1988); Brian D. Ingraffia, *Postmodern Theory and Biblical Theology: Vanquishing God's Shadow* (Cambridge: CUP, 1995); Anthony C. Thiselton, *The Two Horizons: New Testament Hermeneutics and Philosophical Description with Special Reference to Heidegger, Bultmann, Gadamer, and Wittgenstein* (Exeter: Paternoster, 1980). On the criticisms by Nietzsche and Heidegger see, Ingraffia, *Postmodern*, pp. 38, 63, 174, 229.

19 Anthony C. Thiselton, 'Some Comments on the Anglican-Lutheran International Conversations', *Chm* 88.4 (1974), p. 290; cf. Anthony C. Thiselton, 'The Theological Scene: Post-Bultmannian Perspectives', *CGrad* 30.3 (Sep. 1977), pp. 88–9; Thiselton, *Two Horizons*, pp. 38–40, 75–6, 84, 248, 205–92.

[20] Robert Knowles, *Anthony C. Thiselton and The Grammar of Hermeneutics: The Search for a Unified Theory* (Milton Keanes: Paternoster, 2012), pp. 444–571; cf. endnote 16 above.

[21] Ward, 'Tribes', pp. 26–7; cf. Thiselton, '1 Corinthians', p. 305; Thiselton, 'Experience-Centred', p. 8; Thiselton, 'Realized Eschatology', pp. 512–5; cf. 520–6; cf. the title of the book by Donald A. Carson, *The Gagging of God: Christianity Confronts Pluralism* (Leicester: Apollos, 1996).

[22] Thiselton, '1 Corinthians', pp. 304–5 cf. 297–8; cf. Thiselton, 'Experience-Centred', p. 8.

[23] Anthony C. Thiselton, *The Hermeneutics of Doctrine* (Grand Rapids: Eerdmans, 2007), pp. xvi–xxii.

6. Distorted Church as the Main Cause of Church-Hopping

[1] John 7:24; Jas. 2:13.

[2] John 16:12–3; 2 Cor. 5:16.

[3] 1 Cor. 14:24–5; Phil. 2:12–3.

[4] Matt. 24:2.

[5] Anthony C. Thiselton, 'Can a Premodern Bible Address a Postmodern World?' (public lecture, University of St Andrews), in *2000 Years and Beyond: Faith, Identity and the 'Common Era'* (ed. P. Gifford et al.; London: Routledge, 2003), p. 127.

[6] Thiselton, 'Premodern', p. 133.

[7] Thiselton, 'Premodern', p. 134.

[8] Thiselton, 'Premodern', p. 138; cf. Anthony C. Thiselton, '1 Corinthians', in *New Dictionary of Biblical Theology* (ed. T.D. Alexander & B.S. Rosner; Leicester: IVP, 2000), pp. 298; cf. 305 (italics ours).

[9] Jürgen Moltmann, 'Theology in the Project of the Modern World', in *A Passion for God's Reign* (J. Moltmann et al.; ed. M. Volf; Grand Rapids: Eerdmans, 1998), pp. 1–21.

[10] Phil. 2:21.

[11] 2 Tim. 3:7.

[12] Hans-Georg Gadamer, *Truth and Method* (trans. J. Weinsheimer and D.G. Marshall; London: Sheed & Ward, 1975, 1989), pp. 9–19; cf. http://en.wikipedia.org/wiki/Bildung (accessed 26 March 2013).

[13] See endnotes 5–8 and Anthony C. Thiselton, 'Address and Understanding: Some Goals and Models of Biblical Interpretation as Principles of Vocational Training', *Anvil* 3.2 (1986), pp. 112–3.

[14] Anthony C. Thiselton, 'The Theologian Who Must Not Be Ignored. Article Review of W. Pannenberg's *Basic Questions in Theology*, Vol. 2', *CEN* (25 Feb. 1972), p. 11; cf. Anthony C. Thiselton, 'Truth', in *The New International Dictionary of New Testament Theology*, Vol. 3 (ed. C. Brown; Exeter: Paternoster, 1978), pp. 894–900; Anthony C. Thiselton, 'Irrational Assumptions of Modern Theology Exposed. Review of T.F. Torrance's God and Rationality', *CEN* (19 Mar. 1971), p. 9; cf. Chapter 5, endnote 19.

[15] Pete Ward, 'The Tribes of Evangelicalism', in *The Post-Evangelical Debate* (G. Cray et al.; London: SPCK/Triangle, 1997), pp. 26–7; cf. Robert Knowles, *Anthony C. Thiselton and The Grammar of Hermeneutics: The Search for a Unified Theory* (Milton Keanes: Paternoster, 2012), pp. 444–571; cf. Chapter 5, endnote 16, and endnotes 5–8 above.

[16] Anthony C. Thiselton, 'The Parables as Language-Event: Some Comments on Fuchs's Hermeneutics in the Light of Linguistic Philosophy', *SJT* 23.4 (Nov. 1970), pp. 437–68; cf. Anthony C. Thiselton, 'Language and Meaning in Religion', in 'Word', in *The New International Dictionary of New Testament Theology*, Vol. 3 (ed. C. Brown; Exeter: Paternoster; Grand Rapids: Zondervan, 1978), pp. 1123–46; cf. Chapter 5, endnote 18.

[17] Anthony C. Thiselton, *The Two Horizons: New Testament Hermeneutics and Philosophical Description with Special Reference to Heidegger, Bultmann, Gadamer, and Wittgenstein* (Exeter: Paternoster Press, 1980), pp. 268–9, 286–7, 335–42, 354–5, 370–9, 379–85, 432–8, 442–4; cf. Matt. 7:12; 22:34–40; Rom. 13:8–10; Gal. 5:14.

[18] Anthony C. Thiselton, 'The Use of Philosophical Categories in New Testament Hermeneutics', *Chm* 87.1 (1973), pp. 87–100; cf. Anthony C. Thiselton, 'Understanding God's Word Today: Evangelicals Face the Challenge of the New Hermeneutic', in *Obeying Christ in a Changing World*, Vol. 1 (ed. J.R.W. Stott; Glasgow: Collins/Fountain Books, 1977), pp. 92–9; cf. 95.

[19] Anthony C. Thiselton, 'Realized Eschatology at Corinth', *NTS* 24 (Jul. 1978), pp. 512–5, 520–6; cf. Anthony C. Thiselton, 'Experience-Centred Religion: Harvey Cox on the Seduction of the Spirit', *CEN* (9 Aug. 1974), p. 8.

[20] Donald A. Carson, *The Gagging of God: Christianity Confronts Pluralism* (Leicester: Apollos, 1996).

[21] Thiselton, *Two Horizons*, pp. 33–40; cf. 245–51; 285–8, 359, 379–85; Thiselton, 'Theologian', p. 11; Ward, 'Tribes', pp. 26–7; Thiselton, 'Premodern', pp. 127–46; Knowles, *Thiselton*, pp. 444–571.

22 Anthony C. Thiselton, 'The Multi-Model Character of Holy Spirit Language', *CEN* (11 Apr. 1974), p. 8.

23 Thiselton, 'Realized', pp. 510–26.

24 Anthony C. Thiselton, 'Some Comments on the Anglican-Lutheran International Conversations', *Chm* 88.4 (1974), p. 290.

25 I am indebted to Nic Tregoning's verbal comments here.

26 See, Knowles, *Thiselton*, especially pp. 444–571, but the whole book addresses this issue.

27 Gadamer, *Truth*, pp. 9–19; cf. http://en.wikipedia.org/wiki/Bildung (accessed 26 March 2013).

28 Anthony C. Thiselton, 'Signs of the Times: Towards a Theology for the Year 2000 as a Grammar of Grace, Truth and Eschatology in Contexts of So-Called Postmodernity', in *The Future as God's Gift: Explorations in Christian Eschatology* (ed. D. Fergusson and M. Sarot; Edinburgh: T&T Clark, 2000), pp. 9–39.

29 Carson, *Gagging*, pp. 13–54.

30 William John Lyons, *Canon and Exegesis: Canonical Praxis and the Sodom Narrative* (Sheffield: Sheffield Academic Press, 2002), pp. 108–15; but see my response in, Knowles, *Thiselton*, pp. 483–530.

31 As in the case of W.J. Lyons; see, Lyons, *Canon*, pp. 114–5.

32 Anthony C. Thiselton, 'An Age of Anxiety', in *The History of Christianity. A Lion Handbook* (ed. T. Dowley et al.; Tring: Lion Publishing, 1977), pp. 597–9, 602–4.

33 Wolfhart Pannenberg, *Basic Questions in Theology: Collected Essays*, Vol. 2 (trans. G.H. Kehm; Philadelphia: Fortress Press, 1971), pp. 199–200; cf. 202–15; cf. Wolfhart Pannenberg, *Basic Questions in Theology: Collected Essays*, Vol. 3 (trans. R.A. Wilson; Philadelphia: Fortress Press, 1973), pp. 89, 99–102; Anthony C. Thiselton, 'Head-On Challenge to Doubt: The Theology of Wolfhart Pannenberg', *CEN* (10 May 1974), p. 8; Anthony C. Thiselton, 'Theology Made Exciting: Review of W. Pannenberg's *The Apostles' Creed in the Light of Today's Questions*', *CEN* (19 Jan. 1973), p. 12; Thiselton, 'Theologian', p. 11.

34 Lyons, *Canon*, pp. 108–15; cf. Knowles, *Thiselton*, pp. 483–530.

35 Knowles, *Thiselton*, pp. 483–530.

36 Thiselton, 'Premodern', pp. 127–46; cf. Knowles, *Thiselton*, pp. 483–530.

37 Anthony C. Thiselton, *New Horizons in Hermeneutics: The Theory and Practice of Transforming Biblical Reading* (London: HarperCollins, 1992), pp. 393–470; cf. 515–6; 529–55.

[38] Thiselton, '1 Corinthians', pp. 297–306; cf. Thiselton, 'Premodern', pp. 127–46; cf. Thiselton, *New Horizons*, pp. 393–470, 515–6, 529–55.

[39] Thiselton, *New Horizons*, pp. 393–470, 515–6, 529–55.

[40] Franz Kafka, *The Trial* (trans. M. Mitchell; Oxford: OUP, 2009).

[41] Christopher Norris, *The Truth About Postmodernism* (Oxford: Blackwell, 1993), p. 40.

[42] Luke 18:19.

[43] Matt. 15:14.

[44] John 10:3–5.

[45] Brian D. Ingraffia, *Postmodern Theory and Biblical Theology: Vanquishing God's Shadow* (Cambridge: CUP, 1995), pp. 38, 63, 174, 229. Ingraffia is not among those who take such cheap shots; rather, his work is to be strongly commended.

[46] Matt. 7:5; John 7:24; 3:10.

[47] Luke 14:21; cf. Norris, *Postmodernism*, p. 40.

[48] See Chapter 3, pp. 58–60; cf. Chapters 4 and 5; cf. John 3:10; Thiselton, '1 Corinthians', pp. 297–306.

[49] 3 John 9.

[50] Anthony C. Thiselton, 'Review of A. Hodes' *Encounter with Martin Buber*', *Chm* 90.2 (1976), p. 139; cf. Thiselton, 'Understanding', pp. 119, 99; Anthony C. Thiselton, 'Predictable, Domesticated and Tamed', *CEN* (8 Feb. 1974), p. 7; cf. Thiselton, *Two Horizons*, pp. 67–8 (italics ours).

[51] Thiselton, '1 Corinthians', p. 305; cf. Thiselton, 'Address', pp. 112–3; (cf. 2 Tim. 4:3–4 – which, in our view, is often now a fulfilled prophecy).

[52] Donald A. Carson, *Revelation 12–14* (Tape 1 of 4). Available from: EMW Cassettes; Evangelical Movement of Wales, Bryntirion, Bridgend, Mid Glamorgan, CF31 4DX.

[53] Luke 4:24, 27.

[54] Thiselton, 'Premodern', p. 127.

[55] Thiselton, 'Premodern', p. 133.

[56] Thiselton, 'Premodern', p. 134.

[57] Thiselton, 'Premodern', p. 138.

[58] Thiselton, '1 Corinthians', p. 298.

[59] Anthony C. Thiselton, *The First Epistle to the Corinthians* (Carlisle: Paternoster, 2000), p. 826 (italics Thiselton's; Thiselton's bold type removed).

[60] See the back cover of Leonardo Boff, *Trinity and Society* (trans. P. Burns; Tunbridge Wells: Burns & Oats, 1988).

[61] See Chapter 5, pp. 96–7; cf. Ward, 'Tribes', pp. 26–7; cf. Thiselton, 'Experience-Centred', p. 8; Thiselton, 'Realized', pp. 512–5; cf. 520–6; 514–5; Knowles, *Thiselton*, p. 530.

[62] Matt. 20:20–8; cf. 1 Cor. 12:1–31.

[63] Thiselton, 'Anglican-Lutheran', p. 290; cf. Thiselton, *Two Horizons*, pp. 205–92; 330–56.

[64] Borrowing Jacques Derrida's phrase, 'white mythology', but attributing our own meaning to it. See, Jacques Derrida, 'The White Mythology: Metaphor in the Text of Philosophy', *NLitHist* 6.1 (1974), pp. 7–74; cf. Christopher Norris, *Deconstruction: Theory and Practice* (London: Routledge, 1982; 2002), p. 81.

[65] cf. Anthony C. Thiselton, 'The Theology of Paul Tillich', *Chm* 88.1 (1974), pp. 96–102.

[66] Thanks for verbal comments from Louise Woolley, Matthew Crockett and Timothy Smith here. See also Thiselton, 'Tillich', p. 97.

[67] In a recent sermon by Revd. David Morrell at Woodville Road Baptist Church, Cardiff, UK.

[68] On art see, for example, H.R. Rookmaaker, *Modern Art and the Death of a Culture* (Leicester: IVP, 1970/1994); cf. Hans Küng, *Art and the Question of Meaning* (London: SCM, 1981); Stephen Little, *...Isms: Understanding Art* (London: Herbert Press/A&C Black, 2004).

[69] Thiselton, 'Realized', pp. 510–26.

[70] Ps. 88:15.

[71] Rev. 13:10; cf. 1 Pet. 4:17.

[72] Thiselton, *Two Horizons*, p. 343.

[73] Roland Howard, *The Rise and Fall of the Nine O'Clock Service: A Cult within the Church?* (London: Mowbray, 1996).

[74] I. Stewart, *Transactional Analysis Counselling in Action* (London; Sage Publications, 2007).

[75] Matt. 15:14.

[76] Thiselton, *Two Horizons*, p. 170.

[77] John 9:41.

[78] Thiselton, *Interpreting God*, pp. 50–1, 53–62, 67–75; cf. Anthony C. Thiselton, 'Communicative Action and Promise in Inter-Disciplinary, Biblical, and Theological Hermeneutics', in *The Promise of Hermeneutics* (R. Lundin et al.; Carlisle: Paternoster, 1999), pp. 133–7.

[79] John 7:24.

[80] Thiselton, *Two Horizons*, p. 403; cf. Norris, *Postmodernism*, p. 15; Matt. 21:31.

81 Luke 18:9–14; 18:14; Mark 10:18; Luke 18:19.

82 Gal. 5:5; Jas. 2:13.

83 This phrase is Thiselton's. See Thiselton, 'Communicative Action', p. 157.

84 Matt. 15:14.

85 Matt. 7:5; cf. Prov. 9:8.

86 Stewart, *Transactional Analysis*; cf. S.B. Karpman, 'Fairy Tales and Script Drama Analysis', *TAB* 7.26 (Apr. 1968), pp. 39–43; cf. http://www.karpmandramatriangle.com/pdf/DramaTriangle.pdf (accessed 26 March 2013). On symbols see Thiselton, 'Tillich', pp. 96–102.

87 Anthony C. Thiselton, *Language, Liturgy and Meaning* (Nottingham: Grove Books, 1975/1986), pp. 3–33; cf. Thiselton, 'Categories', pp. 97–8; cf. Knowles, *Thiselton*, pp. 330–3.

88 This phrase is cited from Norris, *Postmodernism*, p. 15.

7. Mission Distorted by Five Distorted Church Cultures

1 Matt. 16:18; cf. 7:21–3; 2 Cor. 11:26; Rev. 21:1–4.

2 John R.W. Stott, *The Contemporary Christian: An Urgent Plea for Double Listening* (Leicester: IVP, 1992), pp. 27 cf. 24–9.

3 Anthony C. Thiselton, '1 Corinthians', in *New Dictionary of Biblical Theology* (ed. T.D. Alexander and B.S. Rosner; Leicester: IVP, 2000), pp. 301–2.

4 Robert Knowles, *Anthony C. Thiselton and The Grammar of Hermeneutics: The Search for a Unified Theory* (Milton Keanes: Paternoster, 2012), pp. 476–550.

5 Jeff Lewis, *Cultural Studies: The Basics* (London: Sage Publications, 2002), pp. 109–24.

6 Anthony C. Thiselton, *New Horizons in Hermeneutics: The Theory and Practice of Transforming Biblical Reading* (London: HarperCollins, 1992), pp. 393–470; cf. 515–6; 529–55; cf. Anthony C. Thiselton, 'Can a Premodern Bible Address a Postmodern World?' (public lecture, University of St Andrews), in *2000 Years and Beyond: Faith, Identity and the 'Common Era'* (ed. P. Gifford et al.; London: Routledge, 2003), pp. 127–46; Thiselton, '1 Corinthians', pp. 297–306.

7 See endnote 6 and also, Anthony C. Thiselton, *The Hermeneutics of Doctrine* (Grand Rapids: Eerdmans, 2007), pp. xvi–xxii.

8. Mission and What Evangelism *Doesn't* Involve

[1] cf. Colin E. Gunton, *The One, The Three, and The Many: God, Creation and the Culture of Modernity* (Cambridge: CUP, 1993), pp. 64; cf. 51–73.

[2] Heb. 12:2; 22–4; cf. Matt. 16:21–8.

[3] Anthony C. Thiselton, *The Two Horizons: New Testament Hermeneutics and Philosophical Description with Special Reference to Heidegger, Bultmann, Gadamer, and Wittgenstein* (Exeter: Paternoster Press, 1980), p. 372; cf. 331; cf. M. Blaine Smith, *Knowing God's Will: Biblical Principles of Guidance* (Madison, WI: IVP, 1979), pp. 85–117.

[4] Heb. 4:15.

[5] Matt. 17:24–7; cf. 15:1–20.

[6] Thiselton has been resisting slogans from as early as 1966; cf. Anthony C. Thiselton, 'A Snappy Slogan, But...', *CEN* (11 Feb. 1966), p. 10.

[7] Thanks to Revd. John Smuts for the 'think profoundly, speak simply' principle.

[8] See YouTube; cf. also, Donald A. Carson, *Bible Interpretation*. Parts 1–4. Tapes WA20-WA23. Word Alive 1993 (Eastbourne: ICC, 1993).

[9] John 3:19.

[10] Thanks for Louise Woolley's verbal communication on this point.

[11] cf. Alan James Torrance, 'The Self-Relation, Narcissism and the Gospel of Grace', *SJT* 40 (1987), pp. 481–510.

9. Mission and Understanding Modernity and Postmodernity

[1] This phrase is cited from Jeff Lewis, *Cultural Studies: The Basics* (London: Sage Publications, 2002), pp. 412–4.

[2] Alan R. Lacey, 'Humanism', in *The Oxford Companion to Philosophy* (ed. T. Honderich; Oxford: OUP, 1995), pp. 375–6.

[3] Lewis, *Cultural Studies*, 412–4; cf. Hans-Herbert Kögler, 'Utopianism', in *The Oxford Companion to Philosophy* (ed. T. Honderich; Oxford: OUP, 1995), pp. 892–3.

[4] Arthur C. Clarke, *2001: A Space Odyssey* (London: Arrow Books, 1968); cf. Arthur C. Clarke, *2010: Odyssey Two* (London: Granada Publishing, 1982); Arthur C. Clarke, *2061: Odyssey Three* (New York: Random House, 1987); Arthur C. Clarke, *3001: The Final Odyssey* (London: HarperCollins, 1997). The cited response to *2010: Odyssey Two* is from

The New Yorker newspaper – see the end-pages of *3001: The Final Odyssey.*

5 Lewis, *Cultural Studies*, pp. 412–4.

6 Ps. 127:1; Mark 14:49; cf. John 10:35.

7 John Gray, 'Enlightenment Humanism as a Relic of Christian Monotheism', in *2000 Years and Beyond: Faith, Identity and the 'Common Era'* (ed. P. Gifford et al.; London: Routledge, 2003), pp. 35–50.

8 Lewis, *Cultural Studies*, pp. 412–4; cf. 413.

9 Lewis, *Cultural Studies*, pp. 412–4; cf. 413 (italics ours).

10 See endnote 4 (italics ours).

11 Lewis, *Cultural Studies*, pp. 412–4.

12 On this point and the previous point see Lewis, *Cultural Studies*, pp. 83; cf. 413; cf. 412–4 (italics ours).

13 Colin E. Gunton, *The One, The Three, and The Many: God, Creation and the Culture of Modernity* (Cambridge: CUP, 1993), pp. 13–6. On "apathy", see comments made by Morgan Freeman's character in the film, *Se7en* (italics ours).

14 On this and the previous point see Anthony C. Thiselton, *Interpreting God and the Postmodern Self: On Meaning, Manipulation and Promise* (Edinburgh: T&T Clark, 1995), pp. 121–44; cf. 105–17; ix–xi; 3–9; 11–7; cf. Anthony C. Thiselton, *New Horizons in Hermeneutics: The Theory and Practice of Transforming Biblical Reading* (London: HarperCollins, 1992), pp. 110–1 (italics ours).

15 Brian D. Ingraffia, *Postmodern Theory and Biblical Theology: Vanquishing God's Shadow* (Cambridge: CUP, 1995), pp. 19–32, on Nietzsche's work, notably *The Gay Science.*

16 F. LeRon Shults, *Reforming Theological Anthropology: After the Philosophical Turn to Relationality* (Grand Rapids, MI.: Eerdmans, 2003); cf. Anthony C. Thiselton, *The Two Horizons: New Testament Hermeneutics and Philosophical Description with Special Reference to Heidegger, Bultmann, Gadamer, and Wittgenstein* (Exeter: Paternoster Press, 1980), pp. 37–8.

17 Hans-Georg Gadamer, *Truth and Method* (trans. J. Weinsheimer and D.G. Marshall; London: Sheed & Ward, 1975 / 1989), pp. 3–9; cf. 362–79.

18 Michel Foucault, *Discipline and Punish: The Birth of the Prison* (London: Penguin Books, 1991), p. 218.

19 Foucault, *Discipline*, p. 218.

20 Jürgen Habermas, *Knowledge and Human Interests* (London: Heinemann, 1972), p. 283; cf. Thiselton, *New Horizons*, p. 384.

21 Gadamer, *Truth*, pp. 291–307.

22 Anthony C. Thiselton, 'Knowledge, Myth and Corporate Memory', in *Believing in the Church: Essays by Members of the Church of England Doctrine Commission* (ed. B. Mitchell; London: SPCK, 1981), pp. 45–78.

23 Thiselton, *New Horizons*, p. 248; cf. Alan James Torrance, 'The Self-Relation, Narcissism and the Gospel of Grace', *SJT* 40 (1987), pp. 481–510.

24 Robert Knowles, *Anthony C. Thiselton and The Grammar of Hermeneutics: The Search for a Unified Theory* (Milton Keanes: Paternoster, 2012), pp. 444–565.

25 cf. Gen. 4:23–4.

26 Thiselton, *Interpreting God*, pp. 127–52.

27 At a rally in Sheffield, UK, in 1985.

28 Col. 2:15; Eph. 6:12.

29 Eph. 6:11; 2 Cor. 2:11.

30 cf. Thiselton, *Interpreting God*, pp. ix–xi, 3–163; Anthony C. Thiselton, 'Signs of the Times: Towards a Theology for the Year 2000 as a Grammar of Grace, Truth and Eschatology in Contexts of So-Called Postmodernity', in *The Future as God's Gift: Explorations in Christian Eschatology* (ed. D. Fergusson and M. Sarot; Edinburgh: T&T Clark, 2000), pp. 9–39; Anthony C. Thiselton, 'Can a Premodern Bible Address a Postmodern World? (public lecture, University of St Andrews), in *2000 Years and Beyond: Faith, Identity and the 'Common Era'* (ed. P. Gifford et al.; London: Routledge, 2003), pp. 127–46; Thiselton, *New Horizons*, pp. 103, 314ff, 393, 398–9; see especially e.g. p. 381 cf. 103.

31 Thiselton, *Two Horizons*, pp. 51–84; cf. Knowles, *Thiselton*, pp. 272–571.

32 Thiselton, *New Horizons*, pp. 330–43.

33 Thiselton, *Interpreting God*, pp. ix–xi; 3–163.

34 See, Thiselton, *Interpreting God*, pp. 73–8; cf. John D. Zizioulas, 'On Being a Person. Towards an Ontology of Personhood', in *Persons, Divine and Human: King's College Essays in Theological Anthropology* (ed. C. Schwöbel and C.E. Gunton; Edinburgh: T&T Clark, 1991), pp. 33–46; cf. Christoph Schwöbel, 'Human Being as Relational Being: Twelve Theses for a Christian Anthropology', in *Persons, Divine and Human: King's College Essays in Theological Anthropology* (ed. C. Schwöbel, and C.E. Gunton; Edinburgh: T&T Clark, 1991), pp. 141–65; Colin E. Gunton, *The Promise of Trinitarian Theology* (Edinburgh: T&T Clark, 1991), pp. 83–99.

35 Anthony C. Thiselton, 'Truth', in *The New International Dictionary of New Testament Theology*, Vol. 3 (ed. C. Brown; Exeter: Paternoster, 1978), pp. 896; cf. 894–901; cf. Thiselton, *Two Horizons*, pp. 362–85.

36 Knowles, *Thiselton*, pp. 444–571.

[37] Thiselton, *Interpreting God*, pp. 145–63.

[38] Paul Ricoeur, 'Historiography and the Representation of the Past', in *2000 Years and Beyond: Faith, Identity and the 'Common Era'* (ed. P. Gifford et al.; London: Routledge, 2003), p. 67.

[39] Ricoeur, 'Historiography', p. 63; cf. 67; cf. 51–68.

[40] See, Christopher Norris, *The Truth About Postmodernism* (Oxford: Blackwell, 1993), pp. 14–23.

[41] George Santayana, from *Chambers Book of Quotations* (ed. R.I. Fitzhenry; Edinburgh: Chambers, 1986/1992), p. 166.

[42] So Norris, *Postmodernism*, p. 18.

[43] Thiselton, 'Premodern', pp. 127; cf. 134; cf. 127–46; cf. Knowles, *Thiselton*, pp. 444–571.

[44] Thiselton, *New Horizons*, pp. 416–39.

[45] Knowles, *Thiselton*, pp. 444–571.

[46] Anthony C. Thiselton, 'Communicative Action and Promise in Inter-Disciplinary, Biblical, and Theological Hermeneutics', in *The Promise of Hermeneutics* (R. Lundin et al.; Carlisle: Paternoster, 1999), pp. 144–51; cf. Anthony C. Thiselton, 'Language and Meaning in Religion', in 'Word', in *The New International Dictionary of New Testament Theology*, Vol. 3 (ed. C. Brown; Exeter: Paternoster, 1978), pp. 1123–46; Anthony C. Thiselton, *Language, Liturgy and Meaning* (Nottingham: Grove Books, 1975/1986), pp. 3–33; Thiselton, *New Horizons*, pp. 127–9; Thiselton, *Two Horizons*, pp. 370–85.

[47] Knowles, *Thiselton*, pp. 140–87.

[48] Thiselton, *New Horizons*, p. 69; cf. 80–141.

[49] Thiselton, 'Language', pp. 1142–4; cf. 1139.

[50] Thiselton, *New Horizons*, pp. 313–21; cf. contrast with 103–41.

[51] Ricoeur, 'Historiography', p. 63; cf. 67; cf. Norris, *Postmodernism*, pp. 14–23.

[52] Gadamer, *Truth*, pp. 3–9.

[53] Norris, *Postmodernism*, p. 15.

[54] John 8:32.

[55] Jürgen Moltmann, 'Progress and Abyss: Remembering the Future of the Modern World', in *2000 Years and Beyond: Faith, Identity and the 'Common Era'* (ed. P. Gifford et al.; London: Routledge, 2003), p. 23; cf. 16–34; cf. Thiselton, *New Horizons*, p. 415.

[56] See also Moltmann, 'Progress', pp. 28–34.

[57] Thiselton, *New Horizons*, pp. 393–470, 535–55; cf. Thiselton, *Interpreting God*, pp. 111–7, 127–44; Norris, *Postmodernism*, pp. 1–14.

58 Donald A. Carson, *The Gagging of God: Christianity Confronts Pluralism* (Leicester: Apollos, 1996), pp. 13–54.

59 Carson, *Gagging*, pp. 13–54; cf. G. O'Collins and D. Kendall, *The Bible for Theology: Ten Principles for the Theological Use of Scripture* (New York and Mahwah, N.J.: Paulist Press, 1997), p. 20; Lewis, *Cultural Studies*, pp. 412–4; Thiselton, *New Horizons*, pp. 83, 100–1, 131.

60 Thiselton, *New Horizons*, p. 401.

61 Lewis, *Cultural Studies*, pp. 267–9.

62 Lewis, *Cultural Studies*, pp. 412–4. On 'training', see Thiselton, *Two Horizons*, pp. 376–9.

63 Thiselton, *Interpreting God*, pp. 127–44.

64 Lewis, *Cultural Studies*, pp. 267–9, 412–4, 83–4.

65 Lewis, *Cultural Studies*, pp. 267–9, 412–4, 83–4.

66 Lewis, *Cultural Studies*, pp. 267–9, 412–14, 83–4; cf. Knowles, *Thiselton*, pp. 425–6; J. Suler, 'The Online Disinhibition Effect', *CP&B* 7.3 (2004), pp. 321–6. Thanks to Louise Woolley for alerting me to Suler's article.

67 Lewis, *Cultural Studies*, pp. 267–9, 412–4, 83–4.

68 Lewis, *Cultural Studies*, pp. 267–9, 412–4, 83–4.

69 Lewis, *Cultural Studies*, pp. 83–4; cf. 267–9; 412–4; cf. Thiselton, *Interpreting God*, pp. 12–3, 121–44; cf. Jürgen Moltmann, 'Theology in the Project of the Modern World', in *A Passion for God's Reign* (J. Moltmann et al.; ed. M. Volf; Grand Rapids: Eerdmans, 1998), p. 14.

70 Thiselton, *Interpreting God*, pp. 121–44; cf. 109; cf. Lewis, *Cultural Studies*, pp. 412–4; Gunton, *One*, p. 35; Ingraffia, *Postmodern*, pp. 31–2; cf. Don Cupitt, *Crisis of Moral Authority: The Dethronement of Christianity* (London: Lutterworth Press, 1972), pp. 9–10, 16–7, 20, 22, 26–9.

71 Thiselton, *Interpreting God*, pp. 121–44; cf. 11–7.

72 Thiselton, *Interpreting God*, pp. 106; cf. 105–10; cf. Thiselton, *New Horizons*, pp. 103–13, 127–9; Ingraffia, *Postmodern*, p. 6; cf. 178–85; cf. Roland Barthes, 'The Death of the Author', in *Image-Music-Text* (trans. S. Heath; New York: Hill and Wang, 1977), pp. 142–8.

73 Dan R. Stiver, *The Philosophy of Religious Language: Sign, Symbol, and Story* (Oxford: Blackwell, 1996), pp. 180–4, 188–92, 243; but see my response to Stiver in Knowles, *Thiselton*, pp. 437–43.

74 cf. Thiselton, *Interpreting God*, p. 113.

75 Thiselton, *Interpreting God*, pp. 161–3; cf. 121–63; cf. 11–7, 41–3 (Thiselton's italics removed).

76 Gunton, *Promise*, pp. 87–8; cf. Derek Parfit, *Reasons and Persons* (Oxford: OUP, 1984).

77 Torrance, 'Self-Relation', p. 484; cf. 481–510.

78 Torrance, 'Self-Relation', p. 492 (italics Auden's, cited by Torrance).

79 Roland Howard, *The Rise and Fall of the Nine O'Clock Service: A Cult within the Church?* (London: Mowbray, 1996), p. 128; cf. 5, 131.

80 See, José G. Merquior, *Foucault* (London: Fontana Press, 1985/1991).

81 See, Carson, *Gagging*, pp. 57–64.

82 Torrance, 'Self-Relation', pp. 484–8.

83 Thiselton, *New Horizons*, pp. 344–50; cf. Thiselton, *Interpreting God*, pp. 127–35.

84 Anthony C. Thiselton, *New Testament Hermeneutics and Philosophical Description: Issues in New Testament Hermeneutics with Special Reference to the Use of Philosophical Description in Heidegger, Bultmann, Gadamer, and Wittgenstein* (Sheffield: University of Sheffield Ph.D. Thesis, 1977), p. xxii, concs., 1.2 – 1.2c.

85 Christopher Norris, *Deconstruction: Theory and Practice* (London: Routledge, 1982/2002), pp. 77–82; cf. Peter Barry, *Beginning Theory. An Introduction to Literary and Cultural Theory* (Manchester: MUP, 1995), pp. 172–5; Thiselton, *Two Horizons*, pp. 314; cf. 304–14.

86 cf. Gen. 3:1–5.

87 Moltmann, 'Theology', p. 14.

88 Isa. 14:13–4.

89 Gunton, *One*, p. 32.

90 Gunton, *One*, p. 32.

91 Lewis, *Cultural Studies*, p. 413; cf. 412–4.

92 Isa. 14:15–7.

93 Torrance, 'Self-Relation', p. 495 (italics ours).

94 Suler, 'Online', p. 321; cf. Torrance, 'Self-Relation', p. 482; Thiselton, *Interpreting God*, p. 113; Anthony C. Thiselton, '1 Corinthians', in *New Dictionary of Biblical Theology* (ed. T.D. Alexander and B.S. Rosner; Leicester: IVP, 2000), pp. 297–306; cf. Thiselton, 'Premodern', pp. 127–46.

95 cf. Owen Jones, *Chavs: The Demonization of the Working Classes* (London: Verso, 2011), pp. 1–12. I am using the term 'chav' differently to Jones – i.e. to describe problem-*behaviours*, not a problem 'class'.

96 The phrase 'problem-families' was coined by Conservative MPs during televised discussions about the London riots of 2011. Thanks to Andrew Smith for communicating verbal insights into the 'counterfeit intimacy' enjoyed by cliques. See also Howard, *Nine O'Clock Service* (see endnote 79).

[97] Thiselton, *Interpreting God*, pp. 11–7, 121–44; cf. Thiselton, *New Horizons*, pp. 393–409; 410–70; 535–55; Pete Ward, 'The Tribes of Evangelicalism', in *The Post-Evangelical Debate* (G. Cray et al.; London: SPCK/ Triangle, 1997), pp. 19–34.

[98] Carson, *Gagging*, pp. 13–54; cf. Gunton, *One*, e.g. pp. 51–61, 64, 180.

[99] Lewis, *Cultural Studies*, pp. 83–4; cf. 412–4.

[100] Lewis, *Cultural Studies*, pp. 412–4.

[101] Lewis, *Cultural Studies*, pp. 412–4.

[102] Gunton, *One*, pp. 13–6; cf. Lewis, *Cultural Studies*, pp. 412–4; cf. endnote 13 above (italics ours).

[103] Lewis, *Cultural Studies*, pp. 412–4; cf. Suler, 'Online', p. 321.

[104] Boff, *Trinity*, p. 3; cf. 106–7; 147–8; cf. Gunton, *One*, pp. 61–6.

[105] Anthony C. Thiselton, *The First Epistle to the Corinthians* (Carlisle: Paternoster, 2000), pp. 416–7; cf. our discussion in Chapter 3 above.

[106] Thiselton, *Epistle*, pp. 338–44; cf. our discussion in Chapter 3 above.

[107] See previous endnote and William L. Reese, *Dictionary of Philosophy and Religion: Eastern and Western Thought* (New Jersey: Humanities Press, 1980), pp. 156–7; cf. our discussion in Chapter 3 above.

[108] Gen. 3:1–5.

Paternoster:
thinking faith

We trust you enjoyed reading this book from Paternoster. If you want to be informed of any new titles from this author and other releases you can sign up to the Paternoster newsletter by contacting us:

By Post:
Paternoster
52 Presley Way
Crownhill
Milton Keynes
MK8 0ES

E-mail
paternoster@authenticmedia.co.uk

Follow us: